B
PACK

WHO WANTS TO BE A
BILLIONAIRE?
THE JAMES PACKER STORY

For Lisa

WHO WANTS TO BE A BILLIONAIRE?
THE JAMES PACKER STORY

PAUL BARRY

ALLEN&UNWIN

Allen & Unwin
83 Alexander Street
Crows Nest NSW 2065
Australia
Phone: (61 2) 8425 0100
Fax: (61 2) 9906 2218
Email: info@allenandunwin.com
Web: www.allenandunwin.com

Cataloguing-in-Publication entry is available from the
National Library of Australia
www.librariesaustralia.nla.gov.au

978 1 74175 974 7

Typeset in Adobe Caslon 11/16 pt by Midland Typesetters, Australia
Printed by Griffin Press, Adelaide

10 9 8 7 6 5 4 3 2 1

CONTENTS

PROLOGUE
UNLUCKY JIM

Is he in financial trouble? Shit, yeah.

Sitting in front of his computer, watching the markets fall, James Packer was haemorrhaging wealth at a rate of $8000 a minute, $480 000 an hour, or $11.5 million a day. And on some days it was even worse. As the financial crisis deepened in early 2009, he put on weight, started smoking again and disappeared from public view. In the space of a year, he had lost his spot as Australia's richest man and waved goodbye to two-thirds of his $6.2 billion fortune.

Friends reported he was deeply depressed, although one or two were busy denying this to the media, and he had good reason to be. In just over twelve months, his shares in three key businesses—casinos, media and financial services—had lost almost $4 billion in value. On top of that, he had dropped another couple of hundred million dollars on sundry other shareholdings in property development and managed funds.

But it was not just the money. He had also walked away from the Packers' media empire which three generations of his family had built up. At their huge Hunter Valley property, Ellerston, Kerry would have been turning in his grave. Not only would he never have abandoned his magazines and Channel Nine so lightly, he would never have got himself into the sort of financial strife that James now faced.

Kerry had always been cautious in business, an arch pessimist, a man who constantly feared the world was going to end, and the global financial crisis had proved him spectacularly right. It was a fair bet he would now be sitting on the sidelines with a pile of cash, waiting to snap up the biggest bargains in a century. James, on the other hand, was counting his losses and wondering how much worse it could get. He had always been a believer and an optimist, impatient with his father's refusal to take risks with the Packer fortune (except on the gaming tables). Now he could hear the old man crowing, 'I told you so'.

James had already incurred his father's wrath with One.Tel in 2001, when he had been sin-binned for months after losing $400 million of the family fortune. That experience had driven him to the very edge of a nervous breakdown and caused him to seek refuge in Scientology. Now he was doing it all over again on a much grander scale.

It was some comfort that he was not the only billionaire to be swamped by the financial tsunami. The man who had dislodged him as Australia's richest man, Andrew 'Twiggy' Forrest, had lost $6 billion in just sixty days as the price of his big mining company, Fortescue Metals, collapsed on the stock market. The nation's richest retailer, Gerry Harvey, had also lost $1.5 billion in the crash. But, unlike James, they both seemed able to laugh about it. As his share price headed south, Harvey admitted cheerfully he was down to his last billion dollars but didn't care a bit, because he never thought he'd have a billion to lose. 'In a way I'm sort of proud,' he said. 'Oh, I lost one and a half billion, what a beauty.'

But James was suffering because he took money so seriously. It was what drove him, what he lived for, what had always served as the scorecard of his success. 'His self esteem is the net present value of his assets,' one friend observed. This was hardly surprising, since money was the only measure his father had ever taught him.

Like Kerry before him, James Packer had been driven by a desire to match his father, to beat him, or at the very least to earn his respect and praise. But his father certainly wouldn't be praising him now.

James had always thought big in business, had always had a vision, had always been ready to take on the world. It was what got him into trouble with One.Tel. And it was what was getting him into strife on this occasion too, but on a much bigger scale.

During his lifetime, Kerry had lost hundreds of millions of dollars on the blackjack tables of the world. Now James was nursing bigger bets than his father ever had, laying out billions of dollars to buy or build casinos in Las Vegas and Macau, and losing even more heavily.

Even when he was at school, James had been familiar with the old saying 'Shirtsleeves to shirtsleeves in three generations', which sums up how family fortunes can be squandered by those who inherit them. James was in fact from the fourth generation of rich Packers, but he had always been acutely aware of the weight on his shoulders. And as this crisis ground on, the burden must have felt heavier than ever.

'I feel so sorry for him,' said one woman who had known him since he was a boy. 'He was a very nice soft young man. He wasn't his father's son and he has spent his whole life trying to get his father's approval. It must be shocking for him.'

Kerry had been very proud of the fact he had never beaten James as a child, as Sir Frank Packer had beaten him. But he had been unable to show his love, however hard he tried. He had bullied and belittled his son even when James was in his thirties and abused him brutally in front of his friends.

Several people who saw the relationship up close believed Kerry was jealous of his son and didn't want him to succeed. He was always ready to blame when things went wrong and never there to congratulate when James did things right, as he did on many occasions over the years.

Despite this treatment, James had stuck it out and chosen to stay. He wanted the power and the money and the chance to show he was as good. But luck was not on his side in the way it had been 100 years earlier for the man who started the Packer fortune. James's great grandfather, Robert Clyde Packer, had made his first million dollars after finding ten shillings at a racecourse, putting it on a horse and winning enough for his passage from Hobart to Sydney.

James had had the misfortune to inherit the Packer empire on the eve of the worst economic crisis since the Great Depression and had not seen the storm coming. He was hardly alone in this, but he had been so desperate to prove himself he had taken far more risks than was sensible.

And now he was about to discover whether it would cost him everything.

CHAPTER 1
MUMMY'S BOY

I want them to know only one thing, really—that I
adore them. I'd do anything for them and they know
that.

At the age of ten, young 'Jamie' Packer was packed off to prep
school in Bowral, in the southern highlands of New South Wales,
to a big old rambling property called Tudor House, which had a
working farm with green paddocks beyond the gardens and playing
fields. A tall boy with freckles, big ears and a big grin that revealed
two rows of protruding teeth, he was five years older than his father
had been when he was sent off to board and apparently a fair
bit happier at the prospect. But he was being sent away from his
mother, nonetheless.

Poor Kerry had suffered miserably from such partings, yet he
clearly felt that a dose of this medicine would do James good.
'I think boarding school is very important for kids,' he told
Michael Parkinson. 'I think particularly for kids who have been

very lucky and had a lot of privileges. I think it's very important for them to learn to get along with other people and other kids, some of them not quite as well off as they are, and to learn their responsibilities.'

In the event, Tudor House probably proved to be a great deal more fun than Kerry intended. There was a creek with yabbies, a dam with canoes, and a wood where the boys could climb trees and make camps. At weekends they were free to roam wherever they wanted, taking their meals along with them. 'On Sunday we would just disappear,' one of James's schoolmates remembers. 'You could go to the kitchen and get a flask of billy tea and some flour, then ride out on the bikes, make a fire and cook damper. We all had cubby houses made out of branches. Most of our free time we would go and work on them.'

James was in a boarding house with fifty boys in five dormitories of ten and precious little privacy. It was like a large close-knit family according to his housemaster, Phillip Richards, whose wife Louise washed the boys' clothes, made their beds and acted as a surrogate mum for two years. Both remember James as vague and absent-minded, 'an expert at losing his socks . . . one of those boys who could shed things as he walked'.

One Easter James went off on holidays, leaving a heap of his stuff strewn about the floor. 'That night,' says Richards, 'we saw Kerry telling a story on television about the time he'd left his tennis racquet behind in Geelong, and how his father, to teach him a lesson, had sent him back on the train from Sydney to retrieve it. Well, we saw this and my wife and I were thrown into a complete panic! James had left everything! His tennis racquet, his cricket gear, his clothes. We just imagined the scene back at the house when he arrived home and Mrs Packer would be going through his bags. We genuinely expected poor James to be knocking on our door in the early hours of the morning. To our great relief he didn't turn up.'

It was no accident that history did not repeat itself because it was Kerry's mission to be much less hard on his son than Sir Frank had been on him. Kerry had endured brutal punishment as a child, received very little love, and spent a huge amount of time away from the family home. And as he told the broadcaster Terry Lane, he was determined not to make the same mistake with his two children, James and Gretel. 'I want them to know only one thing, really—that I adore them. I'd do anything for them and they know that. They know they're loved . . . That doesn't mean I don't put them over my knee—I do, but I hope fairly and never in anger. It's a belief that when you've done something wrong you've got to pay a price. Then we talk about it after it happens and say, "It's paid now, but let's learn the lesson and not do it again."'

As James grew older, and more of a rival, Kerry found it impossible to avoid competing with him and slapping him down. But in these early days, he appears to have been a good father and James a happy, confident, cheerful boy who got on well with everyone. In almost all the official school photographs he's wearing a wide, easy smile, in stark contrast to the famous photo of Kerry, taken at the age of five, in which he is sitting on a step in the garden, staring sadly into the lens.

At Tudor House, James was at ease with his teachers, popular with his peers and excelled at just about everything. He played for the Firsts at rugby and cricket, and captained the school at cricket and tennis. He was a senior chorister, starred in the school play and won prizes for most subjects. Academically, he was also above average, especially at mathematics, which was taught by the headmaster,

Bob Darke. 'He was a pretty smart fella,' Darke remembers, 'who grasped the concepts quickly. He *understood* the subject.'

He was also quite definitely not dyslexic, despite the claims he and Kerry made over the years. In his last year at Tudor House James won the reading prize, which involved all the contestants standing up in front of the school and reading aloud from a piece of literature they had never seen before. 'James could not have done that if he was dyslexic,' says Darke, who was one of the judges. Furthermore, he played the lead role in the school play, *The Flying Pieman*, for which he had to learn lines and sing solos. He would have struggled with that had he been dyslexic, according to Richards, but he was 'great, he carried the show'.

For all the freedom that Tudor House allowed its boys, it was an old-fashioned school with a set routine, as befitted an institution that had educated an Australian prime minister, Malcolm Fraser, and a Nobel Prize-winning novelist, Patrick White. 'We had classes all day,' one of James's schoolmates recalls, 'then sport and play, dinner, prep, showers, bed and lights out. Saturday evening there was always a movie in the hall. There was a projector and a rough sort of screen up on the stage and we'd have to sit on these cold steel chairs, but you could bring a blanket in to keep warm, and it was always fun.'

The film show was also precisely choreographed according to Alan Caradus, the teacher who ran it. 'The boys would have showers at 4.30 p.m., then they would get ready for dinner. Dinner was at 5.25 p.m. They came out of dinner at 5.55 p.m., went across and got their woollen blazers, then lined up in the gym with their eiderdowns over their shoulders and their teddy bears under their arms. Then they paraded down the aisle to their seats, these cold metal seats. Then they watched the film.'

James, who was one of a select band of projectionists, would sit up in a little box at the top of a metal ladder, ensuring that nothing went wrong. Sadly, there is no picture of him clutching his eiderdown and teddy.

Even as a ten-year-old, James stood out from the crowd because he was taller than most of his classmates and because his father was Kerry Packer. It was hard to get lost in the background when your cricket bat was signed by every member of every team in World Series Cricket. It was hard, too, if you arrived for your first day at school in a chauffeur-driven Jaguar, with another chauffeur-driven Jaguar carrying your luggage. But James was obviously inured to all this. Bob Darke was struck by how composed the young boy was on his first day. While all the other kids tugged at their parents, asked questions and demanded attention, James sat cross-legged on the floor outside the headmaster's study playing quietly with a toy. He was 'a very self-contained little boy,' says Darke. 'He didn't cry when they left.'

One possible explanation for this is that he knew it would do him no good to cling to his parents. Only a couple of weeks earlier, James had been sent to a cricket camp at Cranbrook School, just down the road from the Packer family home, and found himself in one of the boarding houses on a Sunday afternoon facing a week away from his family. Also in the dormitory was a keen young cricketer called Malcolm Knox, later the *Sydney Morning Herald*'s cricket correspondent, who was struck by how desperately unhappy he was:

We were unpacking when a pasty, freckly boy dumped himself on the next bunk with his bag. The boy sat there and cried. My grandmother made his bed for him. She and my mother helped him sort out his clothes. He sat with his face in his hands and kept

crying. I don't know if he moved from the bed at all. That night
. . . I fell asleep to the sound of my lonely neighbour's weeping.

The boy, of course, was James Packer, who was upset at being abandoned by his parents. He was gone the next day.

It's hard to know how much to make of such an incident, but
it is a constant theme in James's life that Kerry thought him too
soft and a mummy's boy. Almost everyone who recalls discussing
James with his father over the years says that Kerry ordered them
to give the boy a hard time, beat him about the head and toughen
him up a bit. If this was Kerry's way of letting his son know he
was adored, it surely didn't work. But after the abuse Kerry had
suffered from his own father, it was probably the only way he
knew.

Certainly, Kerry found it hard—if not impossible—to give
praise, so it wasn't surprising that James craved it from others. One
boy at Tudor House remembers him chasing the headmaster after
a maths lesson 'to offer his knowledge of the eight-times table',
which he then began to recite unasked. 'He was eager to please,'
says the schoolmate, 'not in a suck-up way, just innocent.'

During his two years at Tudor House, James was visited every
fortnight by his mother Ros—a 'warm', 'wonderful' woman—who
came by car and stayed at Milton Park with Kerry's cousins, the
Baillieus. His father came down once a term and always arrived in
the Channel Nine helicopter, touching down on the playing fields,
which had to be cleared so it was safe for him to land. This was
another thing that marked James out from his classmates. The only
other person who had ever arrived this way was Rupert Murdoch
when he flew up one day in the Channel Ten helicopter to see if
the school was right for Lachlan. It wasn't.

As soon as Kerry's chopper came to rest on the oval, the big man would jump out to be greeted by Bob Darke, a formidable figure in his own right, who always went down to meet him. 'I liked Kerry tremendously,' Darke says. 'I found him straightforward and interesting to talk to, but then I didn't have to do business with him.'

On his visits, Kerry only ever bothered to deal with the boss, talking to James's housemaster just once, apparently in error. 'I think he mistook me for someone else,' says Phillip Richards. 'The subject of the conversation was how I could win my fortune betting on the races. It went something like, "First, always go. Second, never bet on the TAB. And third, only ever bet on horses that are 6-1 or 7-1." I'm not a betting man, I've only been to the races once in my life, so I never took advantage of his advice. And he never made the mistake of speaking to me again.'

Naturally, Kerry played a leading role in the Fathers and Sons cricket match when it came around at the end of the year. And, naturally, he created a lasting impression, especially after landing his helicopter on the square before captaining one of the sides. 'He came out to bat and proceeded to whack about ten fours and sixes in a row off the two eleven-year-old boys bowling to him,' says Geoffrey Boyden, whose father captained the opposing side. 'After a short while, he said, "That's enough" and walked off the pitch. You would have thought he would have given us some catches or made us run for the ball and then done a good job of getting out without making it look deliberate. But that obviously wasn't Kerry's style.'

'He didn't bother running much, just hit a lot of boundaries,' Tudor House's cricket master, Ken Walker, recalls. 'He was smoking back in those days—most of the fathers did—and I remember him in the slips taking a purler of a catch with a smoke hanging out of his mouth. He didn't look like a sportsman or an athlete, but he had very good hand-eye coordination.'

Kerry's showing-off did not endear him to many people, and some teachers gave James a hard time because of it. Others suggested the boy was getting preferential treatment, and more than his fair share of prizes, because his father was so rich and powerful. In James's last year at Tudor House, these critics were given some ammunition when he was made joint school captain. Some asked how he got the job, others why he only got half of it. The position had been split like this only three times in thirty years.

James would not have been considered at all in a good year says Bob Darke, who adds that he was confident and a natural leader but had little time for the stragglers and liked being the centre of attention. 'Was he above himself? No. He wouldn't have dared be above himself with Kerry in the background.'

If any favouritism was shown, it wasn't to reward Kerry for donations to the school, because he made none. But after James left he did become a benefactor, telling Darke he wanted to start a Frank Packer scholarship to help children from poorer families. By the time the headmaster had worked on him, Kerry had agreed to finance two years at Tudor House and eight at King's School, Parramatta, paying all fees and boarding costs, plus skiing trips and excursions and a clothing allowance. 'We had a policeman's kid, we had farmers' kids, we had a minister's kid, a single-parent child,' says Alan Caradus, adding that part of the deal for the lucky recipient was to have dinner with the Packers.

The scholarship lasted for fourteen years—from 1981 until 1995—before Kerry became convinced that he was being taken advantage of. The shop assistants at David Jones, where the scholarship students were asked to shop for their school needs, would bring out the most expensive items if they knew he was paying, says Darke, and Kerry always believed that the boys' parents added things on for themselves. For some reason he always suspected the world was out to get him.

However happy James was boarding at Tudor House, he did not want to be exiled from home for six more years of senior school, and with Ros's help he won a reprieve. In January 1980, at the age of twelve, he started as a day boy at Cranbrook in Sydney, where Kerry had been thirty years before. His first-year photo there shows him kneeling in the front row with his collar askew, squinting against the sun, looking like a real-life Ginger Meggs.

But while he was now only 500 metres from the family home he no longer enjoyed a charmed life. Cranbrook had five times as many pupils as Tudor House and he was right at the bottom of the heap. Instead of starring in the school production of *Oliver* he would be just one of Fagin's chorus. And instead of playing for the First XV at rugby, he was turning out for one of the weakest teams in his year.

Academically, he was also back in the pack, winning none of the prizes, cups and awards that had piled up in Bowral. One teacher remembers him as 'halfway down the class or worse' and says he was 'full of himself, lazy and a chatterbox'. Another who knew him well says he didn't take his studies seriously, didn't do his homework and scored regular detentions. A third confirms 'he just wasn't interested'. James's own account is that he 'bludged' his way through without distinction.

After his 'brilliant career' at Tudor House, this was a huge disappointment to his father, who became angry and upset as the years went on at how badly his son was doing. Claiming that James was in danger of being expelled, Kerry's explanation was that his son must be dyslexic, as he had been. James's teachers were equally certain that he was not, because he could read, write and spell perfectly well. Nevertheless, Kerry was so sure of his diagnosis that he hauled in a specialist from South Africa to help. According to one of Kerry's close friends, the expert's remedy was to put James in a hanging chair and whirl him round to spin the dyslexia out of him. It seems extraordinary that Kerry could have trusted such quackery, but the friend is adamant he did.

When Kerry wasn't blaming dyslexia for James's inadequacies, he was accusing Cranbrook of failing him: Gretel was doing well at Ascham, he told friends, because the teaching there was better. It didn't occur to him that his daughter (who was actually winning prizes) might be smarter or more diligent than his son. Nor did he consider the fault might be his, in that he never missed an opportunity to tell James to forget about university. It was a long-held Packer tradition to ridicule academia and Kerry upheld it with vigour. All James would do there, Kerry told friends, was mix with a bunch of amateurs who knew nothing about the real world, pick up dangerous left-wing ideas and learn how to smoke marijuana. Consequently, James had little incentive to excel.

When it came to cricket, James came closer to living up to his father's expectations, even though it was an impossible task. Kerry was convinced his son could be a champion but was sure he needed to be toughened up first. Here, his main weapon was a baseball-training machine, bought in the USA, which could be adjusted to swing or bounce a cricket ball at terrifying speeds of up to 120 mph, 20 per cent faster than Brett Lee and Jeff Thomson at their best.

It was Kerry's idea of relaxation to wind this contraption up to its full speed and go into bat, whacking the balls as hard as he could.

'Turn the fucking thing up,' he would shout to whoever was operating it. 'Turn the fucking thing up. It's not fucking fast enough.'

Usually, the man at the controls was former English Test all-rounder Barry Knight, who came over every Saturday morning to the Packers' Bellevue Hill compound in Sydney's eastern suburbs to coach James and his father in the net Kerry had built on his disused helipad. When he was teaching James, Knight liked to wind the machine back to a safe speed for a fourteen-year-old boy, but Kerry was always insisting he turn it back up. 'What are you trying to do?' he would ask. 'Turn the boy into a wuss? He's a man, he can face it.'

Kerry always wanted to outdo his son in these sessions, to show who was best. And while James tried hard to rise to the challenge, matching it with Kerry could be suicidal. On one occasion, Kerry was desperate to use a new bat that had just been flown in from England. It had been raining that morning and the fake grass covering the pitch was still wet and slippery, but Kerry was adamant. 'I don't care,' he said, 'I want to use the bat!'

'It was about the tenth ball, over 100 mph as usual,' says Knight, 'and you know sometimes you get those frozen moments? I saw the ball frozen in mid air, heading straight for Kerry's chest. It hit him square in the side underneath his arm. He wobbled but didn't fall. "Sorry!" I said immediately.'

Kerry's first reaction was to smash his brand new bat as hard as he could against the cyclone fence in a fury of pain and anger. Then he came marching out of the net, straight at Knight, who thought he would be the next to get hit: 'I was a grown man at the time, but he still hadn't said a word and I was pretty scared having him bearing down on me. But to my relief he walked straight past me and into the house.'

'What do we do now?' Knight asked James.

'I don't know,' James replied.

Knight decided to follow Kerry into the house, to apologise and ask if he was OK.

'No fucking excuses,' came Packer's reply. 'It was my own fault.'

It was part of Kerry's character that he had to be top dog, and there was no better way to prove this than by daring visitors to take him on. One weekend he challenged Clive Lloyd, the West Indian Test captain, to face the machine at its maximum 120 mph. 'Not a chance,' said Lloyd. 'You can't do it. It's too dangerous.'

'Yes you can,' said Kerry, who promptly marched into the nets to show him, before emerging triumphant to goad the West Indian captain again. 'Come on,' he said to Lloyd. 'You're the batsman.' But still the Test star refused to play.

With a father like this, there was no way James could do anything other than fall short. But by the time he was seventeen he had become a decent cricketer and was opening the batting for Cranbrook's First XI. Occasionally, his father would come to watch and sit on the upper level of the ground, away from the other spectators, with the inevitable result that James would play badly. Normally, he was a flamboyant, attacking batsman, but when Kerry was around he went on the defensive because he was so desperate to impress. If James did get runs, Kerry would bask in the glory. But if he got out, which he commonly did when his father was watching, Kerry would swear and go home.

Normally Kerry didn't go to away games, but when James was selected for the Combined Associated Schools XI—which was more than his father had ever achieved—the old man was sufficiently impressed to jump in the Mercedes and trek up to Barker College on Sydney's Upper North Shore. James promptly came out to open the batting and face the first ball of the match, which turned out to be a bouncer. Despite all the hard work with the ball machine, and the hook shots he had been practising with Knight, James was beaten for pace, got a top edge and was caught behind. Out first ball!

'I could see James marching off the field towards his dad to go and explain himself,' says Knight, 'so I followed him up there. Kerry looked pretty unimpressed, and although it wasn't funny at the time, it's pretty funny in retrospect. He said, "I don't go this far on my holiday. What am I going to do now?" He made his way back to the car park and to the Merc, and he got Ken Callendar [the *Daily Telegraph*'s racing correspondent] on the phone and spent the rest of the day betting on the horses. You could see the car up on the hill in the car park, the front door open and Kerry's leg sticking out. I tell you, it was some ride home in the car. I don't think there was one word spoken between us between Hornsby and Double Bay. And Kerry never came to an away game again.'

Naturally, the harder it was to impress his dad, the more James wanted to do just that. He trained twice as hard as the other boys, on top of his Saturday morning coaching, and took it all very seriously. 'Things meant a lot to him, perhaps more so than other boys, and certainly more than he wanted to let on,' says another well-known English cricketer, Peter Roebuck, who coached Cranbrook's First XI while James was there. 'He had the usual swagger and feigned nonchalance of a young boy, but I could tell he was really very serious about being successful, at cricket and I suspect in general.' James would tell Roebuck half-jokingly that he was the third generation so he would inevitably bring the great family crashing down. 'He was proud of being a Packer,' Roebuck recalls, 'but at the same time he was wary of what was expected of him. I remember saying to him once, "James, you're going to have to deny your father one of these days," and James said, "I know, but not yet."'

But if James carried the burden of Kerry's expectations and had to cope with the bar being set impossibly high, he did not suffer the brutal childhood his father had endured. Kerry was hard on him, says Knight, but never aggressive. 'He could be severe, but he was also fair. And James was a very well-mannered and lovely boy, anyway. He certainly didn't answer back to Kerry. No one did. He just wasn't the kind of man you talked back to.'

Knight used to stay and chew the fat with Kerry after their coaching sessions, sitting in the big study with its leather couches and banks of televisions and remembers it as the perfect home environment. 'He was very tactile and loving with his family. Gretel would come in to say hello and Kerry would always kiss her and ask how she was. Ros would often be gardening, and I remember sometimes she'd leave a plate of raw green beans, topped and tailed, on a plate in the kitchen for James to eat after the coaching session. She obviously wanted him to grow up healthy. In many ways they were the sort of classic Happy Family on the Hill.'

A similar impression might have been gleaned from the set of family photos Kerry kept on his desk in Park Street or from the family album the *Australian Women's Weekly* published after his death in 2005, which showed a beaming, benevolent father playing in the swimming pool with Gretel or having fun on the farm up at Ellerston. And family friends would have confirmed that Ros was a home-loving, devoted mother. She was quiet, down to earth, with no pretences and 'did a wonderful job bringing up those two kids', says one.

But life at the Packers' wasn't always idyllic. Those who spent time in the family circle in the 1980s have shocking memories of Kerry's behaviour. 'He was a dreadful bully and had terrible tantrums,' one friend remembers. 'Everyone was in fear of him and everyone was on tenterhooks when he was around.'

Another recalls an incident towards the end of the 1980s when Kerry sat down with his polo players for a buffet lunch at Ellerston. 'Kerry looked at the curries and quiches on offer and snarled, "I'm not eating any of this shit. Get me a fucking hamburger." Then, while we all sat waiting for his meal to arrive, he picked up a big silver candelabra from the table and started waving it around, asking Ros, "Where the fuck did we get this anyway?"'

Not surprisingly, in view of this behaviour, James was terrified of his father and would occasionally warn friends, 'Dad's really upset today. Whatever you do, don't argue back.' Certainly, James never did.

For his last year at Cranbrook, Kerry sent James back to board so he could concentrate on his Higher School Certificate, in which his prospects were not good. At first, Kerry demanded the boy be put in the toughest house, then he changed his mind and instructed the school to put him in Street, where he himself had been. Finally, he got annoyed because the school was too soft on him. And for once he may have been right. Fabian Muir, who was also in Street, recalls the Packer family butler bringing a bottle of vintage Krug champagne to the boarding house to settle an argument about whether or not it was superior to the 1980 Dom Perignon.

Stories like this made James famous at Cranbrook and he attracted a coterie of fans. 'There were a few hangers-on around him, sycophants, basically,' says Muir. 'There was this almost ridiculous obsequiousness around him, people laughing at every joke he made,' says another schoolmate more bluntly.

James would be dogged by this problem throughout his life. 'I think he had a weakness for being influenced by others,' says Muir. Or, as the other schoolmate puts it, 'He was quite sheltered and susceptible to being conned.' It was a conclusion many would reach over the years: that James was a nice guy but easily led.

This is something one could never have said about Kerry, whom Cranbrook's teachers found to be a loud, crass and aggressive parent. One master recalls him 'swearing his head off' down at the school oval with some of his World Series Cricket stars, with students nearby, making no attempt to moderate his language. Another says Kerry made no attempt to hide his womanising. 'James would tell us when things weren't great at home,' he recalls. 'He'd say, "Sorry, I'm not too good today. Dad's back with the mistress."'

'I don't think James always admired everything Kerry was about,' says Muir. 'He had great love and esteem for his father and he looked up to him, but there was this other side that he found unattractive and difficult to deal with.'

And never was it more difficult than in September 1984, during James's penultimate year at school, when the Fairfax-owned *National Times* published confidential case summaries from the Costigan Royal Commission into the Painters and Dockers Union. These included an explosive dossier on the 'Goanna', a high-profile 'Sydney businessman' whom Costigan's investigators suspected of involvement in tax evasion, fraud, pornography, drug-running and murder. Two weeks later, Kerry Packer confirmed what many already suspected by outing himself as the Goanna and going on the attack, with the help of his young corporate counsel Malcolm Turnbull.

Even though James's father was eventually cleared, the uproar the entire affair created would have been hard enough for the seventeen-year-old to handle, but it was made even worse because Kerry became so depressed he contemplated suicide. On top of that, Cranbook's school magazine decided to publish its own Goanna cartoon. Twenty-five years on, all copies of the offending issue of the *Cranbrook Chronicle* have been destroyed so it's impossible to judge whether its joke was funny. But those involved have not forgotten the trouble it caused.

The *Chronicle* normally came out on a Thursday afternoon when James was at cricket practice, but the session was washed out by rain and a pile of magazines was dumped in James's house before the eagle-eyed headmaster, Mark Bishop, was able to stop distribution. James took a copy home to Kerry, who was furious and rang the school to tear into the headmaster. Teachers and prefects were immediately instructed to confiscate all copies, many being snatched from boys' hands as they walked out the front gate. The students who had produced the magazine were then ordered to cut the back page off every copy. All were convinced they were going to be expelled.

The entire episode was made worse when the *Sydney Morning Herald* ran a story about the incident, which helped convince Kerry it was a Fairfax plot. He was aware that the history master, David Thomas, whose job it was to supervise the magazine, was married to a member of the Fairfax family, and he now insisted that Thomas be sacked.

There are not many people who have stood up to the Packers over the years, but Cranbrook's School Council did just that. It informed 'Mr Packer' that it alone took decisions about who was on the school's staff, then offered him a sop by suggesting he ring the master in question and seek an apology. One can imagine how terrifying this experience must have been for David Thomas, who told his colleagues that Kerry had threatened to send someone round to take care of him.

Sadly, history does not relate how James's school career ended. Cranbrook stopped publishing its pupils' Higher School Certificate results in 1984, which was probably just in time to spare James's blushes. Suffice to say, he was not in the merit list published by the Board of Studies. One friend remembers him scoring below 200 (out of a possible 500), another has him in the high 200s. Either way, it was nothing to brag about and his father would not have been pleased.

CHAPTER 2
FUCKING STUPID

That's a fucking stupid idea . . . No one but an idiot
would suggest that.

Kerry was forever telling James's teachers at Cranbrook that the
boy was 'too soft' and needed to 'work in a bloody salt mine' to
toughen him up. But since there were no salt mines in the Packer
empire, Kerry opted for the next best thing, which was to send
James jackerooing for a year on one of his huge cattle stations up
north. And so it was in February 1986, two months after leaving
school, that James found himself bumping down onto the private
airstrip at Newcastle Waters in the rugged but beautiful Barkly
Tableland, halfway between Alice Springs and Darwin.

Kerry had bought the 10 000 square kilometre property in 1983
after falling in love with the place while recuperating from the first
of his many heart attacks. The owners had taken him on a grand
tour, across the Kimberley and out to the islands, and Kerry had
adored every moment, not least because he could shoot anything

that moved. He had paid $6 million for it, then spent millions more on new fences and artesian bore holes and restocked it with 25 000 Brahmin heifers to produce big, fast-growing, drought-proof calves. Finally, he had built a lavish eight-bedroom mansion with a 20-metre high steel roof that could be seen flashing in the sunlight from miles away.

When James arrived there were about thirty people living on the station, with a mechanic, an accountant and a few domestic staff at the homestead and everyone else out bush in two stock camps up to 120 kilometres away. James was sent to one of these, which consisted of a caravan and camp fire and not much else. There was no electricity, no radio contact, no mobile phones and, of course, no women. As head stockman Lindsay McLean put it, women were 'nothing but trouble'.

In these primitive conditions, James and his fellow jackeroos camped out for two months at a time, helping to muster 45 000 head of cattle so they could be branded, castrated and weaned. It was hard, dangerous and physically exhausting work because the animals were big and wild. Branding a calf, for example, involved two men putting a leg rope on the animal and wrestling it to the ground, then stamping its flesh with red-hot metal.

The horses were a handful, too, especially for inexperienced riders like James. But the worst of it was the heat. This was harsh country with daytime temperatures reaching 40° Celsius. Rated as 'uncomfortable for humans' 200 days a year, stockmen would sometimes be in the saddle without a drink for seven hours at a stretch—although not at the height of summer.

Even for boys from the bush it was pretty hard yakka, but for a city kid like James it was a whole lot tougher. He was tall and thin, with muscles that hadn't been hardened by manual work, and he now found himself working sixteen hours a day, seven days a week, for eight weeks on end. Fresh out of school and just eighteen years old, he was also forced to take care of himself for the first time. Like the other jackeroos, he had only his saddle, his swag and a couple of pairs of jeans and T-shirts, which he had to wash in a horse trough if he washed them at all. There was no butler with canapés and Krug and no TV. Nor was there much sitting around the fire singing songs and spinning yarns. By the end of the day they were all too tired to do anything but wash, eat, have a cup of tea and collapse into bed. They couldn't even have a beer because the camps were dry.

Brian Nillson, one of the head stockmen, remembers James being green and immature when he arrived. 'He hated the early starts and he hated washing in the turkey nests', which were big mounds of earth filled in winter with freezing cold water. 'In fact, he hated being there,' says Nillson, 'and he was not shy about telling us. He thought we were cavemen, living one thousand years behind the times.' But he soon learnt to handle a horse and he never shirked the work.

It wasn't long before James opened up to his new companions, telling them he had wanted to go to university but had been forced by Kerry to come to the university of life instead. So they painted a big sign on the camp caravan saying 'College of Knowledge' to remind him. They also played tricks, waking him once in the middle of the night and turning on the generator and lights to make him think it was morning. But for the most part he was treated like everyone else, in that he was neither bullied nor shown any favours.

At the end of each spell out bush, James and the other jackeroos would ride back to Newcastle Waters, filthy, thin and totally exhausted. Without stopping to eat, they would drive straight to the nearest 'town' of Elliott, which had a school, a post office and a petrol station, and dive into the only pub. Hardly any of them could hold their drink, especially after two months' abstinence, and James was no exception. With two beers inside him, he became 'hard to handle' according to Nillson. 'He would puff out his chest and he certainly knew who he was.'

The highlights of the year were weekends in Tennant Creek, for the rodeo and races, and Katherine, for the annual show, which jackeroos spent getting drunk or trying to get laid. 'I can't tell you what happened in Katherine,' says Nillson, 'but James ended up asleep on the bar in Tennant Creek. And I can tell you the barmaid wasn't too thrilled.'

Back at the homestead, James lived in the stockmen's quarters where he had a private room with a wire bed and mattress but no sheets or air conditioning. It stank, too, because the stockmen didn't wash their clothes that often. But even if his status as the owner's son didn't score him a bed in Kerry's magnificent mansion, it did win him a favour from the housekeeper, Liz Rae, who took pity on him and did his washing.

The station manager, Dick Wilson, remembers James as 'one of the most well-mannered lads' they ever had. Wilson took him down to the local lake one day to water ski with the other jackeroos, and was struck by how polite he was. While all the other boys fought over who should go first, James sat quietly, waiting his turn until everyone had finished. He then asked whether he might have a go. 'He was well brought up,' says Wilson. 'There was a lot of his mother in him and she was one of the nicest women you'll ever meet.'

Ros Packer impressed everyone by bringing up a cake from Sydney to thank them all for looking after her son. Kerry, however, had far more important things to do than trek up to the Territory to see his boy. But when he fell sick in London in late 1986 and was rushed into hospital to have a cancerous kidney removed, James flew to England to be by his side, using the crisis as an excuse to cut short his sentence.

Looking back on the experience a few years later, James admitted he did not enjoy his time in the Territory, but was sure it had been good for him. Typically, he also managed to praise his father for sending him there. 'There have been times when my pampering has been taken away,' he explained to Peter FitzSimons in 1994, 'where Dad actively tried to make my life, for short periods, difficult . . . but he was doing it to make it easy for me to keep my head on my shoulders, and to make me realise the way most of the world lives.'

Kerry also made sure his daughter Gretel understood what life was like for common people. While still at Ascham School in Sydney's eastern suburbs, she did work experience at the *Australian Women's Weekly*, making tea, running errands and catching the bus to the office, even though Kerry drove there with his chauffeur. She then worked in the kitchens at Ansett, preparing food from 5 a.m. A year older than her brother, she was a gentle, intelligent person who was given a much easier time than James by her father. But she was also a girl, so Kerry did not see her as a rival, and she was never going to inherit the family fortune, so she did not need to be toughened up. Kerry was adamant that Gretel would get married and stay at home, as all other Packer women had done. And James was just as keen to ensure she never took his birthright.

One family friend says both children flirted with the idea of doing something else entirely—that Gretel wanted to be an actress and James a producer—and claims they enrolled in a drama course while Kerry was overseas. But there was no chance of them getting their way. Kerry wanted James to learn how to look after the Packer billions and was determined there should be no distractions.

Most sons of dominant fathers are lucky enough to find relief—through travel, university or a job outside the family business—but James's year in the Northern Territory would be the closest he ever came to getting away, and this was decreed and arranged by his father at a place where everyone did his father's bidding. It was hardly breaking free. 'Kerry led James by the nose from a very early age,' another family friend observes. 'They were extremely close; in fact they were too close. It's sad he didn't go to university or get a broader education, because his whole life has been about business and materialism. All he cares about is creating wealth and making money because that's all Kerry ever taught him. And he didn't have a lot of options, because he had to do what he was told.'

James's education would include lessons from some of the smartest people in finance and politics, such as James Goldsmith, Jim Wolfensohn, Jacob Rothschild, Malcolm Turnbull and Neville Wran. But he also had to knuckle down and learn the family business, as Kerry had done thirty years before, and this began in earnest in 1987 when he clocked on at Channel Nine's *Today* show as a researcher. After that, he moved on to sell ads at the *Bulletin* and then the *Women's Weekly*. Typically, Kerry told Graham Lawrence, ACP's advertising director, to 'beat him up and make his life a misery', issuing similar instructions to the *Bulletin*'s Peter Miller to give him 'a good flogging'. But, just as typically, neither did what they were asked because there was no knowing how soon their battered trainee might become a vengeful proprietor, especially with Kerry in poor health.

James took life easy, much as his old man had done thirty years earlier. He turned up for work every day, but didn't bust a gut and soon found advertising pretty much sold itself. 'All he had to do,' says Miller, 'was ring up and say "I'm James Packer" and they'd say, "Great, come on over."' He was polite, charming and a good salesman, and Kerry's son, which was probably enough to clinch the deal on its own. Occasionally, his father inquired how he was doing, and sometimes he was told. One junior employee jumped into the lift with Kerry one morning and blurted out that James was having fun. 'He's not supposed to be having fucking fun,' the boss roared back.

But Kerry was keen for his son to enjoy himself in traditional Packer fashion, telling his executives in the bar one night that he had bought James a couple of hookers for his birthday and sent them down to Perisher to show the boy a good time. One of Kerry's closest friends tells a similar story in which James supposedly fell in love with a girl who seduced him, only to have his father reveal afterwards that he had hired the young woman himself. Kerry did this sort of thing 'all the time', according to a family friend.

Back at the office, however, James was cutting a swathe through the female staff without any help. One woman who worked alongside him says he spent half the time on the phone checking his shares and the other half chasing her. He was ten years younger than her but not in the least put off. He was charming and persistent, and refused to take no for an answer. And she was not the only one he was chasing.

But if there were echoes of Kerry in this alpha-male behaviour, James was actually very different to his father. He was soft at heart, took life seriously and was touchingly naive. He confided to one girlfriend that he had given up drinking so he wouldn't kill too many brain cells because he wanted to be prime minister and needed to be in tip-top shape when the call came.

James was encouraged to dream such dreams by his mother and sister, who thought he was so brilliant he was capable of anything. 'Ros was a real Lady Macbeth,' says one Packer family friend. 'She adored James and wanted her son to be king.' His grand ambitions were also encouraged by the extraordinary life the Packers led, which was reminiscent of royalty. According to staff who worked at Bellevue Hill over the years, Kerry's every whim had to be catered for. Each morning, there would be a delivery of fresh fish and oysters to the kitchen, even though the master of the house wasn't fond of seafood, in case he decided he wanted to eat them for dinner. Every night, the cook would also roast a joint of beef and a leg of lamb for the same reason.

For his part, James would wake up to discover the butler had put the morning newspapers by his bed during the night. He would fly to Ellerston from the beach house at Palm Beach on Sydney's northern peninsula and take it for granted that his wardrobe arrived before him. Staff would pack up his clothes, put them in the chopper and hang them up again by the time he was ready to change. Back at Bellevue Hill, his valet would fill the cars with petrol and turn them around in the driveway so they were facing in the right direction when he wanted to leave.

Kerry did his best to add reality to this fairytale life by keeping James on a tight rein financially in the hope that he would work for his living and not squander the family fortune. But he was never as tough as Sir Frank had been. The old tyrant had insisted Kerry knock on his office door to collect his wages and had confiscated half his pay to cover rent at Bellevue Hill.

Kerry was also torn by conflicting desires. On the one hand, he wanted to show his children he loved them; on the other, he wanted to ensure they weren't spoilt, which was an impossible task when he had billions of dollars in the bank. Consequently, he lurched from one extreme to the other. He bought Gretel a secondhand Mazda 323 with 100 000 km on the clock for her first car, then gave her a $290 000 Cartier diamond choker and an unbelievably lavish party for her twenty-first birthday. Similarly, he gave James a new Mercedes Sports when he came of age as a reward for not smoking, but baulked at paying for a party. Or so said Rene Rivkin, who claimed to have footed the bill for James's twenty-first because 'his father was too mean to give him one'.

The flamboyant stockbroker became friends with James in the late 1980s after Kerry press-ganged him into teaching the boy about the risks of investing. As Rivkin told the story, Kerry phoned one day to announce, 'I'm sending my fucking son over and I want you to lose him some fucking money on the stock market so he understands the fucking value of the fucking dollar.' But as so often happened with Kerry's instructions, Rene ignored them completely and made money for James instead. Worse than that, he became almost a surrogate father in Kerry's long absences abroad. James told friends naively that he was impressed by Rene's family values. Kerry told his mates more bluntly that Rivkin was a 'poofter' and he feared James might become one too.

Rene was surrounded by beautiful young men who lounged around on his boat, roared about in his cars or used his money to trade tips on the stock exchange. And outsiders were suspicious about the role they played in the stockbroker's life. Kerry clearly shared these suspicions but, according to Rivkin, was also jealous of his relationship with James, which is why he was eventually banned from seeing the boy. 'It gave his father the shits that we got so close. And so his father withdrew permission to be up close to me,' Rene told Andrew Denton in 2003.

A friend of the Packers, who knew all three in the 1980s, believes that Kerry 'didn't like the competition and didn't like Rene's ostentation. Kerry did whatever he wanted, whenever he wanted, with his mistresses, his prostitutes and his gambling, but he did it privately and discreetly. Rene probably did 1/20th of what Kerry did, but he ensured everybody knew what it was.'

Rivkin regarded Kerry as a good mate, and was shocked and saddened by his banishment. But he was not the first to discover the Packers could toss friends away when they no longer had a use for them. One old acquaintance believes James had a similarly lopsided view of loyalty. Outside his inner circle, who were almost all boys he had been to Cranbrook with, he found it hard to develop real friendships and tended to drop people without warning. But with so much money, it was always hard for him to know who were his friends and who was just sucking up, as an incident in London illustrates.

In 1988 James was sent to the United Kingdom for the next stage of his training. His arrival was heralded by a big dinner party at Annabel's, the swanky Mayfair night club owned by billionaire businessman Sir James Goldsmith and John Aspinall, whose son Damian was one of the hosts. The two rich kids had much in common: they had powerful, dominant, difficult fathers, had failed to shine at school and were desperate to make their mark. But things still got off to an awkward start. As Aspinall later explained, 'An English twat who had never met Jamie before said, "I would like to propose a toast to Jamie, not because of who you are and how much you've got, but because you are a true friend." At this point, everyone rose to their feet except Aspinall, who declared loudly, 'I am not your friend. I have never met you. I only came here because of who you are, what you've got and how much I can get out of you.' Far from being upset by this rudeness, James was amused. Acknowledging a fellow king of the jungle, he marched around the table to shake his new friend's hand and tell him, 'You are the only genuine one here.'

James had not been in London long before he found himself ringside at one of the world's biggest takeover fights, in which his father joined forces with James Goldsmith and Lord Rothschild to mount a $28 billion bid for British American Tobacco (BAT). And as the battle unfolded, he was taken in hand by Goldsmith's abrasive right-hand man, Al Dunlap. Nicknamed Rambo in Pinstripes because of his brutal approach to business, the brash American was the ideal person to teach James what 'tough' really meant.

Dunlap found his student polite, respectful and eager to learn. He sat in meetings, took notes and asked questions afterwards, telling his mentor, 'I want to learn from you because Dad says you're the best.' One of Dunlap's plans at the time was to shut down a tyre plant in Ohio and sack all its workers. James asked why he had to be so hard on people, to which Al replied it was the way to succeed in business.

James stayed at the Savoy Hotel with Kerry while his father was in town and spent the rest of his time at the Packers' new estate in Sussex, playing polo and partying with his upper-class mates. Being the son of an Australian billionaire, his exploits soon filled the gossip columns. *Tatler* noted that he and Damian Aspinall co-hosted a Mad Hatters Tea Party at which topless girls hurled 3500 cream buns at the guests. The tabloids, meanwhile, published photos of him with a succession of attractive young women, including TV-AM's weather girl, Ulrika Jonsson, whom Kerry's old friend Bruce Gyngell 'discovered', and Tania Bryer, who eventually replaced Jonsson in front of the weather map. To Dunlap, it seemed the girlfriends were James's main concern. One night he turned up on his mentor's doorstep in a shocking state and announced bleakly, 'My life is over. I've broken up with Tania.'

By mid-1990 James was back in Australia, following respectfully two steps behind his father as they marched into Channel Nine to repossess the network from Alan Bond. And soon after that he was back on the *Today* show, where it became clear he did not share Kerry's love of television. As the months went by, the 'work experience billionaire' came to the office less and less. According to the show's executive producer, Steve Wood, James didn't enjoy being there one bit: 'My feeling was he hated it and wanted to know why the fuck he was there.' It was also obvious that he was not going to become a TV mogul. 'He didn't like it, he didn't get it, he didn't try to understand it,' says Wood. 'And Kerry was so good at television he was on a hiding to nothing. The last thing he needed to do was try to compete with his father in TV.'

Wood never told Kerry about James's lack of commitment and his boss never asked, which was just as well. 'The old man was incredibly tough on him and James was under his thumb,' Wood recalls. 'He was very careful what he did in front of his dad. He never smoked in front of him and I rarely saw him drink, but he did both to excess when his old man wasn't around. Was he scared of Kerry? Yeah, absolutely. Kerry treated James like he treated anybody else. He swore at him and called him a fucking idiot.'

It wasn't just at the office that Kerry behaved like this. James was given the job of organising entertainment for a party at Ellerston around this time and enlisted the manager of a famous Australian group to help. When the proposals were put to Kerry, he let rip at his son. 'That's a fucking stupid idea,' he told him. 'Why on earth would you want to do that? No one but an idiot would suggest that.'

Later that year, in October 1990, Kerry nearly died on the polo field at Warwick Farm in the semi-final of the Australian Open Polo Championships. His heart stopped for seven minutes and he was extraordinarily lucky to survive. Those who observed James coping with the crisis as his father lay lifeless on the grass were struck by how calm he appeared while he attempted to get Kerry's personal doctor, Bob Wright, on the phone, and by the way he seemed to take command of the situation.

Kerry later accused his son, half-jokingly, of wanting him dead, telling people with great relish, 'This young bloke was standing over me, waving me goodbye.' And perhaps he was closer to the mark than he realised. At best, Kerry was a difficult person to live with. At worst, he was impossible. And it was hardest for James because his loyalties were cruelly divided. Like many sons, he was desperate to win his father's love and approval. But he also loved his mother. Not only did Kerry bully Ros and treat her abominably at times, he also conducted an open affair with his young mistress, Julie Trethowan, whom he had been seeing since the early 1980s. James was hugely confused by this and unsure what to do. He would go out with his mother to the movies one night and with Julie the next, because he felt sorry for both of them.

There was no question Ros knew of Julie's existence and of Kerry's many other affairs over the years because he regularly spent nights at his penthouse in the Toft Monks Tower in Elizabeth Bay, which he kept staffed with a cook and butler. On occasions Julie also played hostess at Ellerston, where people would arrive for the weekend not knowing who was going to greet them. It was confusing for everyone, but especially for Packer's executives. Kerry would show up with Ros one night and Julie the next. Al Dunlap's wife Judy found it particularly distasteful. 'I liked Ros. She put up with a hell of a lot,' she says. 'I didn't particularly care for Kerry. We saw a lot, and that's why I didn't like him.'

Some maintained that Ros didn't leave because she loved Kerry and wanted to keep the family together. Others claimed she had threatened divorce in the mid-1970s, when he was entangled with Ita Buttrose, and had warned she would fight for custody of the children. James, for his part, told friends, 'Mum couldn't leave Dad.' But it was not clear whether Kerry's rage or Ros's loyalty to her family stood in the way of this course of action.

Whatever the truth—and no one but Ros knew for sure—it was a mystery that she stayed and a mystery how James managed to cope with it all. He loved his mother unreservedly, but admired his father and craved his respect. It was a conflict he would struggle to resolve until Kerry died.

CHAPTER 3
HIS FATHER'S SON

Jamie was a ludicrously gentle boy. He was also very
self-effacing. He has gone through a metamorphosis and
is now very much his father's son.

A week after his near death on the polo field, Kerry was back at
Warwick Farm to watch the final of polo's Australian Open. Sitting
in the back of his big white BMW, he was surrounded by TV camera-
men and reporters wanting to grab a picture of him and to ask about
his Lazarus act. As a scrum formed around the car, Packer's driver
managed to slip through and accelerate away, but he had gone only
20 metres before he was ordered to stop. Kerry flung open the rear
door, jumped out and came towards the startled media pack almost
at a run, homing in on the nearest cameraman. 'I'll tell you how I'm
feeling. Leave me alone, get out of my way,' he said, as he shoved his
hand into the lens and sent the cameraman spinning to the ground.

How the TV footage failed to make it onto Channel Nine's
Spectacular Dummy Spits will always be a mystery. The last time

the world had seen Kerry Packer he was lying on a stretcher, fat and freckly with tubes in his nose and an oxygen cylinder under his chin. Now he was charging at a TV crew like a large wounded animal. And he was not finished yet. Seeing another cameraman filming his attack, Kerry turned to grab the camera and rip out the tape. One of his minders then stepped in to punch the man twice, sending him crashing to the ground. Dizzily, the cameraman staggered to his feet and threatened to call the police, only to be told, 'Go ahead. Make my day.'

Despite his apparent immortality, James's father was by no means a good bet to make it through the next few years. He had lost one kidney to cancer and was still in some danger that the disease might spread. He had also suffered two major heart attacks and was doing everything he could to bring on the next. He smoked sixty cigarettes a day, lived on a diet of milkshakes and hamburgers, with the odd Fanta thrown in, and was 30 kilograms overweight, all of which combined to push his blood pressure sky high. Worse than that, there was a history of heart disease on both sides of his family. Aged fifty-three, he was one year younger than his grandfather Robert Clyde had been when he died of heart problems, and the same age his mother Gretel had been when her heart failed. Only his father, Sir Frank Packer, had lasted beyond sixty, and he had spent the last ten years of his life in terrible health. So Kerry's chances of living into the mid-1990s or beyond were slim, and he knew it. Consequently, he was determined to have as much fun as he could in the time he had left.

In the months that followed, he pulled back from the day-to-day running of the business and was rarely seen at ACP's Park Street headquarters or Channel Nine. Even when he was in Australia he often spent only two days a week in the office, flying down from Ellerston on a Sunday night and flying back again on Tuesday. More often he was overseas, gambling, golfing, playing polo or chasing women. In his absence his right-hand man, Trevor Kennedy, was left in charge of the shop. But when Kennedy departed in mid-1991 to run the Tourang consortium, which was spearheading Packer's bid for Fairfax, Kerry was forced to find a replacement.

He settled for James Goldsmith's sidekick, Al Dunlap, who had impressed with his ability to sack people and close companies during a brief spell working for the Packers in Australia in 1989–90. The big man invited Dunlap over to breakfast in his suite at the Savoy Hotel in London and told him bluntly that the Packer empire was in danger of collapse because the Australian economy was in such a mess. 'I'm losing everything,' said Kerry. 'I need you to come back and sort it out, and you're not leaving this room until you say yes.' Dunlap's brief was to knock the empire into shape so it could be handed over to James, and to train the boy up as quickly as possible so he was ready to assume the crown if Kerry died. After three hours of discussion, Al was ringing his wife Judy to ask whether she fancied another trip Down Under.

When he arrived in Australia, it seemed to Dunlap that he was only just in time. Cash was flowing out fast, the business was billions of dollars in debt and, in his opinion, on the fast track to bankruptcy. 'It was like the Roman Empire was collapsing,' he says. 'We had 401 companies and no one knew what they all did. Kerry had just gone out and bought things. There was a fluorescent lamp manufacturer in Hong Kong, a shipbuilder in Amsterdam. It was astonishing.' Dunlap promptly set about getting rid of 300 of these companies by closing them down or selling them, and shedding hundreds of jobs in the process.

Dealing with situations like this had earned Dunlap a reputation as the best turnaround man in the business and had made him millions along the way. It now won him a new nickname, Chainsaw, for the way he went about clearing everything in his path. With his gold Rolex and chunky gold signet ring, he was soon hated by almost everybody he dealt with. Richard Walsh, who ran the Packers' magazine division, thought him the 'most uncivilised, inhuman person' he had ever met and 'an absolute abomination', a man who appeared to enjoy firing people and liked to do it personally. James, on the other hand, both liked and admired Dunlap, and was impressed by his lack of emotion in taking hard decisions. 'He has shown me how hard you can push people,' he said.

This is important because Al was one of James's most important mentors. For two years in the early 1990s, the two men were daily by each other's side.

Nowadays, Dunlap is retired, in his seventies, and somewhat in disgrace. In 2002 he was charged with fraud by the US Securities and Exchange Commission and forced to pay US$15 million to the shareholders of Sunbeam, a company that received the Dunlap treatment before going bankrupt in 2001. He lives in Florida behind high, wrought-iron gates that part automatically as you approach. Half a kilometre up his private drive, which is flanked by oaks and magnolias, there is another set of gates, guarded by a pair of life-sized bronze lions. He is well known as a man who feels at home among predators.

When I visited him in February 2008 he came to the door in black slacks, a white shirt and grey silk jacket, which he quickly removed and folded when he saw I was more casually dressed. He then grabbed me and took me on a lightning tour of his life.

Dunlap is an ex-marine and a graduate of America's elite military academy, West Point, and has the gun, cap and uniform to prove it. The walls of his study—which is like a shrine to his life—are covered with pictures of thirty or forty famous people alongside Al, in loud blue jackets, loud red jackets, tuxedos or tennis gear, always with the biggest smile and always to the fore. He's there with Ronald Reagan, Norman Schwarzkopf, Al Haig, George W. Bush's brother Jeb, and a host of other famous figures, including Australia's John Howard. There's even a snap of Kerry Packer.

Also on display are testimonials from some of the big US companies he pulled back from the brink, including one from the directors of Scott Paper thanking Al for saving the company from oblivion and creating US$10 billion worth of shareholder value. Judy, Dunlap's wife of more than forty years, met him at Scott, in her home town in Wisconsin, when he was sacking scores of workers in the late 1960s. She cried when she found out how brutally he was treating the people she had been to school with, but chose to marry him in spite of her tears and has been by his side ever since. She is a charming, warm and intelligent woman, despite being Al's number one fan, and it is hard to believe he can be quite as bad as he is painted when someone such as Judy supports him.

Dunlap has been described as 'an asshole . . . a creep . . . a psychopath . . . a despicable human being' and more besides. Reviewers of the very unflattering 2003 biography *Chainsaw* have gone even further. One labelled him 'an hysterical, violent sociopath who, if his life had turned slightly differently, might well have ended up in prison, a mental hospital, or an early grave'. Another observed that at Sunbeam he 'ruled through total intimidation and with the exception of his right hand man, listened to nobody but himself'. A third said, 'Think of the most egotistical, arrogant, selfish, greedy,

low-class and verbally abusive manager from hell you can think of
. . . Al Dunlap is all of these things, and maybe more.'

Perhaps no man can live up to such a billing, or perhaps he has
mellowed over the years, but he didn't strike me as the monster his
enemies make out. He's crude and brash, with an ego that would
light up Manhattan, but he's smart and good company—in small
doses—even if all his stories glorify him. And his account of his two
years with the Packers is a real insight into the way they operated.

Dunlap's dictum was, 'You are not in business to be liked . . . If
you want a friend, get a dog.' And when he arrived in Australia in
1991 to work for Kerry, he was taking no chances. He brought two
long-haired German Shepherd dogs that had to spend six months
in quarantine. By the time they were out, he was at loggerheads with
his new boss. The clashes began when Al started removing Kerry's
friends and hangers-on from the Packer payroll, and continued
when he banned a whole lot more from the Packer-owned Perisher
ski resort, where half the regulars appeared to be having fun at
Kerry's expense. 'By the time you finish, I'm not going to have any
friends,' Kerry complained, only for Dunlap to snap back, 'The way
things are, you can't afford them.'

The next clash came when Al turned his attention to head office
and slashed the number of staff at Consolidated Press Holdings
from seventy to thirteen. One accountant was axed the day he
finished valuing a company asset for sale. He had a new house, a
mortgage and a new baby, and was being pushed onto the street
after fourteen years of loyal service. A long-serving driver was
sacked without warning, handed his money and sent home. Kerry
asked dryly if he and James were next on the list. When told they
were safe, he quipped, 'Oh, that's nice. I can go home and tell Ros
that me and the kid still have a job.'

For a time, the two men managed to avoid serious head-on conflict because Kerry was away playing polo or busy trying to buy Fairfax, and because he had hired Dunlap to get rid of dead wood and realised pain was necessary. But when Al started sharpening his axe to cut back Kerry's personal expenses, a fight was inevitable. 'The money he was spending whole towns could live on,' says Dunlap. 'He was gambling hundreds of millions of dollars on currency markets and he lost huge sums. I'd be trying to cut costs and get rid of billions of dollars of debt and he'd be doing all this crazy stuff. He was one of the largest traders in the world. I thought it was reckless and I told him. We had a helluva battle. It wasn't pleasant, but to me it was lunacy.' The two men almost came to blows. 'I thought he was going to sock me,' says Dunlap. For the next three days Kerry cut him dead and refused to speak to him, a sign of things to come.

James was stuck in the middle of these two dominant males as they banged heads, beat their chests and shouted each other down. He had always hated conflict and he tried his best to prevent it now. When Dunlap proposed something, he would try desperately to rein him in so his father wouldn't get angry. When that failed, he would try to persuade Kerry that Al was right and it had to be done. Dunlap would decide to sack a hundred people and James would protest, 'Dad won't like this, Dad won't like that'. Then he would go home and try to sell the idea to his father and Kerry would explode. It was a painful and difficult position to be in, being bullied and shouted at from both sides. And there was no escape. The three men occupied offices side by side on the third floor in Park Street, with Dunlap's office joined to James's via a connecting door. The apprentice was supposed to be at his master's elbow at all times to learn the trade.

Only on rare occasions did James succeed in getting Al to back down, and one of these involved Dunlap's attempt to close the Hyde Park Club, the gym in the basement at Park Street run by Kerry's mistress, Julie Trethowan. James asked Al if he could hold off for a day to give him time to talk to his father about it. The following morning James arrived with news that Kerry wanted the club to remain open because it made a profit, which Al told him was bullshit. James's next gambit was to claim that all the Packer executives were members and that its losses were funded by the private company. And when Dunlap wasn't moved by that either, James finally came clean: 'Well, you can't close it down because my father has a special relationship with Julie.' For once Dunlap backed off.

Sometimes, it all seemed too hard for the boy. One day he walked in to Al's office and said: 'I've been thinking, and this just isn't worth it. You chewed me out all day yesterday, then I got home and Dad chewed me out all last night. I've had enough.' Dunlap replied: 'What's your problem? You're the only son of the richest man in Australia, you're going to inherit billions of dollars when he dies. And you're telling me it isn't worth it?'

'It was like a light went on in his head,' Dunlap recalls. 'He looks at me and he says, "OK then, what do you want me to do?"'

After Dunlap had been there for nine months, James was promoted to General Manager of Consolidated Press Holdings and given a seat on the Channel Nine board. But whether his father intended him to wield real power was not clear. 'Kerry would eyeball you to say, "Forget he's my son, he's going to take orders from you,"' says Richard Walsh, 'and you'd think, "Yeah, right". So he's a trainee on one hand, but he's also about to become Australia's richest man.'

'James would not get in when others got into work,' recalls Walsh, 'and he wouldn't do the things he should be doing. Sometimes he had an excuse—Kerry would be chewing the fat with him or had whisked him off to play polo in Argentina—other times he didn't. It was hard to give him tasks because you didn't know if they would get done. Did you wait for him to start meetings or not? It was a difficult period.' It was difficult, too, because James had firm ideas about how the business should be run, and was determined to have his way. He believed, for example, that it was wrong for each magazine to sell its own ads, as had long been the case, so he insisted they start selling advertising space as a group. Peter Miller, who had become advertising sales director, thought it was a bad idea and left, as his predecessor, Graham Lawrence, had already done over a similar disagreement with James about incentive payments.

At least Miller's departure was amicable. James didn't shout, swear, read the riot act, throw him on the street or make his life miserable, as Kerry might have done. He was professional and respectful and even gave Miller a farewell party. But James was adamant that it was his way or the highway, and he was already showing the familiar Packer trait of seeing the world in black and white, with no shades of grey. It was yes or no, stop or go. People could be divided the same way: for him or against, friends or enemies. No one was neutral. As it turned out, James's recipe for selling ads was not successful, even though he had been 100 per cent convinced it was the way of the future. Some of his colleagues were already concluding he was impressionable and too easily led.

James's elevation to General Manager was a signal to others that they should comment on his coming of age. Kerry's former lieutenant at Channel Nine, Sam Chisholm, gushed to *The Sunday Age*'s

Muriel Reddy that James was a wonderful boy who embodied 'the best of his parents' fine qualities: a rare combination of his father's business acumen and his mother's personal charm'.

'He has flawless manners,' Chisholm continued, no doubt bolstering his career prospects should he decide to give up running Britain's BSkyB for Rupert Murdoch and return to the fold. 'I think he is very able indeed. He is numerate. He is not the world's most punctual human being at times but I find it hard to fault him.'

A more independent Phillip Adams, who had no desire to work for Packer again, told Reddy more sagely: 'Jamie was a ludicrously gentle boy. He was also very self-effacing. He has gone through a metamorphosis and is now very much his father's son.'

Trevor Kennedy, who by this time had fallen out with Kerry over his failure to capture Fairfax, said much the same. 'He is very cynical for a young man. He is very much under the influence of his father. I don't think we have yet seen the real James Packer. His mother is a wonderful and warm human being, and we hope that he has absorbed some of her characteristics.'

On the face of it, Adams appeared to be right: Kerry had always believed that people were out to get him—his employees (his journalists in particular), the media in general (and especially the ABC)—and he had passed this creed on to his son. So James was suspicious of outsiders and convinced that loyalty was the most important virtue: loyalty to mates, loyalty to the tribe, loyalty to the Packers against the world.

But not everybody was so sure the transformation was complete. Typically, Al Dunlap was one of those who worried that James wasn't tough enough to take Kerry's place. He was not alone in reaching this conclusion. One of Channel Nine's publicists in the early 1990s thought James 'a bit of a mummy's boy' who was too soft to be in charge of billions. 'He seemed like a nice guy who'd ended up in the wrong family,' the publicist recalls. On one memorable occasion James had the stunningly beautiful Jennifer Flavin in tow, during a brief period in which she had broken up with Sylvester Stallone, but 'he kept pandering to her, asking if she wanted to go to the toilet, and talking to her in baby language'.

Flavin was one of a string of models and starlets whom James dated around this time, causing Dunlap to tell him to spend less time chasing Penthouse Pets and take his vocation seriously. 'You have to determine whether you are a James or Jamie,' he warned. 'If you want to play polo and take out a different model every night, you can continue to be Jamie. But if you want to learn how to run a business you have to become James. And James, I believe you can be a world-class executive if you want.' But a much bigger impediment to the young man's development was his relationship with his father. 'Kerry was very tough on young James,' says Dunlap. 'He was such a dominant human being, he just overwhelmed him. James would speak up and Kerry would stamp him down. I told him, "It's wrong, you should be proud of him".'

'I'm sure that in his heart he really loved James but he damn well didn't show it,' Dunlap adds. 'Kerry was never the sort of father who would say, "Great day, well done, son." He was more inclined to point out the things he had done wrong, to bawl him out. James desperately wanted his father to be proud of him. He spent a lot of time wondering if he was succeeding.'

Judy Dunlap recalls James showing up at their door several times, 'distraught' after an argument with Kerry. 'He was intimidated by his father but he wanted to be like him. He was always trying to live up to Kerry but Kerry was always raising the bar.'

In January 1993, Dunlap's spell as James's mentor came to an end when the inevitable bust-up with his boss finally occurred. He and Kerry had moved on the troubled Westpac Bank a couple of months earlier, picking up a 10 per cent stake and getting the support of another large shareholder, AMP, for radical changes after the bank announced a record loss. They had already secured two seats on the board and persuaded Westpac to dump its managing director, Frank Conroy. But they wanted much more. At their first board meeting Packer and Dunlop demanded that 10 000 of the 39 000-strong workforce be sacked, that the bank pull out of North America and Europe and that $20 billion of properties or loans be liquidated. On top of this, they insisted that the bank's chief executive should report to a committee chaired by Al Dunlap, who would see all this through. When their fellow directors rejected these demands, Kerry flew into a rage, pushed back his chair and stormed out of the boardroom. As they descended in the lift together from the 28th floor, a furious Dunlap turned to Packer and told him, 'I couldn't believe the excessive display of stupidity.' And he was not talking about the people they had left behind.

Whether it was Kerry's or Al's fault that it all went wrong—and opinions differ—there was no way the two men could keep working together. For six months they had barely spoken to each other, and now there was open hostility. Kerry told Al his time was up. 'If you go on any longer,' he said, 'you'll be firing me.' Dunlap rang Sir James Goldsmith for advice and was told it was fine to leave because he had done the job. And so he headed for the door, with Kerry's size 14 boot imprinted on his backside as he departed.

On Dunlap's last night in Australia, Ros and James took him and his wife Judy out to dinner to say goodbye, and thanked him warmly for everything he had done, which according to Al amounted to increasing the Packers' net worth by $1.2 billion and saving the empire from financial disaster. Two years later, in 1996, James wrote his mentor a formal letter saying he would never forget the lessons he had learned and promising he had never 'spoken ill' of him or 'disrespected his memory'.

The two men have met only once since then and no longer speak.

CHAPTER 4
CHIP OFF THE OLD BLOCK

I don't *give* guarantees to governments, I *get* them.

Two weeks after the flare-up at Westpac, Kerry and James flew out to the Utah snowfields to meet an American banker, Brian Powers, at his ski lodge and offer him Dunlap's job. Kerry told Powers the pay was good, there was cash to spend, and they would have fun together. Part of his brief as managing director would be to get James ready to take over the Packer empire in five years' time.

Powers asked the young man, who had been silent as his father made the pitch, what he thought about it all. 'I agree with Dad,' he said. 'He has a lot of respect for you.' Powers took all of three minutes to negotiate a package and promised Kerry a definite answer by the time he touched down in Australia.

Powers was smooth, smart and aristocratic, and about as different as one could get from Dunlap. Tall and conservatively dressed with grey hair and glasses, he had run the Hong Kong trading house Jardine Mathieson in the 1980s, before heading to San Francisco to be an investment banker with Hellmann and Friedman. He had first met Kerry in 1982 over dinner at Packer's home in Bellevue Hill and had been left in no doubt about his new boss's capacity for cruelty. One of the other guests was TV personality David Frost, who was heartbroken because his wife, Lynne Frederick, had just left him, and Kerry had spent the evening being absolutely brutal to him.

The next day Powers had sat in Packer's office and listened to a 45-minute monologue about a disastrous real-estate venture Kerry had got into on the Gold Coast, at the end of which the big man turned to him and asked what to do.

'I've no idea,' Powers replied.

'What do you mean you've no idea?' Packer snarled. 'You know something about real estate, don't you, what the fuck should I do?'

'Kerry, I know nothing about the Gold Coast. I've never even been there,' Powers told him coolly, 'and the fact that you want to ask me what to do about property there tells me you know nothing about real estate.'

It was the start of a friendship cemented by a spell in the trenches together in 1991 when Packer and Powers were both in the consortium bidding for Fairfax. And it now became closer. Kerry was soon boasting about the 'exceptional rapport' he had with his right-hand man—matched only by the understanding he had shared with Harry Chester, who had been a mentor and father figure to him in the 1970s. 'He is doing a terrific job,' Kerry told *A Current Affair* in 1995. 'He's managing director; he's running the business day to day; and we talk for an hour, maybe two hours every day.'

In practice, the two men rarely saw each other face to face as Kerry still spent nine months of the year overseas, trying to live each day as if it were his last. But they talked constantly because the Big Fella never let go of the reins, whether he was in London,

Las Vegas or on his boat, and they never had a major argument in the five years that Powers ran the business. The price of this, according to James, was that Brian didn't push Kerry hard enough.

After his spells overseas Kerry would come back to Australia, according to one executive, and 'piss in all the corners, like a dog, just to show he owned the place'. Typically, this involved challenging decisions that had been made in his absence and abusing the people who had made them. One or two executives found this funny because it was 'so staged, so predictable, such a performance', but most were terrified, and James was among them. He was quite incapable of standing up to his father, but delighted when someone else did it for him. One senior executive remembers weathering one of Kerry's storms and turning to see James beaming with pleasure. Another executive will never forget receiving a call from James to join him in a restaurant in Sydney's Double Bay, and arriving to find the boss's son riotously drunk, extremely loud and on the verge of being expelled by the proprietor having, as he put it, won his first ever argument with Dad. This historic celebration took place around 1997 when James was almost thirty years old.

James, of course, was not alone in being cowed. Almost everyone except Brian Powers was bullied or humiliated by Kerry, and no one except Powers really stood up to him. Some felt they could play the role of court jester and joke around, but hardly anyone dared oppose their master's views and none prospered if they did. As one insider puts it, 'We were all shameless sycophants to his face, but there was no end to the insults once he was gone. I could never understand why people stayed around, why they put up with it.'

Money was a big part of the answer: Kerry paid people well and could own them as a result. But there was another force at work, which might be described as abused-person syndrome, that makes victims incapable of escape from their tormentor.

Fortunately, James got on well with Brian Powers, who had the office next to him (Kerry was on the other side), and was able to use him as a human shield. Instead of arguing with his father directly when suggesting a new idea, James could go through the connecting door and persuade Powers to do it for him, something Powers was good at. For his part Powers was impressed by James's abilities, which included an extraordinary facility with numbers. James could do sums in his head that most people could only do using a calculator, and he could recall strings of figures from a spreadsheet even if he had only glimpsed it a couple of times. Powers, who had spent his life 'surrounded by people with Phi, Beta, Kappas from Harvard', had never met better.

It is hard to chart James's progress to power in the Packer empire over the next few years because in one sense Kerry never relinquished control until he died. But he was a member of the team that ran the business from the day Powers arrived and, according to the American, was 'in 99 per cent of the debates' with Kerry about its direction.

In 1994 he was given charge of his first project, which was to bid for Sydney's first legal casino where the Packers were leading contenders. But it soon became clear that Kerry did not intend to let him run the show or make the key decisions. At the launch of the bid for the casino licence—notable for its flashing lights and scantily dressed models—it was James who made the opening pitch. But as soon as he had finished, it was Kerry who stood up to deliver the important message that he was in charge and expected to win. 'I've picked this team to give you the best bloody casino you can get,' he told the assembled group of senior bureaucrats who would make the decision, 'and if they don't give it to you, I'm going to kick 'em up the arse.' His audience was left in no doubt about who was really calling the shots or what Kerry intended the outcome to be.

It was not surprising that the Packers considered themselves favourites because Kerry had the clout and connections to deliver the prize, and plenty of money to buy a licence that would produce $600 million a year in revenue. But just in case anyone failed to realise what was expected of them, he got James to deliver a reminder to the New South Wales Liberal government, which also served as a primer for the boy in how the Packers treated politicians. As soon as the starting gun was fired, James phoned one of Premier John Fahey's ministers to say, 'The old man told me to ring ... this is the message. If we don't win the casino, you guys are fucked.'

Kerry's attitude to the contest was captured even more pungently in a memorable exchange with the New South Wales Casino Control Authority (CCA) in early 1994, by which time the original field of six applicants had been whittled down to two. Concerned that the casino's 20 per cent tax rate would make it impossible to earn a quid from high-rollers—because VIP players had to be offered special deals—Kerry wanted to put a proposal. Why didn't he and the government do a deal to forget the tax and just split the profits 50/50? It was an audacious suggestion, but the big man sold it superbly. According to one observer, who had expected him to be a thug and a bully, he was heroically charming and extraordinarily persuasive.

The two head bureaucrats from the CCA, Christopher Cullen and Lindsay Le Compte, listened to Kerry's sales pitch and asked an adviser to respond. The adviser pointed out that there would be problems with the regulator making money out of the casino but there was also a risk the profits would be diverted into marketing—on Channel Nine or in Packer's magazines—which could leave the government with 50 per cent of nothing. The adviser ventured that perhaps Mr Packer might guarantee to hand over a decent sum of money to the government every year.

There was a brief silence. An entirely changed Kerry Packer then launched into his reply. Pulling himself up to his full height and leaning towards the unfortunate adviser, who was of Mediterranean appearance, he said something like, 'You fucking little dago cunt, I don't *give* guarantees to governments, I *get* them.' And he followed this with a stream of invective of truly world-class proportions. When the tirade finally died down there was a silence as the assembled company drew breath. 'So, I suppose we take that as a no, do we, Mr Packer?' asked the chairman.

The story has probably been embellished over the years, but there is no doubt that Kerry felt governments should favour him, especially when handing out licences to print money. So it must have been a huge shock in May 1994 when the CCA gave the nod to Packer's rival, the American operator Showboat and its Australian partner Leighton Holdings, who had offered $80 million more for the licence.

It was also a setback the Packers were determined to overcome. According to an ABC-TV *Four Corners* investigation in 1997, Kerry and James immediately phoned Fahey's ministers to tell them what they thought of the decision. They then approached the winners and suggested the spoils be shared. Three days after the CCA's decision, the property developer John Boyd, who was a close friend of Kerry's, rang Leighton's chief executive Wal King to say the Packers would prefer to 'co-operate' and not 'fight'. When King asked what on earth he meant, Boyd backed down and ventured that 'fight' was the wrong word.

But two weeks later, the mud started flying. The *Australian Financial Review*'s Pam Walkley was rung by an informant who told her an important package was on its way. 'Remember how George Herscu won, then lost, the first Sydney Casino licence back in 1986?' the anonymous caller inquired. 'Well, the same thing could happen to Leighton.' Soon afterwards, a manila envelope landed on her desk with documents from the Royal Commission into the Building Industry that revealed Leighton's involvement (along with almost every other major builder in New South Wales) in collusive tendering for building contracts.

Kerry's media mate, Alan Jones, also started slinging dirt. According to Dick Warburton, chairman of the winning Sydney Harbour Casino consortium, 'Jones was on the radio just about every morning, attacking Leighton and Showboat, saying how pathetic and incompetent they were. But it was the personal abuse of Wal King that was so bad.' However, this was just the beginning. Three months after the Packers had failed to get their way, an even more powerful assault on the prospective licencees came from another faithful Packer ally, the New South Wales branch of the Australian Labor Party.

On 12 August 1994, the New South Wales Opposition leader, Bob Carr, called a press conference to demand an inquiry into the licensing decision and to hand out copies of a confidential Louisiana State Police report alleging Showboat had links to organised crime. Specifically, the report claimed that Louie Roussell III, Showboat's partner in a floating casino on Lake Ponchartrain near New Orleans, was in business with the brother of a one-time Mafia boss. It was pretty flimsy stuff for a number of reasons. First, because the revelations had not prevented Roussell from winning two casino licences in Louisiana; second, because his supposed connections to the Mafia were tenuous in the extreme; and third, because none of it incriminated Showboat in any way. But Bob Carr was adamant that the Casino Control Authority should launch an immediate public inquiry nevertheless.

As the *Sydney Morning Herald*'s Ian Verrender and Colleen Ryan observed tartly:

> A has a business partnership with B, who owns a bank which employs C, whose brother D runs a tomato canning company which used to be owned by E who is dead now, but when he was alive was alleged to be a Mafia figure. Therefore, A is tainted by associations with the Mafia. Sound ridiculous? Bob Carr doesn't think so.

The ALP leader refused to reveal where he had obtained the report, except to say it was from public sources. Louisiana State Police disputed this strongly at the time, and three years later Captain Ronnie Jones assured *Four Corners*'s Sally Neighbour even more forcefully the report was never publicly available. 'For whatever reason, those documents got out and they should not have gotten out. He [Bob Carr] may have some information in there which is publicly available but some of the information in those documents should not be in his hands. He may not be responsible as the person who took it from our file, but somebody took some of those documents from our file and made copies. And they should not have had access to those things.'

Captain Jones subsequently withdrew any suggestion that the report had been stolen. But it was still a mystery how Bob Carr had got hold of it, and he declined to shed light on the matter even when asked formally by the CCA, to whom he refused to give evidence. James also denied the Packers had obtained the report or were running a campaign to discredit the licence winners. 'It is not our fault if the probity of the Leighton-Showboat consortium comes under question,' he protested to reporters, adding that it was Bob Carr 'who announced his doubts about the Showboat group'.

But, as ABC-TV's *Four Corners* revealed, the Packers' fingerprints were all over the story. Several hours before Carr held his press conference, Kerry's political bagman, Peter Barron, had been briefing journalists by phone from Packer headquarters. Ian Verrender noted the conversation verbatim and passed the transcript to *Four Corners*, which re-enacted it three years later using actors' voices:

> Barron: 'I'm fucked if I know how they could have licensed this mob. How is it that they haven't found out any of this stuff? Roussell's old man was in bed with Carlos Marcello and the Mafia.'

Barron then suggested he had detailed knowledge of the damaging material and had known about the allegations for some time.

> Barron: 'I mean, I've had it for a while and I have been wondering what to do with it.'

The Packers' man also appeared to know that Bob Carr's office was just about to release a copy.

> Barron: 'Look, I heard Bob Carr is probably going to come out and hold a press conference this afternoon with some of this stuff.'

Voice at the other end of the phone: 'What, the Mafia connections?'

Barron: 'Yes, but don't ring him and ask him about it or mention my name. This is all off the record . . .'

At the very least, the conversation demonstrated that the Packers' political odd-job man knew about the contents of the Louisiana State Police report several hours before Bob Carr released it to the public. But if Barron was actually telling the truth in claiming he'd had the report a while, he may well have had a much greater role in the affair. Either way, Barron and Carr's office were obviously in close touch on the matter.

Two months later, the Packers and the ALP were working hand in glove again. With the Casino Control Authority's inquiry into Bob Carr's allegations in full swing and the licence again up for grabs, the ALP's most senior gaming adviser, Charles Shields—a lawyer with contacts in the gaming industry and a history as a private investigator—was sent to the USA at the Packers' expense to dig more dirt on Showboat. In October 1994, Shields spent two weeks in New Orleans, New Jersey, New York and Los Angeles and was paid $15 000 by the Packer organisation for his trouble. His brief was to interview journalists and gaming experts and locate witnesses with evidence against Showboat. Job done, he headed back to Australia and turned over his results to Peter Barron.

In her 1997 program, *Four Corners* reporter Sally Neighbour confronted Shields in the street to ask how the Packer trip had come about, who had paid him and whether the ALP knew about his mission. He refused to tell her. By that time Shields had become chief of staff to the New South Wales Gaming minister, Richard Face, in a new Labor government.

Kerry also tried to get his television network to weigh into the battle. Sometime in 1994 (almost certainly during the CCA inquiry), Channel Nine's head of News and Current Affairs, Peter Meakin, got a call while he was drinking in the bar at the network's Sydney headquarters. It was the boss, ringing from Las Vegas, where it was early in the morning, to say he wanted Meakin to 'turn over' Showboat for breaching its licence conditions in Louisiana. Showboat managed a riverboat casino on Lake Pontchartrain that was required by law to sail while people were gambling, and he had discovered it wasn't leaving its moorings.

'It's a bloody good story,' Kerry told his executive. 'Those bastards are breaching their licence. Why would we want them in Australia? Get down there and do a story about them.' Meakin said he would check it out.

'Don't check it out. Just do it,' Packer demanded.

'Kerry, is that an instruction?' Meakin inquired.

Packer replied, 'I didn't ring up to have a conversation at that level.'

Channel Nine did in fact run a story on the riverboat casino and reported that Showboat's multi-million dollar paddle-steamer had been badly damaged by a sunken log in its first month of operation and was staying in port because it didn't want to risk the safety of its passengers. 'Kerry had omitted to mention that bit,' says Meakin. Nor had he mentioned that other operators were refusing to cruise the lake for the same reason.

Despite all their efforts to swing the process their way, the Packers failed to overturn the Casino Control Authority's decision. In December 1994 the inquiry chairman, Murray Tobias QC, ruled there was no evidence to connect Louie Roussell III to the Mafia and no evidence to suggest that Showboat was unfit to hold the

Sydney casino licence. However, he did bring down adverse findings against Wal King and Cyril Vella, who ran Leighton Holdings, and barred the company from having any role in the management of the casino, in which it held a 5 per cent share.

The Packers were furious, but despite immediately beginning legal action to challenge the decision, they were not surprised. James had already complained that the deck was stacked against them and that justice was being denied. Just after the inquiry opened in September, he told the *Sydney Morning Herald*'s Peter FitzSimons that the Packer consortium should have already been given the licence because Leighton had 'broken the rules'. He also claimed that the press would have been clamouring for this to happen had it been anyone other than his family involved. 'I don't think that the press wants to get on a bandwagon of helping the Packers,' he protested, 'even if they think we're conceptually right . . . because they say Kerry's got enough, and because at certain times certain elements have had rows with him. It gets personal.'

It was rare for James to talk publicly and even rarer for him to open up in the way he did to FitzSimons (who was working for Nine at the time, and whose wife Lisa Wilkinson edited *Cleo* magazine), but anyone who has ever met the irrepressible ex-Wallaby would know he's a hard man to say no to. And James may have felt at ease because FitzSimons was a big, boofy rugby player. In any case, the budding tycoon volunteered as much about himself as he has ever done, with insights into his family, his upbringing and his outlook on life, much of which was parroted from his 'dad'.

Asked by FitzSimons why he wouldn't just put his father's billions in the bank and live off the interest, the twenty-seven-year-old James replied: 'I'm an ambitious person. I mean, if I did that . . . I would self-destruct, in the sense that the decadence would be too strong an attraction for me. Whether that be in the form of gambling, fast cars, alcohol, drugs, whatever it happens to be . . . I think the lure of that lifestyle would be too strong.'

But perhaps he exposed the real reason when he said: 'If I sat back and decided to sell the product of my father and my grandfather's work, like a leech, you know I wouldn't be able to look at myself in the mirror . . . I want to be able to look at my father in ten years' time and say, "I'm proud of you, and you should be proud of me."'

James had always been desperate for his father's admiration and had talked about making money ever since he left school. And now that he was in a position of power, he was besieged by people offering him deals. It's an old adage that money makes money and James was able to benefit, even though Kerry gave him none, because he had the Packer name.

One of the most persistent petitioners for his attention was a lawyer called Theo Onisforou, who was working his way up from nothing to become the multimillionaire he is today. At university, Theo had been paid by Malcolm Turnbull to take notes in lectures, and he now made himself indispensible to James. They first met in the late 1980s when James was booked for speeding and looked like he might lose his licence. Theo, who was recommended as someone who might get him off, saw his opportunity. 'He sucked up to him in a big way,' says a former Packer executive who remembers Onisforou at a polo match at Warwick Farm standing behind the goal, waving flags when someone scored.

Theo also ingratiated himself with James's sister Gretel and with Kerry, who ordered a reluctant Trevor Kennedy to hire him. In no time at all he was inside Packer headquarters, making himself unpopular. Nowadays, no one seems quite clear what his title was, but most give him character references that would make Al Dunlap blanch. One senior Packer executive remembers him as a sycophant, and one of his oldest friends, who fell out with him in the 1990s, says he was rude and self-centred and had little consideration for others.

But just as James could see good in Al, he now took a shine to Theo, and the two became good friends, perhaps because Onisforou was so good at what he did. 'He was one of those people you just *knew* was going to make money,' says one entrepreneur who did business with him in the early 1990s. 'He and James did heaps of developments together. Theo found the projects, James's name produced the money. It was a fantastic arrangement. Theo borrowed the money from the bank, got James to guarantee it, then split the profits 50/50. Theo was absolutely incredible at property, so all the developments did well, and James had some real spending money for the first time in his life.'

Almost all the deals were in residential property in inner Sydney, and all made handsome profits. Soon, FAI Insurance's Rodney Adler, who knew James from Cranbrook and was also a friend of Rene Rivkin, was roped in to provide more firepower, and other lucrative projects followed.

By 1994, James and Theo had made enough to throw $3 million into a new investment fund called Strategic Pooled Developments run by Melbourne stockbroker Andrew Kroger (brother of Liberal Party powerbroker Michael Kroger). And this money made more money. One of the fund's notable successes was a stormwater treatment company called CDS Technologies, which was floated on the Australian Stock Exchange in early 1997, multiplying its initial investment twelvefold and delivering around $4 million to James. Another windfall came with the sale of Melbourne-based Portfolio Partners in 1999, netting James a further $2 million.

But the best opportunity of all fell into James's lap in August 1994 when he was invited to invest in One.Tel, a new mobile phone company run by Jodee Rich, who had dazzled the financial world in the 1980s with his cutely named computer company, Imagineering. A multi-millionaire at twenty-six, Rich had been greeted as a genius by the financial press, 'The youngest and richest self-made millionaire this side of the Indian Ocean'. At its zenith, Imagineering controlled 50 per cent of the Australian home computer market and was doubling its sales every year. But it grew too far, too fast, and after briefly lighting up the sky Jodee's rocket ran out of fuel and crashed to earth, losing more than $100 million for its shareholders.

Jodee had walked away from the wreckage of the company with his pride badly dented and his reputation in tatters, but by late 1994 he was convinced mobile phones could make him a second fortune. In the United Kingdom, several smart entrepreneurs were already making a mint by buying network access from big phone companies and reselling it under a different brand name. Jodee reckoned he and his marketing maestro at Imagineering, Brad Keeling, could do even better in Australia. All he needed was a big phone company to give him a start.

It took Jodee just one meeting to convince Bob Mansfield, the new chief at Optus Communications, that it was a great idea and to be commissioned to write a business plan. A few weeks later, he came back with a sixteen-page outline for Project E, written in almost incomprehensible bizspeak, promising to 'leverage the customer base' and 'customise the end-user interface'. This was enough to get him the go-ahead, on condition he find a corporate backer to bankroll him and (one hoped) stop him repeating the mistakes he made at Imagineering, where he had never listened to anyone warning him to slow down.

At Bob Mansfield's suggestion Jodee had already talked to James Packer, who had tried unsuccessfully to get Brian Powers to invest some of the family fortune. Jodee had also talked to Rodney Adler, who had put up money in the early days of Imagineering. Adler liked the idea but knew nothing about telephone companies, so he flicked it on to one of his business analysts, Diane Nolder, who was soon exposed to the full force of Jodee's persuasive powers. Nolder had seen hundreds of deals come across her desk, but reckoned this was one of the best and Jodee one of the most inspiring entrepreneurs she had met. He was so sure of himself, so knowledgeable and so passionate that she was certain he would make One.Tel work.

With Adler and FAI now backing the project enthusiastically and James Packer waiting in the wings, Rich was able to negotiate an extraordinarily generous deal with Optus, giving One.Tel low call rates, subsidies for every handset, $170 for every connection to the network and an extra $120 'loyalty bonus' for each new customer it signed up. It was a far better deal than any of Rich's rivals had carved out, and it just about guaranteed that One.Tel would succeed. The only mystery was how it had come about. One possible explanation is that Rich and his chief negotiator Ted Pretty (later number two at Telstra) were sharper than the guys at Optus. 'We were young, naive and they took us to the cleaners,' says one former executive. Another is that Optus wanted to woo Kerry, who was a shareholder in the fledgling pay-TV operator Optus Vision and had options to invest in its parent. Rightly or wrongly, Kerry was convinced he deserved the credit for One.Tel's special treatment.

With Rich's new venture now looking like a sure thing, James tried again to get his father to back it, then decided to invest

$250000 himself. But he now found Jodee reluctant to share. Stiff letters went back and forth, and James would have missed out had Rodney Adler not intervened to persuade Rich that the Packer name was good for business.

In May 1995, One.Tel's new 'fun and friendly' phone service was launched in brand new offices at the top of the Castlereagh Centre, just down the road from Sydney's Martin Place, with a red, wooden phone box at centre stage. James wasn't there. He was away from Sydney, fighting another battle for the Packer family, this time over rugby league and pay-TV.

CHAPTER 5
THE BLOODING

These are the words that sum it up: pay-TV, power,
money, commercial greed.

On a warm day in February 1995, in a private box high above the
Sydney Football Stadium, Kerry Packer reached out his hand to
Ken Arthurson, the man who ran rugby league in Australia, and
told him: 'Son, I give you my assurance that I will be doing no deal
with News Limited without your approval. And if I get knocked
over by a bus tomorrow, these two guys have heard me say it.' As
he spoke, he gestured toward James and Brian Powers to confirm
that they would keep him honest.

It was with these words that the war between the Packers and
Murdochs over the control of the TV rights to rugby league was
ratcheted up in a saga of betrayal, deceit and the triumph of money
over friendship and loyalty.

Arthurson was 100 per cent sure that Kerry was a mate and a
man he could trust. But the ARL chief was about to learn what

happens to business morality when hundreds of millions of dollars are at stake. Young James was going to learn the lesson, too, for this was to be his blooding in business. He would lead the Packer forces into battle and, when time came to make peace with the enemy, it would be his job to tell Arthurson that Kerry's promises counted for nothing.

The war over Murdoch's plans for a new Super League was, of course, only incidentally about rugby league and much more about pay-TV, where the Packers and Murdochs were fighting for a billion dollar market. In the UK, Rupert had used Premier League soccer to pull in the punters and turn BSkyB into a money-making machine. In Australia, he was hoping a slimmed-down rugby league competition would do the same thing. But there was no way Kerry was going to stand by and let the Murdochs create a powerful pay-TV monopoly which could become a serious rival to Channel Nine.

Kerry knew the battle for the pay-TV market would be a gladiator-ial contest with only one winner, and he had tried very hard to be on Rupert's team. But in late 1994 he had been dumped from the powerful PMT consortium (which comprised the Packers, Murdoch and Telstra), and had been forced to join forces with Optus Vision, which was also planning to invest billions of dollars in pay-TV. Now the Packers' strategy was to build something big enough to make Rupert join them again. And keeping hold of the TV rights to rugby league—which rated higher than anything else on television—was going to be the key to success.

Among those who were involved with the game, feelings about Murdoch's plan for a new Super League were mixed. The big clubs loved the idea because they would make far more money than they had in the past. The small clubs opposed it because most of them would end up being history. If News Limited's vision were to be realised, ten of the existing twenty clubs would disappear. But it was among the game's supporters that emotions ran highest. Rugby league was a sport with fierce tribal loyalties, deep-seated rivalries and 100 years of glorious history. It was a working-class game under attack from the big end of town. It was the little Aussie battler against money, power and commercial greed. It was Rupert Murdoch trying to steal their game.

The ARL's general manager, John Quayle, says he knew for two years there would have to be a shake-up because News Limited was keen to replace Winfield as the game's main sponsor and was already working with the ARL. The ban on tobacco advertising was due to come into effect at the end of 1995, and News was planning to pour in millions of dollars to fill the hole. But in return, Murdoch's men were clearly going to demand a share of the action.

After months of rumours that something was afoot, Quayle and Arthurson finally demanded a meeting with Rupert's deputy, Ken Cowley, in early November 1994 and were told News wanted to create and televise a new, elite twelve-team competition in Australia that could 'take rugby league to the world'. 'I love the game,' Cowley assured the two men, 'and I want you to know that I'd never do anything to harm it.'

Arthurson and Quayle said they would be happy to talk as the ARL needed the money and would be delighted to have both the Packers and the Murdochs supporting the game. But there was one small problem: the TV rights had already been sold to the Packers until the year 2000, and the ARL was bound to honour that commitment. Cowley told them this wouldn't be an obstacle, because News only wanted pay-TV rights and Channel Nine would still have the free-to-air rights to a stronger competition.

But he soon discovered he was dreaming. Within a couple of hours, Cowley was phoning Ken Arthurson to tell him, 'I've been to see Kerry but I didn't get much joy. In fact he almost threw me out of the office.'

'It was pretty colourful,' Cowley later told Roy Masters. Kerry stormed around his office, threatened to 'paper the wall with writs', and said he would welcome a fight because life had become boring. He then told Cowley to 'piss off' and marched him to the lift.

Not surprisingly, Cowley was shaken and angered by this reception, but he was not deterred. He told Quayle that News would go it alone because it was a waste of time talking to Kerry. Three months later, on 6 February 1995, the day after Kerry's promise to Arthurson at the Sydney Football Stadium, Cowley came to a meeting at the ARL's headquarters to sell the idea to the clubs and tell them what he had already told the league's bosses: that he loved the game and would never do anything to harm it.

Considering that Super League threatened to wipe out half the clubs there, the sales pitch went down pretty well. But when Kerry Packer marched in an hour or so later to give his response, it was clear where allegiances really lay because he was greeted by cheers and applause. For the next fifteen minutes, the 'Big Fella' held the sixty delegates enthralled with his trademark mixture of charm and menace, telling them that he had the TV rights, that he would not sell them to anyone and would 'sue the arse off' anybody who tried to take them away. Murdoch's supporters were so intimidated by this performance that not a squeak came from the floor, even though the Brisbane Broncos, the Canterbury Bulldogs and Cronulla-Sutherland had already decided to jump on the Super League bandwagon.

The next day, Cowley repeated the mantra in his own newspaper, the *Daily Telegraph-Mirror*. He told readers that he loved rugby league and would do nothing to harm it. More importantly, he reiterated the promises made to Arthurson and the clubs that there would be no rebel or breakaway competition. This was all hogwash, of course. Since his ejection from Kerry's office three months before, Cowley and his fellow News Limited executives had been planning to sign up clubs and players in secret, if necessary. And they now set about doing exactly that.

By the end of March 1995, Murdoch's men had a detailed plan of attack with charts and daily schedules listing who would go where and which players they would sign. Flights and hotel rooms were booked in false names so word would not leak out. There was even a war room from which the 'blitzkrieg' would be controlled. The key was 'secrecy, suddenness and deception', the Federal Court's Justice Burchett later concluded, with 'complete capitulation the objective'. If everything went to plan, it would be over before the enemy knew what had hit them. The ARL and the Packers would surrender. As President Nixon's aide Chuck Colson put it, 'When you got 'em by the balls, their hearts and minds will follow.'

The assault began on the evening of 30 March when players from the Canterbury Bulldogs were rounded up after training and bussed to a nearby hotel. There, Lachlan Murdoch and John Ribot, Super League's new chief executive, offered them contracts worth up to $300 000 a year—two or three times their current pay—plus a signing-on fee of up to $100 000. They were told they could not ring their families or agents and could not take the contracts away. By the end of the night, seven players had joined the new rebel competition. They were given crib sheets instructing them to deny they had talked to News and to promise they would honour their contracts with the ARL.

Earlier that evening, six clubs—Canterbury, Cronulla-Sutherland, Canberra, Auckland, Brisbane and the Western Reds—had faxed the ARL to say they were defecting to Super League. Quayle, who had been expecting the letters and stayed behind at the office until he received them, arrived late for a farewell party in The Rocks clutching these declarations of war.

Despite all the secrecy, the Packers had been given veiled notice of the coup by Ken Cowley, who came to Brian Powers's house a couple of days before the raids to offer a deal. His message was that Super League was already a fait accompli so it was pointless to resist. He went on to offer Channel Nine the television rights to the competition for the price it was currently paying, which was roughly the deal Kerry had rejected four months earlier. Powers didn't turn down the offer flat—it was financially attractive and there were huge risks in fighting a war with Murdoch. But Kerry didn't pause to consider it. His instant reaction when Powers phoned him in London: 'Tell them to fuck off.' Powers hung up thinking, 'That's why I like him.'

Despite this warning that Super League would go ahead, Kerry still didn't believe the attack was coming. He thought his position impregnable. A couple of days before the raids, he took the new chairman of Optus Vision, Geoff Cousins, to lunch and told him not to worry. 'Son,' he said, 'it's not like World Series Cricket where all you need is a couple of teams. You can't do that with rugby league. You've got to have at least eight teams; people get injured all the time and you need back-up. Super League is just not going to happen.'

But for once he was wrong. And as a result, his side was ill-prepared to fight back. Early on April Fools' Day 1995, as the Saturday editions of the *Daily Telegraph-Mirror* and other News

Limited papers trumpeted victory, the Packer forces gathered in Park Street to decide on a response. Despite all his previous bravado, Kerry was ready to throw in the towel. 'You'll never beat Rupert, we might as well give up now,' he said gloomily, adding that it would cost far too much to take Murdoch on. But Geoff Cousins and Frank Anthony from Optus Vision were adamant that surrender would be even more expensive. Putting in a quick call to their new head of sport, Tom Barnett, they asked how easy it would be to sell pay-TV subscriptions without rugby league. Barnett told them it would be impossible. 'We either had to fight or fold the tent,' says Cousins. 'There was no way we could sell a pay-TV service to the punters if we didn't have footy.' And without pay-TV, Optus Vision's parent company would not be able to fund the cable network that would allow it to take on Telstra in the lucrative fixed-line telephone market.

Kerry did eventually agree to join the fight, on condition that Optus Vision paid most of the bills. Powers, Cousins and the Packer team then walked a few blocks across Hyde Park to the ARL headquarters in Phillip Street, where James was deep in talks with Quayle and Arthurson. An emergency meeting of the ARL board had been called for noon, and Powers was able to deliver the news that Optus Vision and Channel Nine would put in $20 million to keep Super League at bay. No one was tactless enough to point out that Optus Vision did not even have a business at this stage. All it had was an empty office in North Sydney and a grand total of five people on the payroll.

By mid-afternoon, the counter-attack was already under way with James leading the charge to re-sign players to the ARL or to stop them defecting. And as Mike Colman revealed in his book *Super League: The Inside Story*, it was James who snatched a key player, Adam Ritson, from the Murdochs' clutches that first weekend. An up-and-coming eighteen-year-old from the Cronulla club, Ritson had been corralled in Perth on Friday night after the game against the Western Reds and offered $150 000 a year plus a $20 000 sign-on fee. Like most of his teammates, he had agreed to pocket the cheque but, unlike them, had refused to sign until he talked to his agent, Steve Gillis.

Gillis, a knockabout sports journalist who had taken to managing players, was still working casual shifts as a sub-editor on the Murdochs' *Sunday Telegraph*. That Saturday morning, he rang the ARL before going to work to see if it would match Ritson's offer from Super League. Before long he was sitting at his desk fielding a call from James Packer, who told him his boy was not to defect. 'He's part of the ARL's plans for next year,' said James, 'and the ARL will be running the comp, do you under-stand?' When Gillis asked why on earth Ritson would knock back a truckload of money 'on a maybe', James replied coolly: 'Steve, you don't know me and I've never met you, but I'm sure you have heard of me and my family and we pride ourselves on our principles and honesty. And if I tell you Adam Ritson will be looked after, he will be looked after.'

Twenty-four hours later, with Ritson being offered even more money by Super League's recruiters, Gillis rang James at home and was told to come around to the Bondi apartment, where he was greeted by Packer in pyjama shorts and a T-shirt, looking like he'd been up all night. James assured Gillis again that the ARL would win the fight, then asked what it would take to keep Ritson safe. Five minutes and two offers later, the men shook on a deal. Moments after that Gillis's mobile rang. The voice on the other end was 'soft, polite and had an American accent'. It was Lachlan

Murdoch wanting to know whether he could sort out Ritson's problem. Gillis told him he was too late and, as Colman put it, 'The ARL was back in the game.'

In fact, Ritson was just one of a stream of players through Packer's apartment that afternoon, with James making the same sort of pitch to each. And he was still going full tilt next morning, by which time he had moved to ARL headquarters where a war room to rival Murdoch's was in operation. For the next fortnight, James worked furiously. 'It was really intense,' says one of his aides. 'We hardly slept for two weeks.' Asked why it was left to James to lead the charge, he answers: 'He was up for it. And Kerry wasn't going to do it, was he?' A key difference between father and son was that James believed in pay-TV while Kerry did not and was never convinced the battle was worth fighting because, whatever happened to Super League, Channel Nine was likely to end up with the free-to-air TV rights.

In those crucial early days, the ARL had three clubs it was desperate to retain: the Canberra Raiders, the Newcastle Knights and the Western Reds. John Quayle remembers visiting the Raiders, the Western Reds and the Brisbane Broncos in one crazy day, hopping onto the Packers' private jet with James at 6 a.m. to fly down to the nation's capital, then stopping off in Sydney on the way to Brisbane, and finally taking a commercial flight to Perth that evening. As it turned out, none of the trips was successful.

The key target in Canberra was the Raiders' star player, Ricky Stuart, who was offered half a million dollars a year and captaincy of the Australian team if he would stay with the ARL. A fervent speech from James helped extract a commitment to consider the offer, but by the time he and John Quayle touched down in Sydney, Stuart was having lunch with Ken Cowley and putting his mark on a contract.

On other days, however, the young Packer fared better. The captain of Newcastle, Paul Harragon, was swayed by a similarly passionate pitch from James and the offer of a job at Channel Nine when his playing days were over. Anthony Mundine, who was playing with St George at the time, was another who was won over by James talking about 'the green and gold' and the honour of playing for Australia, which would be denied to anyone joining the rebel cause. 'James was good,' says Geoff Cousins. 'The players liked him and trusted him because he knew the game well and he was really persuasive.'

James was by no means the only one doing the talking, but he was there to twist arms if necessary, as was the Packers' Mr Fixit, Graham Richardson, who had been phoned at home by Kerry that first weekend and asked to go down to the ARL to help out. 'Richo was leader of the pack,' one insider later recalled. 'He was so passionate, so driven. I've never seen anything like it, but then I've never seen anything like what was going on all around us.' Nor had anybody else.

According to Arthurson, 'It was a mad, bad time ... It was just like war. It was war.' Young players were being called in to sign contracts for two or three times their existing salaries, to do what they were already doing: to play the same game, with the same team, at the same grounds. They were walking out holding cheques for more than they had ever dreamed of. 'We were dragging kids into the office and saying, "Here's half a million dollars, now sign,"' says Cousins. 'There were kids of eighteen, barely out of school, who were getting $100 000 shoved at them.'

Across town, in an office just over the road from Murdoch's newspapers, Lachlan and his Super League negotiators were doing the same. After three weeks they had signed up almost 200 players, or two-thirds of the number they needed, but the ARL had nailed down even more. 'When we started, we were ... very behind and unplanned,' Richardson told Peter FitzSimons, 'but we changed up to top gear very quickly and signed 600 players at phenomenal pace.' In these first three weeks, Richardson drove up and down the motorway from Sydney to Newcastle countless times to 'plead and beg with footballers and officials' not to defect. He was used to doing dirty jobs, he admitted, but even he started wondering how it had come to this.

'Richo was going round with a bag of money to the ones who were wavering,' says Cousins. 'I remember him coming up at one point and saying, "I need a few million dollars for the referees." I told him, "No way. There's no more, we've spent enough."' But there was reason to be desperate. Players and clubs were asking why on earth they should knock back News Limited to stay with Optus and the ARL. 'You don't even have a business. Why should we trust you?' they asked. To which Cousins would reply bravely, 'Well, we don't have a business yet, but we will.'

'It was the toughest job I've ever done,' he says of his time in charge. 'For the first six months the whole business was on the brink of failure every minute. Optus had paid the government $600 million for the licence to build a cable network and all the local councils were up in arms. We had legal challenges all the time and we just had to tough it out.'

There was an even bigger legal battle to tough out, however. The day after launching its raids, News Limited had asked the Federal Court to strike out 'Commitment Agreements' that bound all twenty clubs to compete in the ARL's competition until 2000, on the basis that these were in breach of the Trade Practices Act.

In reply, the ARL was suing the rebels for breaking their contracts and News Limited for inducing them to do so.

Graham Richardson was supremely confident his side would win. 'Super League won't be here in 1996,' he proclaimed. 'It won't be here in 1997, it won't be here in 1998, it won't be here in 1999.' But Kerry was not so sure. A natural-born pessimist, he had never wanted to fight Rupert Murdoch in the first place and was now keen to cut a deal. Brian Powers also wanted to make peace and suggested to Ken Cowley that a broad-based accord would benefit both sides. In early November 1995, a couple of weeks after the court hearings began, he and Kerry popped into Murdoch's London office for a chat with Rupert and his deputy and, in the space of just 45 minutes, agreed to settle the Super League war and carve up the Australian media between them.

The first deal in this secret pact was revealed two weeks later when Channel Nine announced it would televise Super League in 1996 if the Federal Court allowed the rebel competition to proceed. Ken Arthurson was devastated. 'It was a breathtaking piece of corporate treachery,' he wrote later. 'Packer had done business with the enemy.' More to the point, he had broken his promise to strike no deal without his old mate's approval.

A couple of weeks later, Arthurson buttonholed James at the ARL's Christmas party and told him how upset he was. Soon afterwards he got a call from Kerry, who claimed not to understand what the fuss was all about. It was only a conditional agreement, Packer assured him, and of no real importance. And in Kerry's eyes this was possibly true because by comparison with the other things he and Murdoch had agreed (which were yet to be made public), TV rights to a competition that might never happen were pretty trivial.

At that London meeting Murdoch had promised to give Channel Nine access to his Fox TV programs and 20th Century Fox movies. He had also agreed to buy a 15 per cent share in the network and sell out of Channel Seven, to put an end to any TV rivalry. In return, Kerry had promised to sell Rupert his 15 per cent stake in Fairfax so Murdoch could launch a takeover. After a year of fighting over rugby league, the two men had remembered that peace in the valley could be worth hundreds of millions of dollars to each of them. 'The impetus for talking,' according to one unnamed insider, who sounded remarkably like James, 'was a realisation that we can beat the shit out of each other, or have an easier time. Super League is a symptom of what happens when we fight.'

But almost before the ink was dry the peace treaty was being torn up, because two powerful forces were blocking the way. The first was the prime minister, Paul Keating; the second was Geoff Cousins.

To take over Fairfax, Murdoch needed Keating's approval to waive the foreign ownership laws that prevented an American citizen from owning more than 25 per cent of an Australian media company. And Keating wasn't prepared to give Murdoch his blessing. More immediately, Geoff Cousins wasn't prepared to let Optus share pay-TV rights for rugby league, which Murdoch saw as an essential part of the deal. 'The Murdochs thought I was a Packer appointee and would do what Kerry told me,' he says. 'But I didn't and I couldn't.' Cousins saw no reason to give anything away because he was confident the ARL would win the court case. And, as corny as it may sound, he believed in the rightness of the cause.

So the deal fell apart and relations between Packer and Murdoch deteriorated even further than before. In the year leading up to the failed accord, Packer had thrown Cowley out of his office and

Rupert had hit back by attacking Kerry in public. 'Mr Packer spends his time travelling, playing polo and other activities,' he had sniped in early 1995, 'while people like Mr Cowley and my son Lachlan go to work every day.' Now, the slanging match got worse because Rupert accused Kerry of 'welshing' on the deal. Instead of pushing Arthurson and Cousins to hammer out a compromise, Packer had been in Argentina playing polo as if he didn't care whether it happened or not. Murdoch told Channel Seven's *Witness* he was 'saddened' by his rival's behaviour. 'I've told the world when people have come to me and said, "Who's this fellow Packer from Australia?" you know, "I trust him, I always have absolutely", so my first reaction was to feel angry and let down.'

As the accusations flew, the decision both sides had been waiting for was finally handed down in the Federal Court after 51 days of hearings. Justice Burchett's 219-page judgment in February 1996 was a victory for the ARL and a thrashing for Super League. It was also damning of News Limited's behaviour, which the judge said was characterised by 'secrecy', 'dishonesty' and 'deceit'. Burchett was particularly harsh on Ken Cowley for his refusal to give evidence and for his repeated (and false) promises that there would be no rebel competition. But Justice Burchett's remedy was even more damaging, because he ordered that Super League be banned indefinitely from holding, promoting or advertising any rival competition, and from recruiting players to take part.

Rupert Murdoch greeted the verdict by telling journalists it was 1-0 at half time and he would wait for the final whistle. But in reality he and Cowley were contemplating surrender. News Limited was spending a fortune, its reputation was suffering and an appeal looked hopeless. So, Ken Cowley and Lachlan Murdoch were dispatched to see Kerry and James in yet another attempt to make peace with the offer Cousins had rejected a couple of months earlier. Straight after they left the Packers' compound at Bellevue Hill, the Optus Vision chief was hauled in for dinner and told by Kerry they would never have a stronger hand. But once again, Cousins refused to budge. He was confident the verdict would hold and saw no reason to give anything away. Kerry rang Cowley that night, and the high-handed manner of his dismissal stiffened Cowley's resolve to fight.

A month later the ARL competition kicked off its 1996 season with half its players missing, and with seven Super League clubs forfeiting matches because they couldn't field teams. Eventually most of the players did return but, in Arthurson's words, 'the season limped along, never seeming quite real'. As long as News Limited's appeal was winding its way through the courts, everything was in limbo. But even when the verdict was finally delivered in October, it still offered no resolution because Burchett's decision was simply overturned and the whistle blew for the battle to begin all over again.

The three full-court judges had agreed on Justice Burchett's reading of the facts but reached entirely opposite legal conclusions. To a layman, it was all quite baffling. 'It was like playing the same team twice, under the same set of rules, with the only difference being a new referee,' Ken Arthurson wrote in his memoirs, 'winning 100-nil the first week, then losing 100-nil the second.'

Shortly after the decision, Graham Richardson told Peter Fitz-Simons that both sides had lost: 'All that any of us can do now is to determine by how much we lose. But we can't win.' It was clear to Richardson there would have to be compromise, 'Otherwise we'll not only beat the hell out of each other, but beat the hell out of the game.' One month later, rumours began to appear that Lachlan and James had held secret peace talks, a suggestion Ken Cowley instantly denied.

As it happened, Cowley had approached James Packer himself at Lachlan's request. In the weeks either side of Christmas 1996, the two junior tycoons met a dozen times at Lachlan's waterfront mansion in Elizabeth Bay, which was the only place they could talk in private. This time it was hard to get their fathers back to the table again, but Kerry and Rupert were finally persuaded to meet just before New Year in New Zealand's Bay of Islands, where Murdoch's $30 million yacht *Morning Glory* was moored for the summer break. Kerry flew in on a chartered plane to the remote northern end of the North Island—where the runway at Kerikeri Airport was too short for his DC-8—and was choppered out to the boat for the day. This time, there was no talk of redrawing the map of Australia. All Kerry and Rupert did was endorse what their sons had already agreed: that Channel Nine would get the free-to-air TV rights to Super League and the Packers would drop their legal action for non-delivery of the Fox movies Murdoch had promised in the November 1995 deal.

It took another three weeks for the details to be finalised and made public. And it was James who then took on the task of phoning Arthurson and Quayle to break the news. 'Ken, this is a call that gives me no pleasure to make,' he told the ARL chief, before explaining that it was a 'business' decision. 'This hurts me, as I know it hurts you,' he told John Quayle, who had by now resigned from the ARL.

For Ken Arthurson it was the last straw. 'Business had come in through the door, and friendship and loyalty had flown out the window,' he wrote, adding that it was 'business, at its worst and most immoral'. The betrayal was bad enough, but the damage to the game was worse. What also bothered him was that Kerry had not mustered the courage to make the call himself. 'I never have thought him a weak person,' he says today. 'But why else would he have failed to do it? I've asked myself that question a hundred times and I still don't know the answer.'

There seemed to be two possibilities. One was that Kerry simply didn't care what his old friend thought. The other was that he wanted James to be blooded in the art of betrayal. But whichever it was, Arthurson was floored: 'Channel Nine's decision dragged me down about as far as it was possible for a fundamentally positive person like myself to go.' Six days after the call from James, he resigned as chairman of the ARL. He couldn't take any more. He had been in the front line for two years, 'confronting more stress, more pressure, more anguish' than in all his fifty years in football. Several times, Quayle had found him lying in the dark on the floor of his office, sheltering from a blinding headache, or had watched him come back from a press conference and collapse into a chair in tears. One evening, the ARL boss had been struck with a stabbing pain in his chest, and had thought he was going to die.

A dozen years later, Ken Arthurson and John Quayle have had plenty of time to reflect on what they might have done differently. Both now believe they should have stood up to Kerry and told him, 'You own the TV rights, but we own the game.' They should have dared him to sue and called his bluff. They deeply regret the hundreds of millions of dollars wasted, the vast payments made to players who didn't deserve it, the friendships broken and the opportunities missed. Both men accept that peace had to come, but remain angry that it was not made before the war started.

Shortly after the ARL court victory in February 1996, several secret meetings took place between Arthurson and Ken Cowley at Rupert Murdoch's Sydney apartment. At one such meeting, Arthurson was offered a five-year contract as an ambassador to Super League on a salary that would have set him up for life. He rang Quayle that night to rue the fact that he couldn't accept it, telling his friend, 'I couldn't do it, could I?'

Six or seven years later, he found himself next to Kerry Packer at a rugby league celebration dinner. They had not spoken to each other since the settlement. By then Packer was sick, and Arthurson decided it was time to forgive and forget. 'I didn't want to be bad friends with him,' he says today. But Kerry felt no need to apologise or explain.

Despite what happened John Quayle bore no grudges against James, and even went to his wedding in October 1999. He remembers the young Packer being passionate about the game and convinced they were right, a point he illustrates by James's attempt, in the thick of the battle, to help South Sydney, one of the weakest clubs in the competition. The Rabbitohs had already received $1 million, along with the other teams in the ARL, but needed more to stay alive. The broadcaster Alan Jones was 'driving him mad' to get Souths some more money, so James asked if the ARL would help out. When Quayle said nothing could be done, James reached into his pocket and wrote out a personal cheque for 'some hundreds of thousands of dollars' to be given to the club. Quayle warned him he might never get his money back, and it seems he never did. 'But that was an indication of how much he cared,' says Quayle. It was perhaps also an indication of how much notice James took of Alan Jones.

Once the Packers and Murdochs had joined forces in January 1997, the Super League war was all over bar the shouting. At the end of that season the two competitions were merged into one, with an agreement to reduce the number of clubs from twenty to fourteen. The Packers picked up free-to-air TV rights until 2000 and the Murdochs got pay-TV rights until 2022.

'What we have done today,' Lachlan Murdoch told the press, 'is ensure the survival and prosperity of rugby league.'

'I think it stinks', said Souths president Frank Cookson. 'It'll be the downfall of rugby league.'

But by this time James and his father had other things on their mind. There was unfinished business to attend to.

CHAPTER 6
UNFINISHED BUSINESS

What the fuck have you said to Dad?

By August 1996, Sydney's new casino had been open for a year in its temporary facility and things were not going well. As the *Sydney Morning Herald* reported, it had 'lurched from one disappointment to another', was 'struggling to attract crowds in all but peak times' and had failed to win 'a crucial tax cut which would allow it to play in the lucrative high-roller market'. Worse still, it had lost its chief executive, put the New South Wales government, the media and its employees offside, and been buried in an avalanche of bad publicity. Its financial results were also so disappointing that Showboat was looking to sell out. And James in particular was keen to buy.

Four months earlier he had been promoted to managing director of the Packers' new public company, Publishing and Broadcasting Limited (PBL), as Kerry took a step back from the business. Brian Powers, who was taking over as chairman, told James as they flew back from China on the Packers' private jet with Kerry looking on, bursting with pride. James was obviously thrilled, although somewhat surprised. 'It speaks volumes for nepotism,' he told an acquaintance who congratulated him at a dinner shortly afterwards. Two years later he was still shaking his head, admitting he had been 'surprised', 'flattered' and 'very touched' to be rewarded by his father. 'He implied a trust in me which . . . was something that meant a lot to me,' he confessed. A trust—and a generosity—which Kerry rarely showed.

In October, this new managing director flew to Los Angeles to meet Showboat's CEO, Gregg Nasky, and shake hands on a takeover deal. Negotiations continued for the next three months, but stayed such a well-kept secret that even the casino's new chief executive, Neil Gamble, was kept in the dark. In January 1997, he told the press categorically that there had been no talks between Showboat and the Packers and there would be none. A couple of days later, James and Brian Powers were on a flight to Los Angeles to dot the i's and cross the t's on the agreement. A week after that, it was officially announced that PBL would pay $340 million to acquire 85 per cent of the casino management contract and 10 per cent of the shares in Sydney Harbour Casino Ltd.

It seemed to be a good deal for both sides—although hardly on a par with getting it for free. Even Dick Warburton, chairman of the winning consortium in 1994, was pleased with the outcome because he felt the Packers would make a better fist of it than Showboat had done. Warburton had several meetings with James and Kerry, including one on the Packers' huge converted icebreaker, the *Arctic P*. And for three months all appeared to be going smoothly, even if he got the feeling that Kerry was less enthusiastic about the deal than James.

But there was still one obstacle to surmount: the New South Wales Casino Control Authority (CCA) had to agree that Kerry was a fit and proper person to hold a casino licence. And this was proving to be a lot tougher than the Packers had expected.

Kerry had gone through this scrutiny back in 1994, at the time of the original bid, and had apparently been given the green light. He had also been cleared by Victoria's regulators in 1992 to be a major shareholder in Melbourne's Crown Casino. But despite that the CCA's boss, Lindsay Le Compte, was not going to let approval go through on a nod. Indeed, he seemed determined to examine Kerry rigorously and do so in public, as the CCA had done with Showboat in 1994. This was not good news for Kerry because the CCA had no intention of being hampered by rules of evidence or natural justice. Anyone who wanted to make allegations about the Packers would be able to do just that.

Probity checks for the most junior casino employees involved taking fingerprints, checking criminal records and trawling through personal and financial affairs. But Kerry was going to be forced to surrender tax returns, bank statements and financial records for himself and some 300 companies and asked to identify and explain every transaction in excess of $5000 over the previous five years. He would also have to turn over records from the various trusts and holding companies that owned the Packer business empire via the Bahamas. And he was certain to be quizzed about his tax dodging, his involvement in bottom-of-the-harbour schemes in the 1980s and his brush with the Costigan Royal Commission in 1984. Finally, the CCA would almost certainly want to ask him about his punting, his massive wins and losses in casinos and the currency markets, and about the company he kept, which was not always entirely savoury.

On 22 April 1997 the man who was to conduct the inquiry, Peter McLellan QC, confirmed the ground rules and made it clear what the consequences might be. 'I am aware of the very significant damage which could be done to individuals or corporations, investors and others by publication of confidential information during the course of the inquiry,' he said, '[but] where the authority is satisfied that it is in the public interest . . . the inquiry will proceed in public.'

Shortly afterwards Neil Gamble got a call from Kerry, who wanted to know what the CCA's investigators had put him through. Gamble said they had looked at his passport and questioned him about every trip he had made in the previous five years. They had also hauled him into their office and asked him about people who had been subcontractors on his house before he owned it. It had been an incredibly intrusive process that had taken several months and, as he told Kerry, his affairs were absurdly simple by comparison.

The Big Fella listened and asked if Gamble's wife had been put through the wringer as well. She had. And this, it appears, was the clincher. The investigators had already started asking Ros questions, and Packer told Gamble he was not prepared to let it continue. Thirty-six hours later, he pulled out of the casino takeover. Or, to be more precise, at midnight on Saturday 1 May 1997, PBL allowed its letter of intent to expire.

Thus the Australian public was cheated of what would have been one of the great spectacles of recent times. God only knows what Kerry would have made of the hearings, but he absolutely hated being questioned about his private affairs and this sort of public examination would surely have caused a massive meltdown. His bristling appearance before the 1991 Senate Inquiry into the

Fairfax takeover, when he said only a fool pays more tax than he has to, would have paled by comparison.

But it may not have been just the probity hearings that put Packer off. He was also having second thoughts about the price PBL was paying. Brian Powers, for one, believes he would have been prepared to endure the agony of the inquiry had the casino been more of a bargain.

This view is backed up by an adviser who was summoned to Park Street and Packer's private bunker in the Hyde Park Club. 'Tell me about the casino, son,' said Kerry, as he took off his clothes and stripped right down. Trying not to stare at the boss's crown jewels, the adviser looked him hard in the eye and tried even harder to concentrate as Kerry asked detailed questions about the take per table, the breakdown of games and the brand of slot machines they would be using. Sweating in his suit, and valiantly trying to focus on the pros and cons of the deal, the adviser's interrogation continued as Kerry immersed himself in the hot tub, then the cold bath, and finally the sauna. Back in the lounge area, where Kerry wrapped himself in a towel and sat down, the poor man's concentration was challenged again when Packer put his feet up on the table, leaving his ample private parts dangling in mid air. 'So, son?' he asked. 'What d'ya think? Should we buy it?' Gulping, the adviser said, 'Not at that price.' Two hours later, he fielded an angry phone call from James. 'What the fuck have you said to Dad?' And the casino deal was dead.

James had been mad keen to go ahead and was now angry at those who had counselled Kerry against it. He believed a great opportunity had been lost. Worse still, the Packers had expended a huge amount of money and effort over the previous three years to win the casino, and all that was now going to waste.

The people at Showboat were also annoyed and surprised that Kerry had pulled out. But there was nothing they could do. There seemed to be no penalties involved for the Packers changing their mind.

The spin to the media was that Kerry had dumped the casino because there was a more valuable prize on offer. The Fairfax newspaper group was up for grabs again, and word was that Prime Minister John Howard had promised it to his friend. The papers happily reported this because it raised all the old fears of the Packers becoming even more powerful.

Kerry had come within a whisker of getting control of Fairfax in 1991 when he had been part of the Tourang consortium with Conrad Black. But he had wanted to capture it for much longer than that, to get his hands on the 'rivers of gold', as his father had described the newspapers' classified ads when Kerry was a boy, and to take revenge on his oldest rivals. The Packers had fought the Fairfaxes in the Sydney newspaper market for forty years while Sir Frank owned the *Daily Telegraph*, and Kerry had a few scores of his own to settle with the organisation that had exposed him as the Goanna in 1984.

But by the mid-1990s, he wasn't nearly so keen to spend the $3 billion that would be needed to bring victory. Unlike his father, he had never fallen hopelessly in love with newspapers, and Fairfax was now almost three times the price it had been back in 1991. However, every so often, late at night, he would get excited about the prospect of another tilt at the windmill. If the *Sydney Morning Herald* attacked him or wrote something he didn't like, he would decide it was time to teach its journalists a lesson or, as he put it, 'take those cunts over'. He dreamed of storming in, sacking a few key people, shaking up the management, showing a bit of leadership and running the place properly. And it was precisely this prospect that worried everybody there.

It didn't take much to make Kerry cross, of course. He loathed being written about, especially if his tax affairs or personal life were being investigated. And even the most trivial trespass was capable of getting him riled.

One story that caused him to go ballistic was a front-page article in the Fairfax-owned *Australian Financial Review* (*AFR*) about a weekend break-in in May 1995, when thieves sliced open the personal safe in his Park Street office with an oxyacetylene cutter and made off with $5 million worth of gold bars weighing nearly 300 kilograms. It remains a mystery to this day how they managed to do it, but they got in and out of the building in less than half an hour, while security guards patrolled outside, and were able to turn off the alarm system and use the lift. According to the detective charged with investigating the theft, it was the neatest job he had seen in thirty-five years in the police force. Clearly, the safe-crackers (who were thought to have flown in from Europe) had been given the inside track, including the information that Kerry was crazy enough to keep the gold in his office in the first place.

The *AFR*'s story, which appeared six months after the theft, suggested that someone close to the Packer family might have given the robbers information. After describing the layout of Kerry's third-floor office and pinpointing the location of the secret safe, it also quoted his personal assistant's account of discovering the theft. But what upset Packer most of all was the suggestion that he liked to gloat over his hoard. 'Very few people within Consolidated Press knew that their boss had a safe in his office, let alone the riches it contained,' the *AFR* told its readers, 'but those who did know say that Packer had a penchant for occasionally taking some of the 25 bars of bullion from his safe just to look at it.' Presumably, this nugget of information had been passed on by the police investigating the theft, but Kerry may have suspected someone from his staff of talking directly to the paper. Either way, it was enough to send him into orbit.

On the day the story hit the streets Richard Coleman, a Fairfax lawyer, got a call as he was eating breakfast at home. It was the switchboard with a 'very rude, very angry man' insisting he speak to a lawyer. Coleman told them to put the caller through and answered, 'Richard Coleman speaking.'

'Well, Richard Coleman,' came the reply, 'it's Kerry Packer here and I'm ringing to tell you you're going to pay for this, you're not fucking going to get away with it. I'm going to sue and I'm going to get my just deserts. I'm just not going to put up with it.'

In one of the most frightening moments of his life, Coleman managed to calm Packer down for long enough to find out what had upset him, promise to read the offending article and ring back. Before long, a grovelling apology was being drafted and Kerry was being told his legal costs would be paid. Looking at the story today it is hard to see why Packer was so furious, and even harder to see why Fairfax was in such a hurry to hose him down, but Packer was one of Fairfax's biggest shareholders at the time and had made no secret of his desire to take control of the newspaper group.

Despite being repelled in his attempt to capture Fairfax in 1991, Kerry had muscled back onto its share register in 1993 by acquiring a 15 per cent stake. He bought more shares in February 1995 and invited himself on to Channel Nine's top-rating news program, *A Current Affair*, to tell Ray Martin he wanted to own the company. Days later he made a similar pitch in the *Bulletin*, telling Trevor Sykes it was the 'perfect scenario' to gobble up

Fairfax and double the size of his media empire, adding with a twinkle that it might take twenty years and be something his grandchildren would do.

It seemed unlikely he would have to wait that long. When interviewed on *A Current Affair*, Kerry told Martin that John Howard was a decent man who would make a good prime minister if he was ever given the chance. A year later Howard was elected and breezed into government promising to scrap Australia's cross-media laws.

The precursor to this was supposed to be a wide-ranging public inquiry. But after six months in office Howard's Minister for Communications, Richard Alston, decided to by-pass this messy and troublesome process in favour of a simpler fix which could get a new law onto the statute book while the Coalition still had control of the Senate. This involved issuing a brief discussion paper and calling for comments, the first of which summed up the pessimists' view of the pantomime. 'As a concerned member of the public,' wrote Stephen Kress of Victoria, 'I would like to see diverse media ownership, not a Packer–Murdoch duopoly. However, since the Government has already obviously done a deal with either or both media barons, this review is merely a farce. I will bet you . . . that by the end of Mr Howard's first term in office, Kerry Packer will own Fairfax.'

It appeared that this prediction was right on the money because Howard and Alston were soon championing a proposal that the Department of Transport and Communications (DOTAC) had not even bothered to include in its recommendations to Cabinet. This would allow 'Australian' proprietors (like Packer) to own one TV station and one newspaper in each major market, while foreigners (like Murdoch) would not be allowed to buy more than 15 per cent of anything. By a strange coincidence, this was also exactly what

Kerry wanted because it would stop Rupert buying Channel Seven and turning it into a more powerful rival to Channel Nine.

By April 1997, when the Sydney casino deal was dumped, it seemed almost certain that Packer would get his way because Howard had been on radio to say the cross-media laws were 'ludicrous' and 'outdated' and the government would get rid of them. The question was whether the Coalition's backbenchers would allow this to happen.

Two months earlier, Howard had summoned a number of backbenchers to The Lodge—including members of the Coalition's communications committee—and found them to be hostile. Almost immediately, the Packers had wheeled their lobbyists into action. Michael Kroger, the Liberal powerbroker, had been hired to chase Coalition stragglers over the line, and Graham Richardson had been sent to harass the Senate. As part of the push, James had also met Richard Alston in Sydney to advance the argument. And Kerry no doubt raised the matter with Howard, whom he saw regularly and with whom he had much in common: they both loved talking cricket and believed Fairfax needed a whipping.

In late April, a couple of weeks after abandoning his casino bid, Kerry paid a formal visit to Howard in Canberra, spending an hour at his Parliament House office. Days later, the prime minister was again spinning the Packer line on ABC Radio's *AM*, describing the cross-media laws as 'ridiculous' and arguing that Australian media companies needed a strong base from which to take on the world. He also admitted candidly: 'Mr Packer . . . would like to buy Fairfax. At the moment he can't, because he owns Channel Nine. We're considering whether that law should be changed.'

By most accounts, Howard and Alston had already decided it should be. However, they faced mounting opposition. On

5 May 1997, the day before the changes were due to go to Cabinet, *The Age* published a letter from eighty prominent Australians, including Malcolm Fraser and Peter Westerway (who as head of the Australian Broadcasting Authority had torpedoed Kerry's involvement in the 1991 Fairfax takeover). Their concern was diversity, the letter said, but as Fraser had often made clear, it was also about the danger of giving more power to Packer. Senior ministers were also worried that voters might see changes in the law as a gift to Kerry. Consequently, Cabinet failed to reach a decision.

But this didn't stop the Packers pushing even harder. The day after the Cabinet meeting—with Kerry in London playing polo—James lobbied senior government ministers at Crown Casino's formal opening in Melbourne. And the day after that, he braved a barrage of lollipops from Ray Martin on *A Current Affair*, who asked whether Fairfax would make a nice Christmas present. James, who managed to slip 'Australia' or 'Australian' into his answers at least thirty times, agreed it would be 'fantastic'. Ironically, the interview provided the perfect example of what people were concerned about: a powerful proprietor using his media outlets to advance his own interests.

James promised that the Packers would take great care of the *Herald*, *The Age* and the *Australian Financial Review* and not interfere. 'Ninety per cent of Australian newspapers are controlled by foreigners,' he told Martin. 'Why, as an Australian media company, shouldn't we be allowed to buy Fairfax, an Australian newspaper company, and grow our business to create a major Australian media company to try and export ourselves to the world?'

It was the first time James had been interviewed on television and the critics were impressed. He was cool, charming, polished and patriotic, and very different from his bullying father, whose appearances always caused such a stir. But it helped that the toughest question he faced was an invitation from Martin to propose to his girlfriend, Kate Fischer. This was the one thing the media trainers hadn't prepared him for and he was momentarily lost for words. 'Oh God, I'm stumped,' he blushed, before picking himself up to say that he was 'the luckiest guy going around'. Every time he went home and felt a bit down he realised he wouldn't trade places with anyone because his life was 'fantastic'.

The Canberra bureau of the *Sydney Morning Herald* wanted James's first TV outing to be the front-page lead. John Alexander, the *Herald*'s editor-in-chief, who had just been sprung sailing with the enemy on the Packers' *Arctic P*, decreed it was not front-page news or even a news story. He then rang James, who was staying at Crown Casino, and arranged for reporters Sally Loane and Glenn Burge to fly down to Melbourne to interview him. Anne Davies, who had been covering the media ownership story for the *Herald* and might have given the budding tycoon a much harder time, was not invited.

The Loane and Burge interview with James did make the front page and filled a fair chunk of the inside of the paper as well. Under the tagline 'Packer's pitch for Fairfax', James was given free rein to explain why it was in the national interest for him and his dad to own the newspaper group as well as Channel Nine. To many, it seemed odd to invite a predator to explain so prominently why he should be allowed to eat the prey. But it was revealing in that James candidly admitted the Packers were doing their best to put pressure on Howard and his ministers. Predictably, he said they would be scrapping the charter of independence that protected Fairfax journalists from the proprietor's political line. 'We would operate Fairfax the same way as Channel Nine,' he said. 'It is editorially independent, and we haven't signed a charter.' As to the Packers' desire to own the newspaper group, if that were in doubt, he said: 'We have always thought it would be fantastic. But it isn't something that we as a family have become obsessed with.' And indeed James had not.

With his father still in London, James also set about lobbying members of the Coalition's backbench communications committee and doing so in most unusual fashion: he went to *call* on them. 'The Packers were hot for it,' says Paul Neville, the committee chairman. 'Jamie flew up to Bundaberg to take me to lunch. I think he was a bit apprehensive about meeting me. He said, "You don't like my family, do you?" I said, quite to the contrary, I have the greatest respect for the Packers and the Murdochs for what they've achieved. This is just about wanting to see diversity in the Australian media.'

James also flew to Brisbane to see Gary Hardgrave, the committee secretary, and spent an hour and a half at his electoral office amid the car yards on the Moorooka Magic Mile. 'I must say I was pretty chuffed to receive a visit,' says Hardgrave, who had been a radio and TV journalist before entering parliament. 'It's not every day that James Packer walks in your front door.'

'He was very blokey, very matey,' Hardgrave recalls. 'There was lots of f'ing this and f'ing that, and he kept thumping his clenched fist into the palm of his hand as he made each point. It must have sounded to my staff like I was being beaten up.'

Hardgrave liked the young man and thought him passionate and impressive in his argument that Fairfax ought to be owned by an Australian company, but the backbencher didn't give ground. 'There was no question that James believed the government should change the law so the Packers could get what they wanted, and I had to tell him we can't do that, we can't change the law just because you want something.'

By this time, Hardgrave, Neville and the other members of the Coalition's communications committee had been summoned to see Richard Alston, who wanted to know if there was any version of the new law they would support. To their surprise, the discussion was not about principles but about what pieces of Fairfax the Packers might have. Would it be all right if they got *The Age* and the *Herald*, they were asked, or would they need to choose between the two? And what about the *Australian Financial Review*? There appeared to be no guiding principle behind these options, apart from finding a way to give Kerry what he wanted.

Neville was baffled by the whole process. 'I could never find out why anyone was doing it,' he says. 'It just helped the already rich and powerful get richer and more powerful at the expense of diversity and competition. And when you asked Alston and Howard what they were trying to achieve they could never give you an answer.'

Hardgrave's conclusion was even blunter. The government wanted to deliver *The Age*, the *Sydney Morning Herald* and the *Australian Financial Review* to the Packers to get more favourable coverage than they had in the past. 'They had that plan, but I wasn't going to be a part of it. I thought it was my job to stop it.'

Richard Alston absolutely denied such motives, telling the Senate that his guiding principle was to 'ensure diversity of opinion'. But it was hard to see how this fitted in with giving the Packers more. And it's a fair guess that hardly a voter in the country would have believed his explanation.

The Coalition's backbenchers certainly didn't. In June 1997, six of them voiced their opposition to the changes at a joint party-room meeting. Brendan Nelson, Joe Hockey and Victorian MP Bruce Bilson all spoke. Then the Prime Minister put his hands up as if to say, 'Okay, that's enough, it's no longer on the agenda'.

But Alston was not ready to give up, and neither was Packer. Later that month, while Howard was in London, the tycoon invited the Prime Minister to his suite at the Savoy Hotel to remind him why Fairfax should be in Australian hands. Soon afterwards, in the hope of assuaging Rupert Murdoch, Alston advanced a new plan that would increase the limit on foreign ownership to 25 per cent and replace the existing cross-media ban with a regime policed by the Australian Broadcasting Authority.

By late July, it was clear the government was hoping to have another run at changing the law, but now the Murdochs intervened. Hearing that action was imminent, Rupert and Lachlan dropped in on the Prime Minister at Kirribilli House to say they would not accept changes to the media laws that gave Packer Fairfax but did not allow them to buy a TV station. It was now clear to Howard that the policy was going to make one media mogul—who owned two-thirds of Australia's newspapers—extremely unhappy.

Out in the electorate the polls were also flashing red, and focus groups were showing the government's media policy was a major factor. Howard rang Neville and Hardgrave, then met Nelson and Hockey in Sydney, and received the clear message that they still weren't happy. Hockey and Nelson would cross the floor if it came to a vote.

Suddenly, it all seemed too difficult. On Monday 1 September 1997, Howard told Cabinet he had decided to give up on the attempt. 'It just got too bloody hard for the government to push ahead with it,' says Hardgrave.

Ultimately James was happy they lost, confiding later to Joe Hockey that he was grateful the deal had been blocked. He had never been remotely interested in journalism for its own sake and possibly had an even lower opinion of journalists than his father did. Asked by a Packer editor in 1996 what he intended to do with his magazines now he was managing director, James replied that he was going to 'leverage the brands' and give away cutlery sets with the *Australian Women's Weekly*. Two years later he was telling his editors they were 'brand managers' and packing them off to a three-day marketing conference with white boards so they could better understand their customers.

As far as James was concerned, journalism was merely something that had to be tolerated in the noble pursuit of making more money. And in his opinion there were far better ways than owning newspapers to make a quid.

CHAPTER 7
DEATH'S DOOR

Operations don't worry me a lot . . . I've had a lot of
them and I believe I'm bulletproof.

While Kerry was busy fighting old battles with the Fairfaxes and
dreaming of his family's golden days when it owned the *Daily
Telegraph*, James was thinking about new media and the next
millennium. In March 1997 he had pushed PBL into starting an
online division to exploit the internet, which would soon be worth
more than all the rest of the Packers' media interests combined.
And three months after that, in June 1997, he had brokered a deal
with Lachlan Murdoch that finally brought peace to pay-TV. This
would also be worth a fortune to the Packers in years to come.

Essentially, James and Lachlan had persuaded Kerry and Rupert
to end the war by dividing the spoils between them. And this was
a fantastic win for the Packers since Murdoch had spent around
$500 million on pay-TV and Super League while the Packers had
spent next to nothing. But the victory was not only James's doing.

Kerry and his team had played their hand extremely well from the beginning. And while it's a complicated story, it is one that's worth telling from the start.

Despite Kerry's desire to stay out of pay-TV and avoid a fight with Rupert, both things had somehow come to pass. In 1994 when the Packer, Murdoch, Telstra consortium fell apart, the old man had been persuaded by James to invest in Optus Vision on the basis that Murdoch would almost certainly agree to join them and they would be invincible. The Packers, however, soon found themselves at war with the newly formed Foxtel, owned by their two powerful former partners.

Kerry felt betrayed by this and claimed he had been lied to. But in September 1994, immediately after being dumped by Murdoch and Telstra, he scored a crucial victory when he sent a team of executives to Hollywood to sign up four of the major movie studios to Optus Vision. Simultaneously, the other four independent studios signed up with Australis, which owned the licence to deliver pay-TV in Australia by satellite. As a result, Foxtel was left out in the cold with no movies (except from 20th Century Fox) and at that stage no sport.

Months before the first shots were even fired in the Super League war, Foxtel had been forced to send Packer's former lieutenant, Sam Chisholm, knocking on Australis's door to pledge a staggering $4 billion over 25 years so it could share the movies (plus Discovery Channel and Nickelodeon) the company had just bought in Hollywood. This seemed like a good idea at the time because Foxtel couldn't have run a pay-TV service if it had nothing to offer its customers. But it was also a burden that Foxtel was desperate to be rid of, and it was what ultimately allowed the Packers to force such a profitable peace.

Within months, Australis was running short of cash and teetering on the brink of bankruptcy because the money it was due to get from Foxtel hadn't started to flow and it hadn't been able to raise sufficient capital. By September 1995, its position was so dire that it was forced to agree on a merger with Foxtel, only for the marriage to be banned by the Trade Practices Commission. Seven months later, in April 1996, Australis was press-ganged into a second deal in which Foxtel would buy back the movie contract for $275 million.

At this point Foxtel was within 24 hours of solving its problem and getting rid of $4 billion worth of baggage, but at the last minute Australis's chief executive, Neil Gamble (who had not yet moved to run Sydney's casino), decided to ring Nick Falloon, head of PBL Enterprises. Gamble, who had played golf with Falloon a couple of times, was hoping for a little sympathy. Instead, he was called down to Park Street and whisked into Kerry's office, where he found his golf partner, James Packer, Brian Powers and the Big Fella in his socks.

'So what's the problem?' Kerry asked.

'I have no money, we're about to go under,' Gamble told him.

'Well, son, that's a fucking stupid way to start a negotiation,' Packer replied, laughing.

Gamble shot back that he had no time for subtlety. 'We sign a deal with News at 11 a.m. tomorrow that will give Foxtel all the programs it needs. What do you think?'

For the next hour Gamble waited in the boardroom while Kerry, James and the others debated what to do. When he was brought back into Kerry's office he was offered a rescue of sorts. PBL would put in money to keep Australis afloat for six months and help it go to market to raise more. In return, it would take a stake in the company, plus first and last rights to buy the Hollywood movies if

Australis went bust. This was Powers's brilliant idea, which proved invaluable in later negotiations with the Murdochs.

Gamble didn't quite know what to make of the deal. If Australis went down, the Packers would have their foot on his neck. But if the company survived, these first and last rights would mean nothing. Besides, anything was better than oblivion, which is what he faced if he sold out to News. So he agreed.

Gamble, Falloon and an army of lawyers worked through the night at the Packers' Park Street offices, knowing they had to have the deal all tied up by morning. At his lawyer's request, Gamble turned off his mobile and rang his wife to tell her to take the home phone off the hook. But at 5 a.m. he used his mobile to call the USA and found himself unexpectedly talking to Sam Chisholm instead. Murdoch's man was having dinner in a restaurant in London and had been ringing all day at fifteen-minute intervals. 'What are you doing up so early?' he asked.

'I'm always up at this time. I'm walking the dog,' Gamble lied.

'How's my deal going?' Chisholm pushed.

'Fine,' said Gamble. 'We're going to sign this morning.'

'That's great,' said Chisholm, and hung up.

PBL and Australis signed the documents at 10 a.m. on 18 April 1996, one hour before News Limited's deadline. Soon afterwards, Australis's chairman, Rod Price, rang Chisholm in London, where it was now after midnight. 'G'day Sam, just called to say we've done the deal.'

'Good,' said Sam, 'that's fantastic news.'

'No Sam, not with you, with Packer,' said Price, before hanging up.

The Australis rescue was a sensational deal for the Packers because it tied up the asset Foxtel desperately needed and made it impossible for their pay-TV rival to escape its $4 billion commitment without mounting a massive legal action. The Murdochs, on the other hand, would now be forced to sue for peace with the Packers over pay-TV or face another long-running war. And after the Super League conflict between the two titans was effectively settled in January 1997, there was little appetite for more fighting.

It was James and Lachlan who first resolved to end hostilities and then persuaded their fathers to fall in behind. Few of the officers in the News camp were happy with the terms of the cease-fire. Ken Cowley was convinced too much was being given away, as were some of the executives and lawyers who drew up the paperwork. And they had a point. The deal gave PBL the option to buy half of Fox Sports—which was already making money—and half of News Limited's 50 per cent share in Foxtel, which would become the most profitable media company in Australia. Better still, it gave both to the Packers at a price that excluded the hundreds of millions of dollars the Murdochs had spent on Super League.

One tycoon who knows the Packers and Murdochs well says Rupert has regretted the surrender ever since. 'Giving up half of Foxtel to Packer has always pissed him off. He has never got over giving so much away. Kerry took advantage of him. He outbluffed him. He spent the least and ended up with the same.'

Typically, Kerry was not so sure he had won the jackpot, perhaps because James had been so important in securing it. He was happy to buy into Fox Sports on the cheap but had no desire to own Foxtel. Pay-TV was still losing millions and Kerry thought it a 'shit business', something he never tired of telling his executives. Consequently, he would need to be rolled if the purchase was to go ahead. But that would be a battle for another day, and Kerry might not be around to fight it.

In April 1998 he took off to Europe as usual to play polo, gamble and have fun. But, after spending the northern summer racing around on horseback, he was suddenly taken sick in London. Three years earlier he had collapsed from a heart attack during a private function at the Hakoah Club in Bondi; now his only remaining kidney was packing up. His doctors were adamant that he had only weeks to live unless they could find him a new kidney. Luckily, his helicopter pilot, Nick Ross, was happy to surrender one of his. Even more luckily, he appeared to be a suitable door.

Ross was not just one of Kerry's employees, he was also a friend. He called the boss 'Father' (which is how sailors in the Royal Navy refer to their skipper) and was known as Captain Whirlybits or Biggles in return. The two men had met in the 1980s when Ross was working as a helicopter pilot at Channel Nine and had immediately hit it off. Ross, who left school at the age of fifteen to join the navy, had trained as a pilot and then knocked around the trouble spots of the world flying choppers, much as Kerry might have done had he not been a billionaire. Both were also 'rascals', as Ross liked to put it, who loved racing fast cars, flying micro-light planes and chasing women. So when Nine was sold to Alan Bond in 1987, Ross had stayed on as Kerry's personal pilot. For the next eleven years he flew the boss wherever he wanted to go, shuttling between Sydney and Ellerston for part of the year and spending the rest of it on the *Arctic P* or in the world's best hotels.

Ross's motives for giving up his kidney were partly selfish, in that he wanted his playmate to be around so they could have fun. But he also reckoned Kerry had been dealt a lousy hand when it came to health and wanted to do something to help. And no one else in Kerry's immediate orbit was volunteering.

Ross had blood and tissue tests taken at the Savoy Hotel, which confirmed he was a good match, and was preparing to be whisked into a London clinic for the operation when Kerry's condition suddenly deteriorated. The chopper pilot was given half an hour to pack a bag and get on the plane back to Sydney, where the Royal Prince Alfred Hospital (RPA) was readying itself for the Packer convoy to arrive.

The head cardiologist at the RPA, Dr Ian Bailey, still remembers his first encounter with his new charge. Breaking all the established rules of patient-doctor relationships, Kerry put his arm round the man who was going to take care of him and told him cheerfully there were two things he needed to know: 'One, I'm very hard to kill. Two, I'm a gambler, and I almost always win.' From then on, Kerry would never waste an opportunity to remind Bailey and his team that he was in charge and they were his servants.

Bailey's reckoning was that Packer would have lasted three days without surgery. His kidney was not working because the blood supply was blocked, and his heart was giving up under the strain. He had fluid in his lungs, was coughing blood, and his body was beginning to shut down. Worse still, his heart was not strong enough to survive a kidney transplant operation. The only option was to get his existing kidney working again by inserting a balloon into the artery that supplied it. Dialysis would then be needed to clean his blood. And if all that went to plan, they could start figuring out what to do next.

Kerry was given an entire private ward that normally held four people (who had been moved to make way for him) furnished with personal effects his butler had brought in. There was an extra-large bed, a giant TV screen and a cocktail cabinet to make it all seem just like home. Before long, the place was also wired for computers so Kerry's staff could keep in touch with his businesses. Despite this royal treatment, or perhaps because of it, the billionaire was a shocking patient. He would refuse to give blood samples and would attempt to walk out of the hospital without warning. According to Dr Bailey, 'He would just yank off his monitors, yank off his oxygen mask, yank out drains and cannulas and head for the door, with all sort of luckless people running behind him, trying to cap and dress wounds.' One night he got as far as trying to hail a cab at 2 a.m. before hospital staff managed to restrain him. 'He could be so, so rude,' Bailey recalls. 'You'd see the eyelids start to flicker, you'd see the bottom lip start to drop, you knew the conversation had about twenty seconds to go and he was going to walk.'

After a week of dialysis, Kerry's kidney was stabilised and the doctors turned their minds to fixing his heart with its blocked arteries and leaking mitral valve. Packer's valve was working so badly it was forcing blood back into the lungs and not allowing enough to be distributed to where it was needed. As a result, he was short of breath, had even higher blood pressure than usual and was at risk of heart failure.

There was no reason why the RPA's doctors could not have fixed the problem, but one of Packer's billionaire friends, Nelson Pelz, who was on the board of Cornell Medical Center in New York, had persuaded Kerry that the operation should be performed by the famous Texan heart surgeon Dr Wayne Isom, considered to be the best in the world. So it was decided to fly him to New York as quickly as possible.

Typically, Kerry was not prepared to lie around and wait for this to happen. The day before his departure, he abandoned his hospital bed and dragged himself off for lunch at Fairfax with Brian Powers and Bob Muscat, who had recently joined Fairfax as chief executive after many years running papers for Murdoch. Muscat remembers Packer pushing the food round on his plate and looking 'as sick as a dog'. Typically, instead of travelling by ambulance, Kerry insisted on going by car, which his driver parked near enough to the Fairfax building for it to be seen by a *Herald* journalist, who reported the sighting in the paper the following day. Somehow or other, Kerry was still well enough to fire off a blistering letter to Muscat accusing him of failing to keep his visit a secret.

The following night, with his plane due to depart at 10.30 p.m., Kerry was entertaining again, playing host to a group of Liberal politicians at his home in Bellevue Hill. He would explain later that he never worried too much about impending operations; he had undergone so many that he considered himself 'bulletproof'. When the time came to leave for the airport, he donned a suit and was helped into his limousine, which drove to Mascot with the ambulance following behind. Conscious that the press knew of his illness and might now have got wind of the reason for his trip, he walked up the steps of his private DC-8 unaided, even though he was spitting blood. Once inside the plane, which was kitted out with a bed, an electro-cardiograph, oxygen and a defibrillator, the blinds were pulled down and he was hooked up to his drips again.

It was 4 a.m. when the plane arrived at Kennedy Airport— which had to be opened up especially because it landed outside the curfew. The pilot had trouble finding the terminal, but when he finally pulled up Kerry, wearing his suit, again spurned the ambulance waiting to meet him. As his limousine drove into the city, he spotted a young man wrapped in a garbage bag huddled against the early-morning chill, and demanded that someone get out and give him a wad of cash. When the limousine pulled into Cornell, Kerry was met by a phalanx of wheelchairs and stretcher bearers.

Again, he refused all offers of help and insisted on walking into the hospital, hauling himself along the corridor, stopping every 30 metres to lean on the wall while a posse of doctors and nurses followed behind ready to catch him. He eventually reached his private suite, where he came face-to-face with Dr Isom, who was trailing a similarly large entourage. There was silence for a moment. Then Packer introduced himself as Dr Bailey and gestured towards the real doctor, saying, 'This is Mr Packer, who is the worst patient you will ever have to deal with in your life.'

An outsize bed, a big-screen TV and all his normal comforts were waiting for him, and he was soon giving the doctors a taste of the behaviour he had warned them about. Having listened quietly as a junior doctor berated him about his heavy smoking, Kerry sat up, ripped off his oxygen mask and jabbed his finger in the man's face, saying, 'Okay, son, you've given me the fucking lecture and I've listened to it, now what are you going to do to fucking fix me?'

Isom and his team were famous for taking the cases others wouldn't touch, but it was still line ball whether or not they would operate because there was a real risk Packer would die on the table. Assessing Kerry's chances as no better than 50-50, Isom decided to go ahead with the first procedure, which was to patch up the original by-pass done by Victor Chang in 1990 by inserting stents and balloons to open up the arteries. A couple of days later he moved on to Kerry's leaking heart valve, which was successfully repaired. The more radical option of a new by-pass operation, which would have involved dragging an artery across from the right-hand side of Packer's chest, was judged to be too dangerous.

While Kerry was going under the knife, several Australian journalists had got wind that he was in hospital and were trying to find out why. But the hospital was even denying that Mr Packer was a patient, perhaps because he had checked in as James Fairfax and had instructed staff to tell callers he was dying. By the time Cornell Medical Center put out a statement saying he had undergone heart surgery, his condition was stable and that they had been asked to say no more, Kerry was already on his way out the door. His two-week stay in hospital was cut short after five days when he decamped to the St Regis, where he took a huge luxury suite with views over Central Park. Naturally, his doctors and nurses moved with him. Ros, James and Gretel were already there, and once again all were under strict instructions not to talk to the press. By the time he checked out two weeks later to fly back to Sydney the media pack had been called off, so nobody knew that his DC-8 and crew had waited for him the whole time.

Back in Australia, James had been running the show on his own for three months without any help from Brian Powers, who had come to the end of his five-year contract and had left in May. Kerry had talked to the American about whether James was ready to take over but had not been convinced by Powers's assurances. 'To be perfectly honest,' Kerry admitted later to the Australian Broadcasting Authority, 'I don't think we ever reached a conclusion, or I don't think I quite reached a conclusion.' But Powers had been determined to leave.

Having at first agreed to stay on a few months to ease the handover, he had decided he wanted to have a go at running Fairfax, which Kerry was still hoping to buy and in which the Packers still held a 15 per cent stake. 'Geez, you would be perfect for it,' Kerry had replied when told. And Powers had departed.

Eleven days later, at his first post-Packer board meeting, Powers had been confirmed as Fairfax chairman. He had started going through the budgets line by line straight away, slamming the brakes on the company's spending and imposing a freeze on hiring.

Not surprisingly, the Australian Broadcasting Authority (ABA) reacted to his appointment by immediately opening an inquiry into whether Powers and the Packers were in breach of the cross-media laws that prevented a TV proprietor controlling a newspaper in the same city. The two relevant tests for the ABA were whether Powers was an associate of the Packers and whether he was in a position to control Fairfax.

As evidence of his continuing association, Powers was still allowing the Packers to pay his rent, golf and tennis club subscriptions and mobile phone bills. He had also been retained by James as a consultant to Consolidated Press Holdings (CPH), the family's private company, on all matters excluding Fairfax, and continued to use his old secretary in Park Street. In addition, CPH had guaranteed a $12.2 million loan so he could buy a 15 per cent stake in the vehicle that now held the Packers' Fairfax shares, the FXF Trust.

There was also some evidence that Powers was in a position to control Fairfax. He had stymied its takeover of the *Canberra Times* and discussed with James Packer an online joint venture between Fairfax and PBL. More generally, he was the most active chairman Fairfax had ever seen, and his considerable ability to get what he wanted had increased in August when the managing director, Bob Muscat, walked out and was replaced by a committee chaired by Powers.

Whether all this amounted to Powers doing Kerry's bidding or to a breach of the cross-media laws was up to the ABA to decide.

Kerry had been too sick to give evidence in July, and when he finally did take the stand on 27 October he was allowed to do so at the Australian Government Solicitor's office in Sydney's Macquarie

Street, so he did not have to run the gauntlet of the media. But this concession neither soothed his anger nor improved his mood. From the start, he was contemptuous, bullying, foul-mouthed and just plain rude. In his opening salvo to the ABA's counsel, John Corker, he said the whole process was 'repugnant in the extreme' and a 'complete and absolute miscarriage of justice', and it got better from there.

The full transcript of Packer's interview has never been published, which is a great shame, because it makes his famous appearance before the Senate Print Media inquiry in 1991 seem meek by comparison. It's hard to do justice to his performance, but his reaction to being told that the ABA was *investigating* his relationship with Powers gives some idea of his hostility.

> Packer: Why wouldn't you be *asking* me? Why would it be on a basis of investigation? Either I'm a truthful person or I'm a liar. If I'm a liar, your investigation . . .
> Corker: No, it's the word the Act uses; we're inquiring into the facts, I think.
> Packer: Investigating, it sounds like a criminal offence.
> Corker: It's not.
> Packer: Well, that's what it sounds like.
> Corker: Well, that's the statutory language.
> Packer: And that's what I'm objecting to.

Moments later, Packer was asked how often he had seen Brian Powers during Tourang's bid for Fairfax seven years earlier. He replied: 'Christ, you're asking me what I was doing in 1991. I don't know. Turn it up.'

Questioned if he was likely to stay friends with Powers, he said he might play golf with him and might then ask, 'What are you doing about getting those arseholes [at Fairfax] into shape?' or 'Have you got rid of any more people?' or 'Is this managing director of yours any bloody good?' But he didn't expect Powers would listen. He had made his views known when he lunched at Fairfax with Powers and Muscat in July, the day before flying to the USA for surgery. 'Did they take any notice? None at all,' he complained. And this was proof, said Kerry, that he wasn't in control. 'If I controlled Fairfax, do you think they'd run the stories they run about me? I mean, I would have thought it was self-evident that I have no damned control of Fairfax.'

When asked why the ABA should believe him, Packer replied: 'Because I am not a liar and I'm telling you I'm not. I do not control Fairfax. And may you be well and truly warned that anybody who pretends to believe or says that I do I will take the most violent objection to, and I will chase you through every court in the goddamned land. I do not control Fairfax and I never, ever have, much as I would like to, and much as one day maybe I will ... at no point in my life, not for one second of one minute, have I ever controlled Fairfax, unfortunately.'

It is unlikely that anyone has treated an Australian public inquiry with such contempt, or used so many profanities. His evidence was littered with words such as 'goddamn', 'stupid', 'fucking', 'crap', 'farcical' and 'nonsense'. And at one point he told the ABA's counsel point blank, 'It's so fucking stupid. I'm sorry for the language, but it is so stupid that you are going through this procedure.'

Kerry also volunteered his views on some of the key players in the Fairfax saga such as director Mark Burrows, 'a merchant bloody banker; they sell out for two bob'; ex-managing director Bob Muscat, 'a weak man ... Rupert's stooge'; and his old friend and right-hand man Trevor Kennedy, who had led the Tourang consortium in 1991, 'he left with no goodwill whatsoever, he left like a dog'. He gave similar report cards to past Fairfax bosses Gardner, Henderson and Mulholland: 'A joke', 'a mean little bastard' and 'an absolute joke'. But he saved his sharpest barbs for Fred Hilmer, whom Powers had chosen as his new managing director. 'I wouldn't fucking hire him as a sweeper,' said Kerry witheringly.

'Can we come to that?' Corker asked.

'You can come to whatever you like,' Kerry fired back. 'For Fairfax to be run by a management consultant I think is just an act of stupidity. I think it's ridiculous . . . He came from McKinsey and he has never run a business in his life. Now, if that is the right criteria for running a newspaper business then I am a Dutchman.'

Reading this transcript ten years on, two things become clear. The first is that Kerry had been at death's door only three months earlier and now appeared to be back to his best. The second is that James had to deal with this sort of performance on a daily basis. It was a minor miracle that he ever stood his ground or got his way.

But what also shines out is the sharpness of Kerry's brain and the revelation that his ardour for Fairfax was cooling. When Tourang was bidding in 1991, the price had been $1 a share and the business 'a goldmine'. Since then, the price had nearly tripled and Fairfax had become hugely vulnerable to competition from the internet. As Kerry explained, it cost a newspaper four or five times as much to print an ad as it did to put it on the internet, so it was obvious where business would end up. And switching to the internet would not save Fairfax because it would only be cannibalising itself and taking $10 for an ad that it had previously been selling for $50. 'I'm not sure what the future of Fairfax is with classifieds,' he concluded, '[but] without classifieds they're a dud business, they're going to go broke.'

When the ABA finally produced its report in March 1999, it essentially accepted Packer's protestations that he did not control Fairfax and was not in breach of the cross-media laws. But its method of reaching this conclusion was controversial. The ABA argued that Powers could not control the company because he was only one of ten directors on the Fairfax board. And on that basis, said the ABA, it did not intend to rule on the question of whether Powers and Packer were still associates.

Behind the scenes, there had been a great deal of drama in reaching this compromise. A draft report ruling that Packer and Powers were associates had been sent to the two men's lawyers, who fired back letters threatening to sue. The ABA's chairman, David Flint—who was a great admirer of the Packers—then wrote his own minority report putting them in the clear. In retaliation, Flint's colleagues drafted a third report finding Packer and Powers in breach of the law. The dispute had promised to erupt into a major public row until word reached the Prime Minister's office and Flint was persuaded to withdraw his report. The dissidents on the ABA also backed down and a fudge was put in place. And in this way the public had been denied a field day.

Kerry left the inquiry with a parting threat: 'I'd love to own Fairfax, I'd love to control Fairfax, I'd love to run Fairfax. And at any point in time I may do it because, you know, I'm only responsible to you blokes while I have a television station, and at any point in time I can sell the television station and do what I like.' But this was more bluster than anything else because he was clearly beginning to have doubts about Fairfax, while James was far more interested in the internet and mobile phones. And in his new role as executive chairman of PBL, James was just beginning to get his way.

CHAPTER 8
THE CROWN JEWELS

James is running PBL nowadays. This is his deal.

The most obvious example of James's growing power was the Packers' decision in October 1998 to go ahead and buy half the Murdochs' share in Foxtel. Kerry was vehemently against taking up the option they had been granted in the peace deal a year earlier because he didn't want to invest money in pay-TV and because James had brokered the deal. But for once the old man was defeated.

As decision day approached, there were several attempts to win Kerry's approval. But with no one able to talk him around, the battle moved to the PBL board where the new head of PBL Enterprises, James McLachlan, put the case for the purchase. Kerry probed, interrogated and needled away, trying to find a chink in the case. James then stood up and argued that they already had a quarter of the free-to-air television market with Channel Nine and ought to have a quarter of the pay-TV market as well, so they could stop worrying about which would win.

With that Kerry got to his feet and said, 'You all know what I think of this. It's fucking bullshit,' and then stormed out. There was an awkward silence but no one followed him out of the room. It was almost certainly the first time that a Packer had been rolled by his directors, or by a son, and Kerry did not like it one bit. Days later he told the ABA crossly, 'I don't think boards matter a damn as long as they don't do anything.' No one could have guessed how raw the comment was.

Despite its significance, James's victory did not mean he had won the war with his father or effected a radical change in their relationship. Kerry retained a veto over most major decisions, and James was still incapable of standing toe-to-toe with him in an argument. Indeed, he still seemed to believe he did not deserve his role as executive chairman of the Packer empire, telling one old friend, 'Look, I've been given this job because I'm Dad's son.' But the fight about Foxtel did reveal a fundamental disagreement between father and son about where the business should be heading and highlighted growing support for James's more ambitious strategic approach.

Despite a willingness to gamble hundreds of millions of dollars in casinos and on the currency markets, Kerry was incredibly conservative and tight-fisted when it came to investing. He bought low and sold high and was only interested in companies that produced a steady flow of cash. His mission in life was to squeeze as much as he could out of his magazines and TV network and make them the best. James, on the other hand, saw a bigger picture. He wanted to expand the business and create wealth for the future, even if it meant taking risks and spending millions. He resented his father for being so conservative, for having no vision and for not being like Rupert Murdoch, who was prepared to take on the world.

As time went on, James became increasingly frustrated with Kerry's caution and refusal to let go of the controls. And this soured his relationship with Brian Powers, whom James felt did not push Kerry hard enough to take risks and accept change. 'It was a very warm relationship at the start,' says one insider, 'but I don't think he had much respect or admiration for Powers by the time he left.'

With Powers's departure Kerry arguably lost one of his allies and James strengthened his position. But James was also left without his most important advocate. Not only had Powers been able to advance arguments on James's behalf, he had also smoothed things over and acted as an emollient between father and son. Now James would have to deal with their differences head on. And Kerry's performance at the ABA showed just how hard that would be.

But as the Foxtel decision proved, there was no longer any guarantee that the father would prevail. It was increasingly James who was setting the agenda, and he was surrounded by smart people who weren't completely cowed by Kerry, people such as Daniel Petre and Jeremy Philips at PBL Online and James McLachlan at PBL Enterprises, where much of the growth was taking place. For Kerry the danger was that he would become isolated as the only one standing in the way of group decisions.

And generally this is how events played out until Kerry's death, with James getting the upper hand when the internet was booming or his father got sick, and losing it whenever Kerry got better or his hi-tech investments got into trouble. It is also what happened in December 1998 with the purchase of Melbourne's Crown Casino. James was mad keen to buy and Kerry just kept knocking it back.

Crown was the dream child of Lloyd Williams, who had given ten years of his life to the project. A 'neat man', as one paper described him, with immaculately clipped hair and nails, spotless lapels and highly polished shoes, he had known Kerry since 1979 and was one of his few close mates. They owned racehorses together, punted on them heavily and then retired to the golf course to plan further betting forays. Kerry was also a shareholder in Hudson Conway, the building company owned by Williams that had put together the bid for the casino licence in 1993, and he had become a founding shareholder in Crown when the initial public offering struck trouble.

The casino opened in its temporary facility in 1994 and got off to a roaring start. Before long, it was earning $100 million a year and had doubled its share price, at which point Kerry sold half his stake and picked up a $110 million profit on his investment. Not for the first time, his timing was perfect because as soon as he got out in September 1996 the shares started heading down.

By then Crown was running late and wildly over budget on its permanent casino and 1000-room luxury hotel on Melbourne's new Southbank. Originally set to cost around $750 million, it eventually came in at three times that price because Williams, the perfectionist, kept changing the design. He was driven and demanding, 'a Cecil B de Mille figure' said one person who worked on the project 'with a total passionate commitment to his dream'.

The new complex opened in May 1997 with a spectacular fireworks display watched by 1200 invited guests, including Victoria's Premier Jeff Kennett. As locals were reminded, it was the largest casino in the southern hemisphere with 350 gaming tables and 2500 poker machines. At $2.2 billion it was also the most expensive, and Crown had been forced to raise an extra $1 billion in capital plus another $1 billion in debt, leaving it saddled with a huge interest bill.

This became a major problem in October 1997, five months after the casino's gala opening, when the Asian financial crisis hit and turnover in Crown's VIP areas, the Mahogany Room and Crystal Club, halved in the space of three weeks. Crown had the biggest high-roller book in the world, relying on it for half its win. It also spent huge amounts of money attracting these high-rollers to Melbourne from overseas, offering free flights in the casino's two Gulfstream jets, free luxury accommodation and generous rebates on their losses.

At first, Lloyd Williams assured the media that everything was fine, dismissing rumours that Crown was losing money as 'the greatest nonsense' he had ever heard. But in December 1997 he shocked the market with an announcement that the casino had lost $39 million between July and November. Worse still, it had breached its gearing ratios and was three weeks away from being declared in breach of its licence conditions. It was also a whisker away from breaking its bank covenants. Amazingly, the management had not told the Australian Stock Exchange, despite having a duty to keep the market fully informed.

With the announcement of the loss came news of a $200 million support package, including capital raising underwritten by the Packers' private company, Consolidated Press Holdings, whose support appeared to be vital if Crown was to raise more cash.

Strangely, the casino's shock loss had been caused by high-rollers actually winning money rather than from any dramatic decline in their spending. This raised the question of whether the business model actually worked. Crown soon confessed to forking out $275 million a year on agents' commissions, freebies for gamblers and rebates on losses, while budgeting to collect only $480 million in winnings. From this it had to pay another

$70 million in gaming tax to the Victorian government and run the casino's VIP rooms. Margins were thus incredibly tight, even when business was booming.

Consequently, Kerry had doubts about whether to buy into Crown's problems at all. He also figured he might get the casino cheaper if he bided his time, and he hoped to pressure the Victorian government into giving the casino a sweeter deal by lowering tax rates. James, for his part, was all for going ahead, as was Brian Powers, who was still running the Packers' businesses at the time. But they were both overruled, and when Kennett refused to reduce the high-roller tax rate in February 1998, Kerry gave orders to pull the pin.

In the event, Crown managed to raise $146 million without the Packers' help, and the crisis passed. But Crown's troubles didn't go away. Another big loss was recorded in the March quarter, and Melbourne's Channel Nine news reported that Lloyd Williams had been forced to resign. This was not true, as it turned out, and Kerry was quick to say so. He had already told Crown's major shareholders that Williams must stay because he was the only person who knew the business and the only one prepared to go into the Mahogany Room at 3 a.m. to shake hands with the high-rollers, who were so important to the casino's survival.

That winter losses continued and the share price slipped further, even though Crown had won a little more breathing space from a couple of regulatory decisions to ease its gearing rules and waive $73 million in fines for not building a second hotel tower. By August 1998, the situation was bad enough for Williams to hop on a plane with James and fly to Kerry's bedside in New York. Depending on which story you believed, this was either to lend support to an old friend or to ask for help.

Crown was again desperate for cash. The share price was down to 29 cents, or just one-tenth of its peak two years earlier, and James was keener than ever to buy. In September, the urgency increased. Crown announced $400 million in write-downs that would again put the casino in breach of its gearing ratios. Consolidated Press Holdings (CPH) now came up with a new rescue deal in which the Packers' private company would pay $425 million to get its hands on half Crown's net cash flow. Lloyd dubbed it 'a wonderful deal' for Kerry and Crown, but some of the casino's major shareholders (including Kerry himself) weren't so sure. 'It's outrageous, it's just too rich' was one verdict, accompanied by a warning that it would only be supported if there was absolutely no alternative.

Six weeks later, with the deal still on the table, Kerry Packer and Lloyd Williams held a joint press conference demanding $150 million worth of concessions from the Kennett government, including a ten-year extension to the casino's monopoly, 1000 extra poker machines, a cut in the gaming tax from 22 to 15 per cent, a cut in the high-roller tax from 12 per cent to 8 per cent and a permanent waiver on building the second hotel tower. Kerry made it abundantly clear that the Packers would walk away from the rescue unless they got what they wanted. Kennett responded on radio by telling Kerry he was dreaming. He also suggested the Packers were just looking for an excuse to pull out.

Two weeks later Kerry withdrew. All bets were off again but, shortly after, Kerry was seen punting with Lloyd at the Melbourne Cup and playing golf with him and Greg Norman at Crown's exclusive Capital golf course.

Despite the two false starts, it still seemed likely that the Packers would end up buying Crown. The casino desperately needed more capital to survive and it was a bargain the Packers could not afford to miss. But Kerry was still digging in his heels. By the time the third rescue bid was finally agreed between James, Lloyd and Kerry in December the casino was at last beginning to trade a little better, so the package had to be pitched at 56 cents per share, about 20 per cent higher than the deal Kerry had walked away from three months earlier.

This time, however, the Packers were going to pick up the whole of Crown, rather than just a piece of the action, and they would also collect some valuable tax losses as the takeover was now going through the public company, PBL. Anyone who knew anything about the Packers knew that their private companies never paid any tax, so the tax losses would have been of no use at all to CPH.

Several people in the Packer camp claimed credit for this new, smarter approach, and for finally winning the prize. Some say that PBL's managing director Nick Falloon suggested it to Kerry, who then claimed it as his own. Lloyd Williams told journalists that James had been pushing for it all along and had finally got Kerry over the line. Certainly, it was James who put the case to the board in a conference call. And, as a delighted Williams insisted, 'James is running PBL nowadays. This is his deal.'

It is said that the third owner of a casino is usually the one that ends up making the money, but the Packers now looked set to prove this wrong. They were effectively getting Crown and its hotel for $1.8 billion, about $1 billion less than it had cost to build. Better still, they were not paying cash because Crown shareholders were accepting shares in an expanded PBL. And thanks to Kerry's delaying tactics, the timing was almost perfect. When PBL finally took possession in June 1999, business was booming again and costs had been cut. Before long, Crown would be making $400 million a year profit before interest and tax, which effectively set its price at four-and-a-half times earnings. There was also $400 million worth of tax losses to make that first slice entirely tax free.

It was as good a deal as the Packers had ever done, as good as selling Channel Nine to Alan Bond and buying it back for a song. But this time it was James, not Kerry, who had driven it. Put simply, PBL shareholders had given up 15 per cent of the company for a casino that would soon earn more than half the group's profit. Crown's shareholders would also do well because PBL's shares would triple in price over the next eight years.

But this was not James's only victory. His $250 000 investment in One.Tel made in early 1995 had just hit the jackpot. And its success had finally convinced Kerry that he should have a punt as well.

CHAPTER 9
MASTER OF THE UNIVERSE

Jodee, I love you. You have bought me my independence. I am practically a billionaire now without any of my father's money.

It had taken One.Tel only a year to become a runaway success and sign up 100 000 customers, or five times as many as planned. And since the stock market was valuing phone companies at $1000 per subscriber, Jodee Rich's creation was instantly worth $100 million. James's share was worth $5 million, or twenty times what he had put in.

It had all come so far so fast. There had been just nineteen people in the office on that first day in May 1995, crowded down one end of the 28th floor of their rented building near Sydney's Martin Place. They sat at secondhand oregon benchtops, with boxes of mobile phones piled up in the corners and dealers queuing to collect them. Everyone worked ridiculously hard those first few weeks, coming in at 5.30 in the morning and getting home at 8 at night. And it never eased off.

Sales had grown even faster than at Imagineering thanks to One.Tel's brilliant marketing, which centred around a scruffy surfer called The Dude. Created by Jodee's brother-in-law, Adam Long, The Dude's purpose was to show potential customers it was so easy to get a phone from One.Tel that even an idiot could do it, and so cheap that even a layabout like him could afford one. With a goatee, and long, straw-coloured hair and dressed in blue shorts, orange shirt and green-checked beanie, The Dude soon acquired a dog and a girlfriend called Jennifer, who was smart and sassy and worked at One.Tel, so she could explain all the company's products.

In those early days it was a great outfit to work for. It was 'fun and friendly', as its motto suggested, and efficient to boot. One.Tel could get new products or promotions up in 48 hours while its big, slow-footed rivals might take three months. And its software systems were brilliant. If you wanted to know how much the babysitter had spent when she borrowed your mobile on a Saturday night, One.Tel could tell you. Customer service was also great: the company was still small and everything worked.

Thanks to Jodee, the vibe in the office was young and hip—a far cry from life at Park Street—with a culture ruled by 'One.Tel's Beliefs and Values', which were a mixture of Deepak Chopra, New Age management theory and self-improvement courses like Est. These laid down strict rules about email (which was not allowed), meetings (which had to be called 'huddles') and groups of desks (which had to be called 'pods' to suggest the way dolphins swam together). Everyone also had to know the One.Tel story in case Jodee Rich made them recite it. Hierarchies were also banned, management was 'flat', and everyone was told to care, share and think positively.

Colourful cartoons covered the lime green, orange, electric blue and sunflower yellow walls. One floor had an underwater theme with fish, octopus and Dude-like snorkellers swimming through tropical seas. Another was painted with flying machines. A third had space rockets. And everywhere there were motivational messages urging the team to 'Make It Better' and 'Give Your Opinions', or reminding them that 'A Happy Team Means Happy Players'.

In many ways One.Tel was like a cult, with Jodee the demigod. But it wasn't just the staff who worshipped at his feet. James was almost as taken with his new-found guru as he would later be with Scientology. Jodee was a mentor, a friend and father figure who was already showing him a new, more positive approach to life. Jodee had a fantastic ability to make people feel special, to make them believe they were the only person in the world who mattered, and he turned the full force of his charms on the heir to the Packer throne. The two men spoke on the phone every fortnight and met once a month to talk about the business. But they also saw each other socially, having dinner with their partners at each other's houses or going out to restaurants in the city.

In July 1996 James invited Jodee and his wife Maxine onto the *Arctic P* for a cruise around the Greek islands. To Jodee it seemed like a Roman court with Packer executives and others (including Liberal lobbyist Michael Kroger) vying for the emperor's favour. The two men also went skiing together and became almost inseparable.

'They were very close,' says Rodney Adler, 'much closer than James and I ever were.' They were also openly affectionate. One man remembers them at Ellerston with a small group of friends, sitting on big leather couches in the Packers' private cinema. Without warning, Jodee leapt on top of James, who was stretched out flat, and began a mock fight. 'They were wrestling like two small boys, in front of everybody else.'

Another who knew them both remembers the pair at Jodee's retreat near Airlie Beach in North Queensland, lying around in the sun, chatting, like brothers or best friends. 'James thought Jodee was wonderful,' this friend recalls. 'He adored his courage, humour, irreverence and vision. And Jodee really cared for James too.'

'James was besotted with Jodee Rich,' another insider suggests. Brian Powers reached a similar conclusion. 'If James has a fault in his judgment it's that he falls in love with people,' he says today. 'It can be a strength and a weakness. If you're going to take big risks you need to back people to the hilt, but if you're the boss you've also got to exercise some discipline if things are going wrong.'

However, at that stage, things were not going wrong. One.Tel was growing fast and making money. Optus was still handing out a $120 bonus for every new subscriber to the network, and this just about guaranteed One.Tel made a profit from its customers even if they never made a call or paid their bills. The Optus bonus gave it a powerful incentive to recruit customers who were not worth having, and this soon became company policy. There were stories of dealers giving out Sim cards on street corners or sending them out in the mail. And failure to validate customers' details or run credit checks was commonplace. 'It was a chronic customer base, full of single mothers, pensioners and schoolkids,' according to one woman who had the job of chasing unpaid bills. On her estimate, 60 to 70 per cent of One.Tel's customers paid late or didn't pay at all. But Jodee did not appear to be worried. With the stock market fixated on how many people were signed up to the network, it made perfect sense to keep pumping up the numbers.

Sooner or later, however, the dream had to end, and in October 1996 a new team at Optus realised One.Tel was taking much more than it was putting back. Tense negotiations followed from which Rich emerged with almost $20 million in compensation. Life then got tougher; the cash tap was turned off. And even worse, Optus started slashing rates and undercutting One.Tel, making survival itself an issue. A couple of big rivals, Digicall and First Direct, went bust. Others had to tighten their belts to stay in business.

The obvious answer for One.Tel was to find a buyer, but no one wanted to pay the $150 million the company was notionally worth. The closest its founders came to cashing in was in mid-1997 when James tried to get the Packers' family company, CPH, to put in some money. Brian Powers sent a couple of bankers along to kick the tyres, but they came away unconvinced. One.Tel had no network and no security. It was also not holding on to its customers long enough to make money from them. Powers went to see Jodee Rich but couldn't get answers to even the basic questions of how much it cost to recruit new customers, how much they spent a month and how long they stayed. Nick Falloon, then PBL's finance director, was also against investing. And both took a severe dislike to Jodee.

So the only way for Jodee and James to redeem any of their investment was to float the company on the Australian Stock Exchange, which is what they did in November 1997, two-and-half years after One.Tel opened its doors. Hardly any shares were actually sold, but enough were issued to value the enterprise at $208 million and make a paper fortune. Jodee Rich was now worth more than $100 million and James $17 million. But there was still no way of cashing in these chips. And One.Tel still faced the problem of how to make the business viable. Jodee had two bright ideas on this front.

The first was to offer cheap long-distance and international calls. By mid-1997, deregulation in Australia and overseas meant that a huge amount of space was suddenly available on international cables at knock-down prices. One.Tel was able to buy calls to the UK or USA for 15 cents a minute and sell them on to its customers for more than double that, yet still offer rates at a fraction of what Telstra and Optus were charging. This was a far better mark-up than the company had ever made on mobiles.

The second was to expand abroad. In 1998 One.Tel went global, opening up in Los Angeles, London, Hong Kong, Paris, Amsterdam and Zurich. This delivered another 100 000 customers, but at great expense. It cost a fortune to set up the offices, run marketing campaigns and sign up customers. And there was now no fairy godmother to hand out cash. By the end of 1998 the company was burning through $50 million a year, and was even more desperate to find a wealthy backer and devise a business plan that actually worked.

Typically, Jodee's answer was to become even bigger and for One.Tel to have its own mobile network. This would cost $1 billion to build and another $500 million to recruit enough customers to make it pay. It was a huge gamble, but there would be huge rewards if it came off: One.Tel would no longer have Optus squeezing it out of business and its marketing would surely pull in all the customers it needed. But where on earth would they find $1.5 billion? James believed he had the answer.

In late 1998 he persuaded Kerry to pay a visit to One.Tel's offices and expose himself to Jodee's charms. The old man was not an immediate convert, but Rich was not disheartened. On the way out, he assured James's father that One.Tel would one day be a billion-dollar business. 'What have you been smoking?' Kerry asked.

Despite failing to find a benefactor, Jodee, James, Rodney Adler and Brad Keeling decided to take the plunge anyway and fork out $9.5 million for the last bit of mobile phone spectrum the government was putting up for auction. 'It was a very entrepreneurial decision,' says Adler, 'a *very* entrepreneurial decision.'

It looked even more like that when they discovered One.Tel couldn't borrow the money to pay for it. 'Jodee and I went everywhere,' says Adler. 'We must have gone to ten or twenty places. We got turned down by an awful lot of people. We were just too much of a risk.' The only answer was to get James and his well-heeled friend David Lowy to dig into their pockets and pull out $5 million apiece. This made it even more urgent to find some wealthy investors, so in December 1998 James went back to Kerry.

This time, for some reason, his father saw dollar signs. Internet and telco stocks were taking off in the USA, and computer geeks starting businesses in garages were becoming billionaires overnight. So Kerry decided it was time to get in the game and stump up $47 million of family money for a 15 per cent shareholding. With 'Dad' on board, James then managed to convince George Soros's former right-hand man, Steve Gilbert, to tip in $54 million from his American venture capital fund.

Better still, Jodee persuaded the big US electronics company Lucent to finance construction of the network and lend One.Tel money to acquire customers, which would cost $300 to $500 a head in dealer commissions and handset subsidies.

Until this point, the company's ambitions had only extended to building a limited network in Sydney and Brisbane. With the Packers' money available, the discussion now turned to covering the entire country, and soon after that came dreams of taking on

Telstra and capitalising on the coming 'convergence' between television, the internet and mobile phones.

But as these ambitions grew bigger, so their funds appeared to shrink. In January 1999 James told Jodee, 'Dad thinks we should get the Murdochs involved.' It would be positive for both families, he said, and bring them together after the Super League war. It would also provide financial muscle for the battle against Telstra, and give One.Tel unrivalled marketing power. Besides, experience had shown it helped to have the Murdochs on side whatever you did. So James had dinner with Lachlan and sold him the idea. Shortly afterwards, the two young guns were boarding the Packer jet with Jodee and Brad to see if they could convince Rupert in New York.

Murdoch's office on the Avenue of the Americas is unremarkable, lacking the huge metal doors and acres of carpet that needed crossing in the fictional world of Evelyn Waugh's famous press baron, Lord Copper. But James would still have felt daunted. Rupert was one of his heroes and billions of dollars were at stake. For half an hour, Jodee and Brad waited outside while their friend made a pitch that went something like: Australia's phone companies were worth around $50 billion and One.Tel could have $10 billion of this if it could run second or third in the race. The company had already showed itself to be brilliant at winning customers and, helped by the Murdochs' newspapers and Packers' TV and magazines, there would be no holding it back.

Two weeks later, almost every paper in Australia splashed the news that PBL and News Limited were sinking $710 million into One.Tel as each took a 40 per cent share. Alongside the story in the *Australian Financial Review* was a photo of James, Jodee, Lachlan and Brad at One.Tel's offices, with James, who had done more than anyone to make the deal happen, looking the least comfortable of the four.

Perhaps he was already contemplating the fact that Kerry was demanding money with menace. A fat slice of the cash being invested by News and PBL was going straight back to the existing shareholders, allowing Jodee, Brad and the others to pick up a nice payout. But poor James had been forced to hand over his $15 million cheque to the family company, even though he had made the initial investment with his own hard-earned savings. James insisted in court in 2005 that he surrendered the money to Kerry of his own volition, saying, 'It was not a hardship for me . . . because I always considered CPH me anyway.'

But Jodee Rich's affidavit in the same proceedings told a different story: that Kerry had demanded the payment as the price for agreeing to let Rich retain control of One.Tel. Jodee says he exclaimed to James, 'You must be joking?', to which James allegedly replied, 'That was the only way I could get him to agree.' Whatever the truth, One.Tel's share price took off now the Packers and Murdochs were backing the company, and before long Kerry had quadrupled his $47 million investment.

One.Tel wasn't James's only shooting star, however. Another of his creations, ecorp, was also enjoying a meteoric rise. This business had started life in March 1997 as PBL Online after James rang Daniel Petre, the ex-head of Microsoft Asia Pacific, and invited him to meet 'Dad'. The three of them had dinner at Beppi's, a dimly lit Italian restaurant in Sydney's Darlinghurst favoured by James's grandfather, Sir Frank Packer, and Petre talked his way into a job. At that time, half-a-million households were connected to the internet compared to 8 million today, and connection speeds were appallingly slow. Petre had assured James and Kerry the business would explode.

The initial idea was to set up sites for Channel Nine and ACP's magazines and then think about how to make money. But in late 1997 Petre convinced Microsoft to form a joint venture, NineMSN, and hand over its internet portal for free. This produced a massive number of hits because Internet Explorer in Australia opened automatically to the new site, which also hosted Hotmail. And after that it was just a matter of finding new businesses to turn the traffic into cash.

The breakthrough came in February 1999 when ecorp landed a second valuable joint venture with eBay, the online auction site. Like so many other dot.coms, eBay had grown from a shed in San Francisco to a multi-billion dollar business in just four years, and was now valued at US$9 billion on the NASDAQ. But again, the Packers managed to get the rights for free. Petre's deputy, Jeremy Philips, buttonholed eBay's chief executive, Meg Whitman, at a conference in San Diego and told her they wanted the Australian franchise. She said, 'Fine, come talk to me,' and then flew out to Australia soon afterwards to meet Kerry. Amazingly, despite its huge potential and zero cost, James still had to work hard to talk his father into investing.

Typically, the old man refused to cough up money for ecorp to acquire other businesses, so in June 1999 James and Petre decided to float 20 per cent of the company on the stock market and raise $160 million. The operation was still little more than a shell, had burnt through $30 million in cash in two years and was losing money. Yet it was sold with a price tag of $804 million, or fifteen times its projected annual sales. Australian investors still thought it a bargain. Even though it was still making a loss, over the next eighteen months ecorp's market value soared sixfold to almost $5 billion at its peak, making it worth more than the rest of the Packer empire, which had taken eighty years to build up.

Ecorp's rocketing share price should have made Kerry deliriously happy because it added $3 billion to the value of PBL and $1.2 billion to his family's net worth. But, instead, it seems to have confirmed his dislike of the internet and everyone associated with it. Right at the start of the venture in 1997 he was invited by Petre and James to watch how it worked, but this only confirmed his belief that it did not. As Richard Guilliatt and Drew Warne-Smith later wrote in *The Australian*:

> Unfortunately, the young executives putting on this demo were using a dial-up connection so agonisingly slow that Big Kerry found himself staring stonily at a blank computer screen for what seemed like aeons. Finally, his patience gave out. 'When you get it fucking working, give me a fucking call,' he growled, turning on his heel. As he exited the room, he turned and added: 'When I switch on my television, it comes on straight away.'

A year later, Kerry was still boasting to the Australian Broadcasting Authority that he had never bothered to learn how to use a computer. And even when ecorp was worth billions, he would still prowl around the office telling people they were wasting their time because no one wanted to sit and look at screens all day.

Not only did Kerry not understand the technology's potential, he also hated the business model because it consumed huge amounts of cash and made no profit. And he hated the fact that others were prepared to pay so much to get involved. He also had a particular dislike for James's new young mates who spoke a language he couldn't understand. Petre (who was in his late thirties) and Philips (who was in his mid-twenties) were each paid $1 million at ecorp and had 35 million options, which at one point made them worth $100 million apiece. Jodee Rich at One.Tel was doing better still.

Since Kerry could never really grasp what this hi-tech generation was talking about, he was wont to interrupt conversations with them to terrorise his PA or switch the subject to how to breed polo ponies. At one such meeting with the head of a management consulting firm, Kerry was lying back in his chair with his shoes off and his feet on the table. Tiring of the jargon, he buzzed for his secretary to 'Get me some fucking cake'. She brought him a slice, then waited while he took a bite.

'This isn't fucking cake, it's shit,' he growled.

'It's cake,' she replied. 'I bought it from David Jones food hall.'

They continued the argument in front of Kerry's visitors—who were not invited to taste the cake—before he resumed the discussion.

'It was just a display of power,' says one of those at the meeting. 'But he also did it because he couldn't cope. It was his way of avoiding looking stupid.'

Kerry was also prone to bad mouthing this new generation to others. When the local head of Lucent came to Park Street in mid-1999 to discuss the construction of One.Tel's new mobile network, Kerry opened the meeting by pointing to James and Jodee Rich and saying: 'Please tell me the truth, Mr Brewington. I don't believe anything these young blokes tell me.' James, who had been Executive Chairman of PBL for a year by this stage, was understandably offended.

Despite Kerry's relentless scepticism, plans for One.Tel were growing bigger by the day thanks to Rupert Murdoch, who had his sights set on conquering the telecommunications world. In addition to an Australian network costing more than $1 billion, Murdoch wanted one in Europe at a cost of US$20 billion, which would really put One.Tel in the big league. Lucent was prepared to finance and build both networks, but One.Tel had insufficient bandwidth in Australia and none at all in Europe, where it would have to bid against some of the world's biggest and richest companies. To give the company more firepower, Murdoch tipped another $200 million into the kitty in November 1999. Kerry sagely passed.

News of the planned European network sent One.Tel's shares even higher, and on 26 November 1999 they peaked at $2.84, making the company worth $5.3 billion. It was now trading at 28 times the price of its November 1997 float and a staggering 750 times its after-tax earnings, which (it would turn out) had been grossly overstated by creative accounting. At these levels, Jodee was a billionaire twice over and James's personal holding was worth $250 million, or a thousand times his initial investment. One.Tel was also in the top thirty Australian companies by market capitalisation. And a glorious future awaited.

According to Jodee Rich's affidavit in the proceedings brought by the Australian Securities and Investments Commission (ASIC) in 2002, James was thrilled it was going so well:

> James Packer said to me on several occasions, 'One.Tel has done far better than I ever expected. It could make me a billionaire in my own right.' And, 'You've given me independence from my father'. And 'Jodee, I love you. You have bought me my independence. I am practically a billionaire now without any of my father's money.' During one of these conversations I recall Mr James Packer telling me that he had told his father One.Tel might one day be worth more than PBL and that this had made his father angry and caused an argument.

The affidavit went on to say that James also told Jodee: 'One. Tel has made me a success. I keep telling them I told you so.' It can only be imagined how pleased Kerry would have been to hear this.

In fact, James was already going around telling people he had made more money than his dad. And, on paper, it was certainly true. At their respective peaks One.Tel and ecorp were worth $10 billion between them, and James had backed both from the beginning in the face of consistent opposition from his father. There can be no doubt that Kerry also knew the score and drew similar conclusions. Indeed, he was so shocked by what was happening in the dot.com boom that he stopped coming into Park Street and no longer attended regular management meetings. For about a year, from autumn 1999 until April 2000, he was conspicuous by his absence. Several insiders say he no longer felt useful because the world had changed so much. They also believe he couldn't bear to see James having so much success.

By contrast, James was becoming more confident and more like his father. With a fair dose of his mother in him, he had always been a milder person than Kerry and had tried hard not to copy the old man. As one senior colleague put it: 'He never bullied people or shouted at them like Kerry did, and he was always supportive.' But there were now signs that he was at last becoming his father's son, that success had gone to his head.

Kerry Stokes has given a hotly disputed account in the Federal Court of a conversation he had with James in late 2000 about TV rights to the AFL, in which James supposedly warned him it wasn't worth bidding. 'I've come to tell you that we're going to take the AFL rights off you,' James allegedly said, following up with a similar warning to Stokes that he could not win the TV rights to rugby league either.

There are other stories around this time of James mimicking his father's behaviour. In March 2000 he had a very public row with the AFL commissioner Graeme Samuel at the Australian Grand Prix. 'He was thumping the table, swearing, using every piece of language under the sun,' says Samuel, who was apparently amused by the young man's aggression. 'Premier Bracks had to come and break it up. He could see we were having an interesting conversation.'

Six months earlier, James had flown off the handle at Bracks himself during the 1999 Victorian election. The Packers had just taken possession of Crown Casino, only to find themselves embroiled in a long-running row over the manner in which the licence had been awarded in September 1993. From the very beginning, there had been concerns about the probity of the process because the winners were very well connected to the Liberal government. Lloyd Williams was a close personal friend of the premier, Jeff Kennett, while his business partner, Ron Walker, was treasurer of the Liberal Party and ex-Lord Mayor of Melbourne.

The ALP had alleged in parliament that Crown had won the licence unfairly by getting inside information on its rivals' bids. Sheraton-Leighton had been the highest bidder and favourite to win until the last minute. Then the deadline was extended, Crown increased its offer by $30 million, and the Packer-backed consortium walked away with the prize.

After digging away for years and calling for a Royal Commission, Labor hammered the issue during the 1999 election campaign. And according to one of Bracks's inner circle, James got so sick of the attacks that he rang the then Opposition leader and shouted down the phone. Like everyone else, he may have thought Labor was so far behind in the polls that this abuse of Bracks could not possibly matter. But he was wrong.

By election day on 18 September Labor had unexpectedly closed the gap. With the result now in the balance, James flew to Melbourne with Graham Richardson for a thirty-minute meeting with the would-be premier to negotiate a ceasefire. They were joined in the room by the ALP's Victorian fundraiser, Dave Feeney, who soon followed up with a phone call to Richardson to suggest a substantial donation might improve matters. Some days later, a cheque for $100 000 from the Packers found its way into the coffers of the Victorian Labor Party.

A week after this meeting, James assured the press he did not anticipate any regulatory problems from the new State government. Sure enough, Rob Hulls, the man who had run Labor's campaign against Crown Casino, did not get the gaming portfolio, and the Royal Commission was forgotten. Three months later, when the ALP held a $1000-a-head gala fundraiser at the Hyatt Hotel, it was James and his new wife Jodie Meares who were at top table seated alongside the new premier.

CHAPTER 10
PLAYBOY MODELS

I'm a man's man. I hang out with the boys . . . If the
words womaniser and playboy come to mind, they
could be right.

James Packer was hardly Australia's most handsome bachelor but he
was certainly the richest, and he had dated a succession of gorgeous
women over the years. Conveniently, his offices in Sydney were next
to one of Australia's biggest model agencies, Priscilla's, and he was
friends with its owner. If he saw a girl he liked on the agency's website
it was a simple matter to score an introduction. And who could turn
him down? Not only was he going to inherit a multi-billion-dollar
fortune, he was in charge of the country's biggest TV and magazine
group. He also drove the latest Mercedes Sports or Porsche Turbo,
could get tickets to any game or concert in town and could whisk you
off in his private jet to the ski slopes or beaches of the world.

But it wasn't just his money and power young women liked.
He was funny and clever and had style. One girlfriend remembers

having a fierce row with him in the car on the way to Palm Beach. As he pulled up at a roadside stall and got out to buy her flowers, she was thinking, 'You're not going to buy me off that easily.' But he didn't just buy one spray, he bought them all and staggered back with his arms full. Another woman who went to a restaurant with him found he had booked all the tables so they could dine alone. It was hard not to be swayed by gestures like this.

But those who got to know him found him a puzzle. He was half like his mother and half like his father, and it was hard to discover the real James. One part of him was sensitive, soft, gentle and romantic, a man who treated women well and desperately wanted a family of his own. The other was arrogant and cocky, and surrounded by blokes who bragged about their conquests and talked disparagingly of women. This James was happiest at home with the boys and a bucket of popcorn, watching action movies like *Rocky* and *Top Gun*.

James's closest friends were all male, had all been to school with him, and still called each other by their nicknames: Cocky (Chris Hancock), Tilley (Ben Tilley), Gynge (David Gyngell) and Ched (Matthew Csidei). James himself was known as Pack. They were a close-knit group, and the only people he felt he could really trust.

One of James's old flames describes them scornfully as 'the brain surgeons' because 'there was so little intellectual activity going on'. In her rather waspish account, they didn't read books—just tabloid papers and magazines—and had done dismally in their school-leaving exams. This was certainly true of Ben Tilley, who had taken five subjects in the HSC exam and scored in the bottom 10 per cent of the state in three of them. It was also true of David Gyngell, whose father Bruce had famously welcomed Australia to tele-vision in 1956. Gyngell, who was dyslexic—just as James claimed to be—had been suspended from Cranbrook for telling the art master to 'get fucked' and dropped out of school at the age of fifteen to work as a janitor at the Rose Bay Surf Club.

Yet neither of these friends was stupid, and both had done well in business. Tilley made millions of dollars owning pubs and collecting debts and was a red-hot card player, while Gyngell had started out selling surfboards from his flat in Bondi and built up a chain of fourteen surf shops under the Beach Culture brand.

Gyngell could be seen three rows behind James in his first school photo in 1980 and they'd been mates ever since. The two men had lived together for eight years; first, with Tilley in a flat near the Packer family home and then in James's apartment overlooking Bondi Beach. With a cook and a cleaner to take care of them, they lived a real Aussie blokes' lifestyle. 'He'd come home and say "G'day mate," and we'd chat,' Gyngell told Daphne Guinness in a rare interview in 1997. 'He'd go to his room, I'd go to mine and watch telly in bed. We wouldn't use the lounge room. We'd have dinner, go to a movie Sunday nights, he'd travel round the world. That's the way we both liked it.'

They shared several girlfriends—though not at the same time—and had similar ideas about women. Gyngell's recipe for a romantic night out, according to Tilley, was 'going to Grandfather's Moustache for a hamburger, then a beer at the East Leagues Club'. Or as Gyngell himself put it: 'I'm a man's man. I hang out with the boys. I love girls and dates, but I've never been a girlfriend guy. If the words womaniser and playboy come to mind, they could be right.' By all accounts, James could have said exactly the same, except that he occasionally got soppy about his girlfriends.

Asked by Guinness whether he planned to get married, Gyngell quipped: 'I've got a daily cleaner and cook, what do I want with marriage?' Then he thought about it and added, 'Not for ten years unless someone bowls me over tomorrow. James is ready for marriage. He found someone who bowled him over.'

That someone was Kate Fischer, who was tall, striking, fun and famous. Kate had hit the limelight at the age of fourteen by beating 6000 others to win *Dolly* magazine's 1988 Cover Girl competition and a modelling contract as a prize. By the age of sixteen she had left home to work in New York, and at the age of twenty made the front cover of *Vogue* before starring in the 1994 film *Sirens* as one of Norman Lindsay's naked nymphs. In between these assignments she had partied hard, ripped off her clothes in public and got herself in the papers at every opportunity.

Looking back on her life in late 1996 at the ripe old age of 23, she admitted she had been like a kid in a lolly shop. 'I just had the best time . . . Limousines, borrowed frocks and paparazzi and everyone paying attention to me, it was great.' But even she could see that her life was crazy. On a typical day, she would eat a cheeseburger at 3 a.m., grab an hour's sleep, wolf down a croissant in the cab en route to a shoot, and tuck into a bag of lollies at 5 a.m. to deal with her headache.

Kate was still doing this when she and James first started dating in 1994 after they met at a modelling contest and started writing notes to each other across the table. In the four months they spent together, James told her she had 'the potential' to be his 'actual girlfriend', but that she was 'too wild'. It was all right, of course, for the Packer men to paint the town red, but it was not good for their partners to have so much fun. James also disliked the fact that Kate was a smoker (even though he was, too, and was always trying to quit). At one point he told her, 'If you don't give up smoking, I'll leave you and we'll never see each other again.' She responded by lighting up a cigarette and saying she would miss him. It was this ballsy attitude that made her so attractive and so different. Unlike the sycophants and flatterers who surrounded James and laughed at all his jokes, she stood up to him. But despite this, or perhaps because of it, they split up and went their separate ways.

Two years later, after a trip to India, Kate came back to Sydney sober, spiritual and more mature, and the romance was rekindled. This time, James told her she was perfect. But now she was the one with doubts because he had remained a playboy. However, she was persuaded to give the relationship a try and moved into his Bondi apartment shortly after Christmas 1996. Soon afterwards one of his ex-girlfriends, Charlotte Dawson, was telling *Who Weekly* she had never seen James so happy. And in some ways they were the perfect match. He was shy, awkward and reserved. She was bubbly, extrovert and fun, the yin to James's yang.

In May 1997, six months after they got together again, James issued a stumbling proposal on national television when Ray Martin asked him if he had a steady girlfriend and did he want to marry her. 'Yes,' said James, 'but I'm scared she'd say no.' A month later, just shy of his thirtieth birthday, he popped the question properly, both to Kate and to Kerry. It was important that his father 'accepted his bride', he said. In late June, they told her friends at a big black-tie dinner at the Horderns' old country house, Milton Park. And within days, the news was everywhere.

They talked of living at Ellerston and bringing up kids. They even picked out names, Jack and Lucy. It was like Camelot, thought Kate. They were going to be a glamorous, power couple, Australia's answer to John and Jackie Kennedy. He would put her on the board of PBL to bring a spiritual side to the company, which he agreed it lacked.

James appeared to be crazy about Kate. There were huge photos and paintings of her in the apartment they shared. And they were all over each other in public, whispering sweet nothings, nibbling ears and canoodling at concerts. 'They were very gooey and very much in love,' Kate's friend Danielle Wallace told *Who Weekly* in 1998. 'I remember when about fifteen of us went to the Billy Joel concert and James was looking at her with these loving eyes and we all went, "Ohhh, how beautiful".'

Others weren't so sure, and worried about James's ability to form a grown-up relationship with a woman. According to another friend of Kate's, 'He called her "little rabbit". And he still talked to his mother over the phone in baby language. I just thought: "Why doesn't he talk properly?"'

Some saw a break-up waiting to happen. While Kate was up dancing next to the stage as Billy Joel played, letting it all hang out, James was sitting in the VIP enclosure glued to his chair. No doubt Kerry would have told him the Packers didn't behave like that in public, and least of all the Packer women.

James tried his best to bring Kate into line with the expectations of the dynasty. He began vetting her assignments and turning down contracts that would not be right for her, that would look like 'Fergie selling Royal Doulton'. He also started cleaning up her modelling and acting portfolio. He couldn't do much about the pictures of her nude in *Sirens*, but she had done a raunchy photo shoot for *Who Weekly* with the renowned celebrity photographer Robin Sellick, and James asked *Woman's Day* editor Nene King to get the photos off the market so they could never be used again. The photo can't be published in this book because James has the copyright, but you can find it in the New South Wales State Library in back numbers of the magazine from 1996 when Kate was chosen as one of Australia's Most Intriguing People.

Sellick has a very clear recollection of how the photo came to be taken (in both senses of the word). It was in 1995, when Kate and

James were not yet an item, and Fischer arrived an hour late for the shoot at her home, apparently straight from a party. She took Sellick into her bedroom, 'threw off all her clothes' and asked what she should wear. Answering the question herself, she donned a pair of black leather thigh-length boots, a studded black leather dog collar and a pair of handcuffs, and nothing much else. Sellick took the photo with her kneeling on the floor in front of her window bars with one hand shielding her breasts. Initially, this was too much for *Who Weekly*, and he was made to go back for another shoot. But a year later the magazine decided to run the original photo, because it was, well, so intriguing.

Six months after that Kate became engaged to James, and the photographer read in a gossip column that James was going to buy back a compromising photograph. Sellick was soon fielding a call from someone at ACP asking how much he wanted for the photo. The woman refused to say how much she was offering; he told her to go away.

Sellick says he and his agent then each received a threatening phone call, warning that he did a lot of business with ACP and would lose these jobs if he didn't hand over the photo. The next day, the original caller came back and tried again to buy the copyright, at which point Sellick told her it was a private matter between him and James: if Packer wanted the photo, he would need to ask the photographer himself.

The next morning, Sellick was flown from Adelaide to Sydney and taken to Park Street, where he was ushered into James's office to meet the young tycoon, who was flanked by Nene King and a lawyer. James was pleasant and reasonable and asked how much Sellick wanted; the lawyer, on the other hand, threatened that the photo wasn't Sellick's to sell. Sellick told James he wasn't interested in what the lawyer had to say, he wanted to hear why James was interested in the picture.

James answered that Kate was 'really worried' about it, and he was hoping the photographer would do him a favour. Sellick replied that he would be happy to hand over the negatives for nothing, but he wanted James to know what had been happening. 'People have been ringing me and my agent and threatening me,' he told him. 'I've wasted three days of my life, and it's been really nasty. It's also been so unnecessary. You could have made the call to me three days ago and I would have given them to you straightaway.'

James was really embarrassed. 'He suddenly adopted this little boy persona,' Sellick recalls, 'as if all this unpleasant stuff was happening and it was beyond his control.' And perhaps this was the case. James may not have had any idea of the threats being made on his behalf. Perhaps, too, it was Kerry who had demanded the photo be canned. It seems unlikely to have been Kate. But in any case, Sellick suddenly warmed to James. 'He struck me as being sensitive and gentle,' he says. 'He was not what I expected at all.'

This may well have been the real James, a soft boy dressed in a hard man's suit. But the family Kate was marrying into was dominated by Kerry, whose sensitivity to women was far more deeply disguised, if it existed at all. For a while Kate got on well with Kerry—he liked spirited women and told others he wanted to 'have a go at her' himself. But it became harder when she became part of the family and saw how he treated Ros. To be a woman in the Packer domain you were expected to know your place and not challenge. Kate refused to accept that role and stood up to Kerry in a way no one else did, and certainly not James.

Kate told friends that Kerry shouted at his son and bullied him unmercifully, except when he was making money. She told tales of her fiancé crying in the shower and of a huge row between him and his father over the Packers' private plane. James had needed to be in Melbourne early in the morning to see Lloyd Williams and Ron Walker about Crown Casino and had taken the DC-8 instead of a commercial flight. Kerry went ballistic and threatened to make him pay the $50 000 bill for using it, calling him 'a fucking spoilt little cunt' and telling him he should use 'fucking public transport' like everyone else.

There were other stresses, too. Kate was into the arts and James was not. He liked business, footy and boxing, and she did not. He loved his mates and she didn't get on with them. But most of all, she adored publicity and attracted it like a magnet, while he loathed the spotlight and would do almost anything he could to avoid it.

In the nearly two years they lived together, and the sixteen months they were engaged, there were constant reports that the match was off. It was reported in the tabloids and women's magazines nine times, but finally it happened. Friends of Kate's say the relationship hit the rocks when James went to Las Vegas with Kerry and she couldn't get through to him. He was always 'asleep' or 'at the tables'. Then she went to New York and was told that James was having a wild weekend in her absence. He was back doing the things he had promised to give up. She had had enough. He made her an offer: 'Marry me. You can have all the money and credit cards you want, and all the glory of being Mrs Packer, but you've got to let me do what I want.' This was not for her. 'You've made your choice then,' he told her. So, in October 1998, two months before it was due to happen, the wedding was called off.

It was all settled as quickly and as quietly as possible. After signing a confidentiality agreement, Kate was given the keys to their Bondi apartment, worth $2.1 million, and told she could keep the Mercedes Sports and big diamond engagement ring that James had given her. She was also given a first-class air ticket out of the country.

There was no statement to the media, as is normal on such occasions, but word of the split soon leaked out to Nene King, who saw instantly she couldn't run the story. 'I just knew he wouldn't want me to write about it,' she said later. 'If I rang James and said, "Can you talk about your break-up with Kate?" I know what he would have said.'

The exclusive went to *Woman's Day*'s arch rival *New Idea*, which splashed the story on its front cover with the headline, 'James pays heartbroken Kate $10 million'. According to 'friends of the couple', James had decided 'he wasn't ready for the commitment of marriage' and couldn't stick to the 'teetotal lifestyle' Kate was insisting upon. His mates also confessed they were glad to see the back of her because she had kept him from them. A year earlier, Gyngell had admitted he wasn't 'madly in love' with her. 'She's a good girl but we've had our disagreements purely because I'm his best mate and she's taken him away from me.'

By the time *New Idea* hit the streets, Kate was catching a plane to Los Angeles. The pressure of being an ex-Packer was too much for her, and she was desperate to escape. James's valet drove her to the airport and dumped her onto the kerb into a scrum of photographers and TV cameras, who gave chase as she strode into the departure hall in a light grey tracksuit and huge, black, Jackie O sunglasses.

It was a perfect tale for the tabloids: billionaire heir dumps fiancée, who flees the country weeks before the wedding. But for some unfathomable reason Rupert Murdoch's *Daily Telegraph* couldn't find room for the story in its sixty-odd pages, despite it being a Monday and a slow news day. It was soon revealed, however, that the article had been ready to go at the front of the paper, only to be pulled at the last minute by editor Col Allan on orders from above. After a phone call from on high *The Australian* had also spiked its story, which was ready to run in a prominent position. The editors of Murdoch's *Herald Sun* in Melbourne and *Courier-Mail* in Brisbane had come to the same conclusion. On and off over the years, the Packers and Murdochs had operated an agreement in which each refrained from running embarrassing stories about the other's personal affairs. Rupert had just left his wife for Wendi Deng, so it was obviously important that the arrangement be back in operation again.

New Idea, which was owned by Pacific Publications, had no such blackout in place. But its new managing director, Bob Muscat, found himself on the end of an angry phone call from young James. Muscat, who had been in the newspaper business for twenty-five years and had just jumped ship from Fairfax, was not in the least perturbed by the rebuke.

Almost as soon as the break-up became public rumours emerged that James had found a replacement for Kate, somebody with whom he had been seen on the slopes at Thredbo and dining out in Sydney. And days after that came photographs to prove it, of James on the beach at Noosa with his new girlfriend Jodie Meares bursting out of a skimpy, string bikini. Kate's friend Danielle Wallace told journalists that Fischer had guessed there was another woman involved, and now it was confirmed.

Jodie was a swimsuit model with even more obvious physical charms than her predecessor. The daughter of a publican from Merimbula in southern New South Wales, she had grown up in Sydney's eastern suburbs and landed her first modelling job at the age of fifteen as the Moove girl, advertising flavoured milk. A likeable, no-nonsense woman, she had made her name with the men's magazine *Inside Sport*, having been on the cover a record five times. Those who knew her said she was uncomplicated, 'one of the boys', and a great deal easier to handle than Kate. She called people 'babe' or 'mate' and got on well with everybody. In addition to modelling (and playing Lara Croft in a TV advertising campaign for Lucozade) she ran her own promotions company, hiring out pretty girls for golf tournaments and major events such as the Australian Grand Prix. She also did stints at Ben Tilley's pub, the Brooklyn Hotel, pulling pints in a bikini in sessions commonly known as Beers with Meares. James could have run into her there, but he might also have met her when she sang in Euphoria, a short-lived 1990s band created by another close schoolfriend, Andrew Klippel.

Once again, James's old flames told the gossip mags he was happy at last: Jodie was down-to-earth and an adrenaline junkie who was much more in tune with his way of life; she liked his mates and they loved her. After six months, she moved into his new three-level apartment on the seafront at Bondi, with its gymnasium, steamroom and private cinema, joining Chris Hancock and his actress wife, Dee Smart, who were already in residence. Then at his thirty-second birthday party in September 1999, less than a year after the break-up with Fischer, the couple told friends they were engaged and would be married within a month. Everyone expressed surprise. There were suggestions she might be pregnant; nothing else seemed to explain the haste. But there was a perfectly good reason for hurrying. Kerry had once again come close to death.

A few weeks earlier, on his way to Las Vegas for a week of gambling and fun with James's friend Ben Tilley (who by this stage had switched his allegiance to the Big Fella), Kerry had suffered another heart attack after a round of golf at Jack Nicklaus's Muirfield Village in Ohio. As he came off the course he experienced sharp chest pains and collapsed, only to be saved again by a defibrillator. On this occasion, however, it was not his portable 'Packer whacker', but a device the size of a matchbox implanted in his chest. Battery powered, the pacemaker sped up the heart when it slowed too much, or acted as a defibrillator to shock it back to normal if it started acting erratically. Paramedics rushed him to emergency at the Methodist Riverside Hospital in Columbus, where doctors diagnosed another major heart attack. But Kerry did not stick around for treatment. As they prepared to admit him to coronary care, he tore off his oxygen mask, ripped out his tubes and ordered one of his staff to get him a limo, which then drove off down the freeway with ambulances in pursuit.

At his villa next to the golf course, Kerry rang his Australian doctors and told them to get over to Ohio at once. Dr Ian Bailey and Professor John Horvath were soon on a commercial flight to Los Angeles, where they were met by a chartered Learjet which ferried them to Columbus. They arrived at Packer's bedside at 3 a.m. to find him asleep with a paramedic staring at reams of print-outs from the machines by his bed. He woke at daybreak to tell them how happy he was to see them, then insisted on showing them the golf course. Within minutes, he was whizzing them around in a buggy at breakneck speed as if he was on the go-kart track at Ellerston.

Once the whistle-stop tour was over, Bailey told Packer he had to come back to Australia for treatment. Egged on by Tilley, Kerry insisted he was going on to Vegas. Eventually he relented. Taking out a cigarette and putting it to his lips, he told Bailey: 'Here's the deal. You light my cigarette and I'll come back to Australia.' Bailey did as he was told, and Kerry did as he promised. Back in Sydney at the Royal Prince Alfred Hospital they would unblock the arteries to his heart with yet another angioplasty and do the same to his main kidney artery, which had also blocked up again.

It was of course understandable with all this going on that James was keen to tie the knot with Jodie as soon as possible. The wedding was set for 23 October 1998, barely six weeks after the engagement was announced. It was the biggest and most expensive bash the organisers had ever been involved in. There was probably little change out of $10 million, with half of that being spent on gold mementoes for the 650 guests and $1 million on Elton John, who flew to Sydney to perform for an hour.

The party was held at the Packers' old family home in Bellevue Hill. (The marriage itself had been conducted earlier before a small group of family and friends, with David Gyngell, Chris Hancock and Damien Aspinall serving as groomsmen.) It was blowing a gale and pouring with rain, and stretch limos kept getting stuck on the hairpin bend at the bottom of the narrow drive. With a queue of cars snaking back almost a kilometre up Victoria Road, revellers had the choice of sitting in the rain for an hour or making a dash through the storm. But once inside, the downpour was forgotten. In the Packers' steeply sloping garden the organisers had created a covered fantasy land with spiral staircases, colonnades and water-falls cascading down from the house. Built from scratch—and thrown away afterwards—the wedding set was constructed on three separate levels with a reception and cocktail area, a big auditorium with stage, dance floor and banks of seats, and a dining area for 700 people with chairs sprayed silver and gold. Custom-made wall-paper with giant tiger-lily motifs covered the walls, $100 000 worth of flowers spilled from the centre of the tables and 250 000 fairy lights sparkled in the night. To complete the effect, Kerry's fabulous $2 million silver collection had been flown in from London.

The food was to die for: lobster tail and sugarcane prawns, freshly shucked oysters, sushi and sashimi, grass-fed fillet steak and charcoal-roasted lamb, followed by strawberry pavlova or berries with double cream, all washed down with 1998 Dom Perignon and 1992 Petaluma Coonawarra. For the smokers, there were $100 Cuban cigars and a consultant to advise which cigar to choose and what wine to drink with it.

After dinner, which was served by waiters in shirts bearing Jodie and James's initials, came the speeches, introduced by James's mate Eddie McGuire. The newly wedded heir thanked his father, his mother and Jodie's mother, but somehow found nothing to say about his bride, who was standing beside him. One old friend says they both looked nervous and unhappy. Others confided that the couple had wanted a quiet wedding, but Kerry had insisted on throwing the party.

And what a party it was. Most of Australia's ruling politicians, including John Howard, Peter Costello and Bob Carr, were among the guests, along with Bob Hawke, Jeff Kennett, Neville Wran, Graham Richardson, Michael Kroger and many more. The New South Wales Police Commissioner, Peter Ryan, was also there, as were Kerry's mates John Singleton and Robert Whyte, and a cavalcade of stars from Channel Nine, most of whom James and Jodie had never met. In fact, the majority of the guests seemed to owe more to the father than they did to the groom.

Not surprisingly, Kerry also took charge of security. He had been adamant that no drugs, cameras or gatecrashers should get past the perimeter, so guests had been admitted by barcode and searched with an electronic wand. He had also assured the hired staff and entertainers that he would break their kneecaps if anything went missing. And to ensure the safety of the VIPs, he had paid for a 100-strong security team, complete with bomb-sniffing dogs and ex-soldiers armed with guns.

Elton John wowed the party with his 1970s classic 'Your Song' (which includes the line, 'I don't have much money') and moved on to 'Can You Feel the Love Tonight' from *The Lion King*, which was the signal for James to lead Jodie onto the dance floor. By this time, she had changed out of her wedding dress and into a body-hugging number from the fashion label Bare, which several guests thought far too revealing.

The next morning, Murdoch's *Sunday Telegraph* ran one posed picture of the bride and groom on page 1, having promised not to publish 'at any time . . . any other photographs of Ms Jodie Meares or any member of the Packer family taken . . . on October 23 1999'. The Fairfax papers opted to go without.

Several days later, the Packers' own *Women's Weekly* brought out a special issue on the 'Wedding of the Decade'. With its cover and sixteen pages devoted to the party, it declared that romance had 'ruled the night'. Sadly, it would not last for long.

CHAPTER 11
A BIGGER BUNNY

We're going to be Kerry's second Alan Bond.

For the newly married James things had never been better. As the next millennium approached, the dot.com boom was reaching crazy heights and his family fortune was growing by the day. Everything he touched was turning to gold. But even as he marvelled at his own brilliance Kerry was in his ear, telling him there would never be a better time to cash in. As 1999 drew to a close, ecorp's market value was pushing towards $4 billion and the Packers' public company, PBL, was worth double that. It was the perfect time to sell up, if they could find someone dumb enough to pay the ridiculous prices that tech stocks were commanding.

It was one of Kerry's famous quips, of course, that you only got one Alan Bond in your lifetime, and he had had his. He had sold Channel Nine to the bouncing entrepreneur for $1 billion in 1987, only to buy it back again three years later at a fifth of the price. But he and James now managed to find an even bigger bunny in Telstra, which came within a whisker of buying the Packers' business empire for an extraordinary $11 billion, or more than ten times what Bond had paid for the TV stations a dozen years earlier.

Most of those involved in the top-secret deal, codenamed Project Patrick, have refused to talk about it ever since. Telstra's former chairman, Bob Mansfield, and chief executive, Ziggy Switkowski, have even tried to pretend it never happened. But perhaps that is not surprising. In the words of one former Telstra director, 'Project Patrick was a fiasco, and management had to be rescued by the board. The whole thing was driven by an overzealous chairman and a weak chief executive who went off and did a deal with the Packers and did not tell the board. God knows how it ever got so far.'

Bob Mansfield, who plays the leading role in this drama, is a salesman with boundless enthusiasm and is regarded by some as a visionary and by others as naive. In 1995, as head of Optus, he had bunkered down with the Packers in the fight against Super League and introduced James to Jodee Rich as a suitable investor in One.Tel. 'He was madly in love with the Packers,' says one ex-Telstra director witheringly. 'He was always talking about Kerry this and Kerry that.'

Mansfield's co-star, Ziggy Switkowski, is a small, neat, likeable man who is far too nice to be swimming with the sharks of corporate Australia. Born in Germany of Polish parents who migrated to Melbourne, he is a brilliant scientist who nearly ended up as an astrophysicist. Instead, he joined Kodak's research laboratory and graduated to running the Australian company before being head-hunted to replace Mansfield as head of Optus Communications. In March 1999, he landed the top job at Telstra.

Ted Pretty, his lieutenant at the national telephone company, plays the main supporting role. A big, brash American with a background in corporate law and one of the founding shareholders of One.Tel, he is the exact opposite of Switkowski. Tall, casually dressed and confident, he was charged with bringing Telstra into the twenty-first century by making telephony, the internet and television converge into one big business.

As the internet boom rocketed ahead and dot.com prices soared into the stratosphere, it had become axiomatic that telephone and internet companies needed to buy TV stations and newspaper groups so they could deliver news and entertainment to everyone's computer screen or mobile phone. James Packer believed passionately in this so-called 'convergence', as did Mansfield, Pretty and Switkowski, who all saw it leading to a hugely profitable future. And this is why the marriage between Telstra and the Packers' media empire almost came off.

It was Pretty's job to go around and talk to Australia's media companies and decide which ones to buy. And he soon made enemies in doing so. He was annoyingly sure of himself and was toting a large bag of money, which every media owner—including the Packers—hoped he would dump on their doorstep, and was upset when he did not.

During the latter half of 1999 Pretty had several meetings with James Packer, Daniel Petre and Nick Falloon to explore the possibility of Telstra buying into ecorp or NineMSN. He then abandoned these talks because the asking price was too high, and the baton passed to Telstra's new chairman, Bob Mansfield, who was due to take office in January 2000.

If anyone could be convinced that the Packers' business empire was a red-hot buy at $11 billion, Mansfield was the man. He was quite convinced Telstra needed to buy a TV network and equally clear it should be Channel Nine. And he seems to have discussed the idea with James or Kerry before arriving at Telstra because he started lobbying Switkowski to support such a deal several weeks before he actually took charge.

By mid-January 2000 Switkowski was also sure Telstra needed to find a big media partner, telling analysts the telephone company would 'morph' into a twenty-first-century multi-media business. A few weeks later he emphasised the need to act quickly, telling the *Sydney Morning Herald*: 'We are all now on internet time, moving at warp speed. Our views today may or may not be relevant a few months down the line.' Little did he know how prescient he was being, for all the wrong reasons. The dot.com crash was only ten weeks away.

Over the next few weeks Switkowski and Mansfield had several phone hook-ups with James and Ashok Jacob, who ran the Packers' private company Consolidated Press Holdings, to discuss a Telstra takeover. And almost immediately problems became clear. Telstra was half-owned by the taxpayer so it couldn't possibly own a casino, and it probably didn't want to own all ACP's magazines. Yet James was insisting on selling the Packer empire in one piece and buying bits back as necessary. Price was also an issue. PBL was trading at $13.50 a share—which was hugely inflated by the value of its holdings in ecorp and One.Tel—and James was demanding a hefty premium on top. He was also driving a hard bargain on details. Whenever negotiations paused so he could run things past Kerry, he came (or was sent) back to the table to ask for more.

Nevertheless, both sides obviously remained optimistic that the sale would go ahead because Telstra's chief financial officer, Paul Rizzo, was asked to prepare a report for the board to recommend whether the purchase should proceed. Rizzo was unaware that his bosses were already discussing the finer details, and was puzzled by the great sense of urgency. He was given just three weeks to finish the job on the basis that James and Ashok had another buyer who was hot to trot. Rizzo was also asked to exclude Ted Pretty from his team, apparently at the Packers' request. However, it was soon clear to him that buying Channel Nine only made sense if one believed in convergence, so it was ultimately Ted Pretty who was sent to Melbourne to work with Macquarie Bank on the case that would be made to Telstra's directors.

The Macquarie team, led by Peter Yates—another good friend of the Packers—was already extolling the virtues of the union, but Switkowski wanted Telstra's managers to back his judgment, and Pretty declined to do any such thing. He told Yates that his assumptions were too optimistic and asked him to change the numbers, then pulled his team out when the banker refused. For his part, Yates thought Pretty was being far too negative.

Rizzo had even graver doubts about the deal. He could not understand why Telstra would want to buy the Packers' magazines and Crown Casino and then sell them back again. Nor could he come at the price. Shortly before Project Patrick went to the board, he demanded a formal meeting with Mansfield and Switkowski and told them he believed Telstra should pull out of the deal.

Despite the serious concerns raised by Pretty and Rizzo, Mansfield and Switkowski called a special weekend meeting of the board to be held at Telstra's Sydney head offices at the end of March 2000. The directors were given very little warning that their gardening or golf was to be interrupted. They, too, were puzzled by the urgency.

The opening pitch was made by Mansfield, who then handed over to Rizzo and his team to take the board through the deal for the next three hours. When Rizzo finished, Mansfield asked everyone to leave the room except the directors, whom he asked in turn for their views. According to two witnesses, John Ralph, Chris Roberts, Ross Adler and Elizabeth Nosworthy all said 'You've got to be kidding', or words to that effect.

'My memory is that the deal was worth eleven to twelve billion dollars and the price was around $17 a share, which was ridiculous,' one director recalls angrily. 'We had quite enough trouble running our own business without running the Packers' as well. And then there was the crazy prospect of the government half-owning Channel Nine as well as the ABC.'

After half a dozen directors had expressed their opposition, Mansfield and Switkowski were asked to leave the room so the board could confer. It was absolutely clear what their decision would be. Only one director spoke in favour of the deal; the rest were against. 'It's very rare for a board to roll the CEO and the chairman,' says one of the directors who led the fight, 'but we did. What pissed us off more than anything was that Mansfield had told John Howard it was going ahead before he even talked to us.'

Half an hour later, Mansfield and Switkowski were invited back in to receive the verdict, but they had anticipated what it would be. With the board poised to roll its chairman and chief executive, Ziggy opted to withdraw the proposal before it was put to a vote. Mansfield then confessed he had already phoned the prime minister to tell him it was off, adding cheerfully that Howard was so relieved he had promised to shout him a beer the next time he was in Canberra.

Rizzo was not in the least surprised that the board knocked back the deal. 'I would have been stunned if the decision had been to go forward,' he says. But when he phoned James to give him the bad news, he discovered that the Packers had been led to believe the sale was in the bag. James was 'flabbergasted, shocked, surprised' says Rizzo, who was unaware that Switkowski had been on the phone to the younger Packer for much of the day trying to reach final agreement on the terms of sale.

Two weeks later James was undoubtedly a great deal angrier that the Packers' second Alan Bond had slipped away because, in early April 2000, the dot.com bubble burst and ecorp's shares fell by 50 per cent. PBL shares also dropped sharply to be worth around half what Telstra had been preparing to pay. The Packers had missed a once-in-a-lifetime opportunity to cash in their chips. Perhaps if they had not tried to drive such a hard bargain they would have pocketed the loot.

But James was quite sure the blame lay elsewhere and, in a manner that suggested he was becoming more and more like his father, he settled on Ted Pretty as the person who had killed the deal. One report said James was 'apopleptic' and vowed to get even.

James was also gunning for Pretty's former business partner, Peter O'Connell, who had worked for the Packers until mid-1999 as the head of PBL Enterprises running the Sydney Casino bid and a string of minor businesses. Like Pretty, O'Connell was also a founding shareholder in One.Tel, but had fallen out with James after criticising Jodee Rich and sold his shares. According to the Packers' version of events, O'Connell had contacted Ashok Jacob shortly after leaving Park Street and offered to broker a deal with Pretty in which Telstra would buy ecorp. He had also allegedly held out his hand for a $10 million success fee. O'Connell's version was that Ashok Jacob had made the approach and asked him to organise the meetings with Pretty, and that no fee had ever been mentioned.

Whatever the truth, O'Connell and Pretty now found them-selves on the end of a whispering campaign that accused them of corruptly seeking to profit from Pretty's position at Telstra. The campaign also took a swipe at Pretty for his decision to buy two Australian internet companies, Solution 6 and Sausage Software, which had cost Telstra millions of dollars in the dot.com crash. By the beginning of May 2000, this scuttlebutt had leaked to the newspapers and there was a tip that Pretty was about to be sacked. Three weeks later the trickle became a flood when the *Australian Financial Review* published a front-page story by Adam Shand which made the corruption allegations more explicit.

It was quite clear to anyone reading the story that Shand (who had been in Jodee Rich and Rodney Adler's year at Cranbrook) had received a detailed briefing from someone in Park Street. His 2000-word article relied heavily on phrases like 'the Packer camp claims', 'the Packer camp felt', and 'the Packer camp was astounded at the collapse of Project Patrick'. But of more concern was that he appeared to have been tipped off about O'Connell and Pretty's private share dealings, which he had chosen to examine in extraordinary detail. As Shand wrote:

> The brawl with the Packers has thrown a spotlight on Pretty's relationship with O'Connell, particularly their dealings in companies related to their formerly-shared consulting-investment company called Hargrave Consulting.

According to Shand, the spotlight's beam revealed one transaction involving Solution 6 where O'Connell's super fund had bought shares six weeks before the company was acquired by Telstra and then sold them at a $52 000 profit. Pretty had been the Telstra executive responsible for this deal and, according to Shand, was quite possibly a beneficiary of the super fund as well, a claim Pretty and O'Connell strenuously denied.

Shand had clearly spent an enormous amount of effort trying to prove that the two men were guilty of insider dealing. And in the process he had gone back several years to examine Pretty and O'Connell's investments in One.Tel.

O'Connell told friends he had supplied details of all his share dealings to the NSW Casino Control Commission and PBL in 1997 during probity checks for the Sydney Casino bid. He believed Shand must have been tipped off about them, either by the commission or by his former employer. However, Shand says he was never in possession of any of these private documents and was able to 'verify' all the trades on the public record. As to how he knew where to look and what to look for, he is not prepared to say, except to admit, 'I did have a source, but it wasn't James.'

As the sparks started to fly, Shand handed over his evidence to ASIC, which looked at the material and decided there was no case to answer. Telstra put a team of forensic experts through Ted Pretty's finances and also came up with a clean bill of health.

Ziggy Switkowski is convinced that the Packer camp was behind the attack. And one executive who was at PBL at the time confirms this suspicion. 'Yup,' he says, 'they were subject to a public campaign. But what else did they expect? James was very angry and disappointed.'

Ted Pretty did not shrug off the attack so lightly. His marriage broke up and he suffered a heart attack. His friend John Singleton, who had had plenty of spats with Kerry, told him to tough it out. Pretty eventually complained to the Packer's point man, Peter Barron. Soon afterwards a meeting was arranged with the Big Fella, who was cordial, charming and the perfect gentleman, perhaps because by this time Pretty was in charge of Telstra's large advertising budget.

Some time later Pretty had dinner with James at his Campbell Parade apartment. He told friends that he accused his host of doing a number on him, to which James replied, 'Well, yeah, but I didn't get what I wanted.'

'But that's a bit rough, isn't it?' Pretty responded.

'Welcome to First Grade,' James is supposed to have replied, an interesting comment given how badly he would deal with similar pressure over the coming One.Tel collapse.

Strangely enough, even as James and Kerry had been trying to sell ecorp and PBL in anticipation of the dot.com bust, they were also placing hundreds of millions of dollars on new hi-tech bets in Australia and overseas. In early March 2000, at the absolute zenith of the Indian stock market boom, James went to New Delhi to buy 10 per cent of Himachal Futuristic, a much-hyped phone company, for $400 million. There is no doubt the adventure was James's idea and that he was the one who was pushing it, but on this occasion Kerry jumped on board almost immediately. According to one PBL executive, he kept telling people how much money he was going to make and 'wouldn't listen to any warnings'.

There was huge excitement in India about the Packers' purchase of shares, with the press reporting it was the biggest foreign invest-ment the country's telecommunications sector had ever seen. And again, it was about convergence: of telephones, television and the internet. Ever enthusiastic about the prospects of making money in this area, James told a press conference in New Delhi that the Packers would launch joint ventures with Himachal in e-commerce and computer software, and export Indian expertise to the world.

Three weeks later James was back in India with Kerry and new wife Jodie to announce that the Packers were punting a further US$125 millon on a new hi-tech investment fund, KVP Ventures.

The launch of the fund was celebrated with two lavish parties, one at the Ashoka Hotel in New Delhi and the other at the Oberoi in Mumbai, at which politicians, Test cricketers, TV stars and pretty women lined up to meet the billionaire and his son from Down Under. With brightly coloured garlands draped around their necks, James and Kerry were serenaded by Amir Singh, a powerful New Delhi politician who told his 'brother' James he was sorry he had not been able to make it to his wedding to Jodie. The younger Packer touched the politician's feet in return and thanked him for all the 'love and affection' his 'older brother' had shown. It is amazing what people are prepared to do for money.

Kerry assured the party-goers that India was 'the place to be' and that he and James were putting their money where their mouth was. By this time even he had caught the internet bug, and he waxed lyrical to a reporter about growth drivers, convergence and the advantages of B2B e-commerce. It did not take long, however, for the Packers to discover they were victims of an Indian Rope Trick.

One of the partners in KVP Ventures—which stood for Kerry, Vinay and Parekh—was a notorious local stockbroker, Ketan Parekh, who was about to face trial on fraud charges relating to a 1992 stock scam. A legendary figure in the Indian market, Parekh was known as the Bombay Bull because he was famous for pumping up prices in information, communication and entertainment stocks. At the launch party he was mobbed by investors wanting to hear his stock tips, one of which was that Himachal's share price would soon go higher because it was 'grossly undervalued'.

In fact, Himachal was one of the most overvalued companies on the Mumbai stock exchange. It was already selling for 110 times earnings, its share price had risen thirty-fold in a year, and it was worth as much as One.Tel in Australia, but had even less to recommend it. Amid all the hype and hope, the Packers' involvement seemed to be the only reason to believe.

Himachal was half-owned by the 'V' in KVP Ventures, Vinay Maloo, who was an accountancy drop-out turned entrepreneurial whizkid. Smooth, charming and often surrounded by pretty women, Maloo liked to dress in black and be ferried around town in a large, black Cadillac. He also had the habit of introducing himself by saying, 'We are Jains. One thing you should know about us, we cannot lie.' He seemed to manage to overcome this cultural handicap.

In 1995 his then very small company had made a ridiculous $34 billion bid for nine regional mobile phone licences. Unable to raise the money, it had been allowed to slip out of the contracts and avoid paying $70 million in penalties thanks to a favour from India's Telecom minister, Sukh Ram, who later resigned amid corruption allegations. Predictably, it was this perceived political clout that the Packers found attractive. Maloo appeared to have powerful connections who could help them get what they wanted, which was a TV network in India. Indeed, they had already dished up the first instalment on this promise.

At the same time as the Packers' private company, CPH, was buying into Himachal, the publicly owned PBL was launching a joint venture with the company to supply three hours of prime-time TV a night to Doordarshan Metro, one of India's public broadcasting channels. The Packers had paid $50 million at auction for this slot, which they planned to call Nine Gold and fill with Hindi soaps and game shows in return for all the advertising revenue. James hoped the one-year contract would become a ten-year deal, which would be as close as any foreigner was likely to get to securing an

Indian TV licence. Maloo, who had already introduced James to several senior politicians, had so far delivered on everything he promised.

But not everyone at PBL was convinced the arrangement would end well. Managing director Nick Falloon was certainly sceptical and so was Kerry. And their fears were justified. Doordarshan's bureaucracy was appalling even by Indian standards, the transmitters were so rundown that half the supposed audience missed out on the signal, and the station managers only seemed interested in pleasing their masters, who turned out to be politicians Maloo did not have in his pocket.

The Packers were also rushing in with too much haste and too little planning. James McLachlan, the head of PBL Enterprises, was given just two days' notice to get on a plane to India and spent the next eight months setting up a TV business from scratch, including commissioning and making twenty-one hours a week of new Hindi-language programs.

Nine Gold finally made it to air in September 2000 and was launched with another celebration at which James was hugged by several more Indian politicians. But the joy was short-lived. The Packers' one-year contract was never renewed and PBL was forced to pull out with losses of between $50 million and $100 million.

By this time the Indian stock market had also fallen through the floor, as had Himachal Futuristic, whose share price collapsed from a high of R2000 to less than R100 by early 2001. Staff in the software and e-commerce ventures had to be sacked and the offices in Australia and the United States shut down. KVP Ventures also shut up shop, having made just four small investments. In total, the Packers appear to have lost at least $400 million of their own money in these Indian ventures on top of the losses in PBL. But it is impossible to be sure of the exact figure because CPH has never revealed details in its accounts.

As for the notorious Mr Parekh, a year after getting into bed with the Packers he defaulted on a $50 million loan from a co-operative bank in Ahmedabad (which promptly went bust). He was arrested on a second set of fraud charges, on which he was still awaiting trial in early 2009. He was finally convicted over the 1992 stock scam in 2008 and sentenced to a year in jail.

CHAPTER 12
HERO TO ZERO

I just can't stand it any more. Kerry gets sick but then he
always seems to get better. I think he has nine lives.

On 4 April 2000, the morning after the dot.com bubble burst on
Wall Street, Kerry bounced into the office looking happier than
anyone had seen him for ages. After two years in which the business
world had gone mad, he had finally been proven right. By mid-
afternoon he had lost more than half a billion dollars on the value
of his shareholdings in One.Tel and ecorp, but he couldn't have
cared less. 'I always told you it didn't make sense,' he bragged.

Two weeks later prices on the NASDAQ plummeted again and
the local market followed suit. By mid-May One.Tel had lost a
third of its market value and ecorp had fallen by half. Despite the
damage done to his wealth, Kerry could hardly hide his pleasure
that James's two stellar businesses had come crashing back to earth.
No longer would his son be allowed to behave like he was a master
of the universe.

It was bad enough for James that his multi-billion-dollar successes were suddenly worth so much less and that Kerry had decided to take charge again, but the tech wreck would now make it harder for mobile phone companies to raise money, and One.Tel needed plenty if it was to get its new $1.1 billion network up and running. Just days before the crash the company had agreed to shell out $523 million for bandwidth, which was ten times what Vodafone, Optus and Telstra had paid at an earlier government auction. PBL had been forced to cough up another $140 million and, as a result, Kerry had become even more convinced the venture was going to end in tears. He told James and Jodee Rich scornfully that they had 'fucked up' by paying too much.

Fortunately One.Tel had been priced out of a similar auction in the United Kingdom, so it would not have to finance the $20 billion network Murdoch had dreamed of building in Europe. But the Australian network alone would stretch its resources to the limit, especially since it would be fighting for market share against Telstra, Optus, Vodafone and Orange, all of which had deep pockets and no desire to lose.

By September 2000 the situation was looking critical, as Kerry had warned it would: One.Tel had lost $291 million in the year to June and had spent $775 million in cash, which was almost all the money the Packers and Murdochs had put in. On top of that, Jodee Rich and Brad Keeling had finally confessed to paying themselves bonuses of $6.9 million apiece, even though the company was losing a fortune. Not surprisingly, there was a blizzard of bad press, the shares fell further and Merrill Lynch issued a report predicting One.Tel would run out of funds and might have to sell its new mobile network as soon as it was built.

In these circumstances, Packer, Rich and Keeling were hauled in to News Limited's offices in Surry Hills to make a presentation to Rupert Murdoch on one of his regular visits to Sydney. Jodee was super confident, as always, and James tried his best to be reassuring. He promised he would get more involved in the business and take extra care of the two families' investment.

Shortly afterwards, James received a rare invitation to lunch at the *Sydney Morning Herald*, where he told his dining companions that Rich was a visionary and a brilliant manager, the business was doing fine and One.Tel's share price would soon rocket skywards again. He seemed passionate, evangelistic and convinced it would come right but, in the view of everyone else there, he was almost certainly mistaken. They were convinced the company was a basket case.

As One.Tel's woes deepened in late 2000, Kerry was taken sick again. He had been in and out of hospital six or seven times in the previous three years and had nearly died twice. Earlier in the year his doctors had taken him to Cornell Medical Center in New York once more, with Nick Ross in tow, in the hope of getting him a heart and kidney transplant. But it had been conditional on finding a suitable donor. 'What I want is a big young negro's heart,' Packer told his doctors, pointing his finger and thumb to his temple. 'And I want the bullet to go right here, so it's in perfect condition.' But even Kerry's billions had not been able to buy that, so he was forced to return home.

He refused to contemplate dialysis, later explaining to *Australian Story* with his usual refreshing clarity: 'You're on a machine lying down in a bed for eight or nine hours a day, three or four days a week. You can't go anywhere, you have no mobility, you have no freedom, and you never get better. All that ever happens is you get a little bit worse . . . and eventually, you die.' So it was now clear he could not last much longer without a new kidney.

In early November, Nick Ross got a call from Kerry's medical team asking him to fly down from Ellerston to Sydney for further tests to ensure he was still a compatible donor and to convince a psychiatrist he was not being coerced. The doctors told him quietly that he could say 'No' and they would concoct a medical excuse so Kerry would never know he had pulled out. Amazingly, he had never discussed his gift with the boss.

Nick and his wife Karin had already booked a holiday to Western Australia, so they decided to go away and talk about the risks. No one had ever died in Australia in forty years of kidney donations, but there was an outside chance that Ross's remaining kidney might eventually pack up and it was a major operation, which always had risks attached. Despite these concerns, they resolved to go ahead.

As soon as they got back to Sydney, Ross and his wife visited Kerry at the spectacular penthouse in Elizabeth Bay where he now lived for most of the time with his long-standing mistress Julie Trethowan. He had deteriorated terribly in the three weeks they had been away. 'He looked shocking, awful, close to death,' says Ross. 'He could hardly get out of his chair.' They sat with him for two hours and talked about everything except the kidney. Only once was the topic mentioned, when Ross described how he and Karin had fed sharks on their diving trip. 'Thank the fuck I'm getting your kidney, not your brain,' Kerry quipped.

The operation was performed at Sydney's Royal Prince Alfred Hospital (RPA), and not just for convenience sake. As Packer later told *Australian Story*: 'One of the few things in life that money does for you is it doesn't restrict you to where you have to go . . . and the people at RPA are regarded as as good as anyone in the world. And

I've checked everywhere in the world.' The actual surgery wasn't the difficult bit. That was just plumbing. The skill was in managing the body's rejection of the new organ with an individually tailored cocktail of drugs. It was in this that RPA excelled.

Because Nick Ross was the first to go under the knife, he was the first to come round. He hobbled down the corridor to see the old man and found him looking 'fantastic, a completely different human being, as if fresh life had been breathed into him'. He was no longer a death mask. There was colour in his cheeks, and he looked better than he had done for years. For six days the pair shuffled up and down the corridor to visit each other, before being whisked off to the Packer compound in Bellevue Hill.

On the way home on his first day out of hospital, Kerry had Ros stop the big BMW at Park Street so he could make a brief appearance in his office. Maybe this was to calm the stock market and show the world he was still alive. Maybe it was because he just couldn't stay away. But thereafter, he trekked into the RPA at seven o'clock every morning for blood tests and a daily cocktail of anti-rejection drugs: even for Kerry Packer the doctors weren't prepared to make an exception and treat him at home.

In the first week of December, he was rushed back into hospital with complications. Ros and James were called to his bedside. Amid the rumours he was dying, one radio announcer told listeners he was actually dead, only to correct the report a few minutes later by which time $700 million—around 12 per cent—had been wiped off the value of PBL's shares.

There were bouts of rejection over the next six months and several times it looked like the old man was going to die. But he managed to pull through. Every time he went back into RPA the four-bed ward reserved for him was cleared and his furniture reinstalled, the newspapers dusted off their obituaries and PBL's share price wobbled. Even his own *Bulletin* magazine conducted interviews so the memorial issue would be ready to run at a moment's notice.

When Kerry wasn't in hospital, to the amazement of his staff he staggered into work. He came in every day, even if it was only for an hour or so. Barely able to walk, he would shuffle the thirty or forty paces from the lift to his office and stop for a rest half way. He just couldn't make it in one go. Yet he was still interfering as much as ever with his son's management of the business. As James, who was executive chairman, later told the One.Tel liquidator: 'My father's been involved in PBL the whole time, whenever his health has permitted it and sometimes when his health hasn't permitted it.'

Even while most of the country was away on its Christmas break, the Big Fella was still busy worrying that One.Tel would go bust. It had gobbled up another $230 million in cash in the six months to December 2000 and had only $100 million left in the bank. When Jodee got back from Airlie Beach in mid-January, he and James were hauled in for a three-hour ear bashing. 'You ran out of cash at Imagineering,' Kerry said, pointing at Jodee, 'and you're going to do it again. I was right and now the markets are telling me I was right. You blokes never listen to me.' From that point on, Kerry and James were sent daily reports on the company's cash position.

Come February, the old man was sick again and back in RPA, yet he still didn't let go, dragging James, Jodee and finance director Mark Silbermann into his hospital room for a detailed briefing. According to Rich, they sat around his bed for almost two hours with Kerry propped up on pillows barely able to keep his eyes open yet apparently taking it all in. His mantra was the same as always: One.Tel would run out of cash, and he didn't believe their assurances that the company was turning the corner. Having finally figured out how to use his computer, he looked up the share price and told them exactly how much money he and the Murdochs had lost.

The stock market was now hearing rumours that the Packers wanted to sell, and James had to hose down those fears. At a lunch convened by One.Tel's broker, Brent Potts, he told the company's biggest institutional backers that the business was doing fine, that it was integral to PBL's strategic vision and that it would be the second- or third-largest mobile telephone company in Australia within five years, with a market capitalisation of $10 billion.

But what James did next only served to shake market confidence further. At the end of March, with Kerry apparently close to death and the family gathered at Bellevue Hill to pay their last respects, James took the opportunity to sack Nick Falloon, who was one of Kerry's longest-serving lieutenants and who had consistently opposed James over One.Tel. Siding with Kerry, Falloon had voiced doubts about the $400 million investment from the beginning, and had declined to serve on the board because he didn't trust Jodee Rich. He had also sought more oversight of the company than James had been prepared to allow.

Falloon had spoken up against other ventures, too. This had been deeply frustrating for James, who wanted someone to support him in battles against his father, or as 'sources close to Park Street' put it, who wanted 'a batsman, not a wicket-keeper'.

Even though the sacking was James's decision, Kerry had been persuaded to sign off on it, which was a surprise because he and Falloon had been close for years. But loyalties and friendships meant little in the Packer empire, as many had already discovered. Ratings at Channel Nine had suddenly started falling and the old man wanted a human sacrifice. 'Dad says we've got to sack someone,' James told a colleague shortly before wielding the axe. He was able to convince Kerry that it should be Falloon's head that rolled.

After nineteen years of loyal service, the Packers' managing director was dismissed by James in a thirty-second conversation. The press release that followed gave no reason for Falloon's departure and made no effort to soften the blow or pretend the parting was by mutual consent. As *The Australian*'s Mark Day noted, quoting one insider's reaction to the execution, 'Kerry was tyrannical, but he was warm as well. James is also tyrannical, but there is little warmth.'

James had been looking for a new right-hand man for at least six months, so Falloon wasn't particularly surprised when the axe fell. But the market was shocked at the news, and PBL shares took a hammering. Media analysts were astounded that James was getting rid of someone who was clearly so good at his job. They were almost as shocked by his choice of a replacement.

Peter Yates was an investment banker who had no experience in television, magazines or management and had never run anything bigger than his team of analysts at Macquarie Bank. According to one insider, he was 'totally the wrong guy, hopelessly out of his depth . . . and just so excited to get the job'. But he was an enthusiast and a believer in One.Tel like James. In November 2000 he dined at James's Bondi apartment with Rich and Keeling and promised a positive report on the company from Macquarie. Published in January 2001, as Kerry's concerns mounted, it valued the company at $3.5 billion, which *The Australian* hailed as 'the most significant endorsement yet from the financial community'. The share price doubled briefly on the strength of the report, allowing Rodney Adler to get his money out before the price resumed its downward slide. Four months later, this supposedly valuable business was dead on the slab.

At the end of March 2001, two days after Falloon's sacking, James Packer and Lachlan Murdoch attended a One.Tel board meeting and were told by Rich and Mark Silbermann that its cash position was at last improving. From a low of $36 million mid-month the balance had risen to $61 million by month's end. The suggestion was that the company had at last turned the corner and would not need more funds. James said later that he emerged from the meeting feeling 'more confident about One.Tel's prospects than [he] had ever been'. Indeed, he was so excited that he turned to Lachlan and said: 'Now we're going to show all those doubters that they were wrong. And we're going to be right on this and we're going to be vindicated.'

Murdoch's response was a non-committal 'I hope you're right', but he too was confident that the company had at last become cash positive. However, as ASIC's calculations would later show, One. Tel had consumed $50 million more in cash during the first quarter of 2001 than it had forecast only three months before. In other words, it was in as much trouble as ever.

Typically, Kerry's pessimism remained unshaken, despite this latest encouraging bulletin from Rich and despite James's conviction that the company would pull through. Two weeks later, with One.Tel's daily cash report showing money still pouring out of the company, Rich was summoned to Park Street for yet another grilling. 'How much cash have you got?' Kerry demanded. 'You are definitely going to run out.' James, who was forced to witness this interrogation, looked so bad that Rich buttonholed Ashok

Jacob to ask what was wrong. Kerry was angry with James, he was told, because he had not kept the old man informed. After the meeting, Rich asked James how he was. 'Shithouse,' he replied. 'Dad's very angry about the share price and he's sure One.Tel will run out of cash.'

Four days later, on Easter Sunday 2001, Rich had dinner with James at his Bondi apartment. James was clearly depressed and complaining that he was 'a third-class citizen again' because his father was treating him so badly. When Rich suggested he might not have to bear it much longer because the old man would probably die soon, James is supposed to have replied: 'I just can't stand it any more. Kerry gets sick but then he always seems to get better. I think he has nine lives.'

Rich claims that James also admitted to having money problems. Having borrowed from the ANZ Bank to buy his stake in One.Tel, he would have to ask Kerry to repay the loan because the shares were now almost worthless. 'One.Tel bought me my independence and now I feel like I've given it all up,' he told his friend. James denies saying this, just as he denies saying that he wanted to walk away. 'I'd prefer to be sitting on the beach,' he supposedly told Rich, 'but I can't. I want to be a billionaire.'

Far from being cash positive, as Rich and his finance director had forecast, One.Tel was now so short of funds it was being forced to juggle its creditors and invent disputes to avoid paying in full. But even this was not enough to stop money pouring out of the company. In mid-April, at Kerry's insistence, two PBL accountants, Darren Miller and Martin Green, started reviewing One.Tel's cash needs. By early May they were warning $100 million was needed, almost all of which would have to come from the Packers and Murdochs.

Kerry was back in hospital again, so it fell to James to call Rich, Keeling and Silbermann into Park Street to tell them they had 'fucked up'. They had promised the market repeatedly that One.Tel was not going to run out of cash, and now it was going to do just that. There would have to be a rights issue at 5 cents a share to bail out the company and Jodee and Brad would have to go, James said, because they had lost all credibility.

Even though Kerry was too sick to be there, he still managed to make his presence felt. He had asked Peter Yates, PBL's new managing director, to warn Jodee that the disaster would cost him 'his right testicle'. Yates, it seems, was only too pleased to pass on the threat, quite possibly in more colourful language than that.

Despite the evidence, James was apparently still convinced that One.Tel had a glorious future. After the showdown with Rich, Keeling and Silbermann he jetted off to the Cannes Film Festival, where Lachlan and Rupert Murdoch were attending the premiere of *Moulin Rouge*, to tell them that another $130 million would be needed to keep the company alive. Asked if there was 'a fundamental problem with the business', James is supposed to have assured Lachlan that it was 'just a timing issue', adding that Jodee didn't even believe the money was needed.

Rich also seems to have been remarkably optimistic about the future, or just good at bluffing. While James was breaking the bad news to the Murdochs, he was telling *The Australian*'s Geoff Elliott that One.Tel was indeed still on track to have $75 million in the bank at 30 June, as its directors had repeatedly promised. Rich was his usual charming self, friendly, smiling and oozing confidence, even offering Elliott a vitamin C tablet as they both had colds. 'Rich knew he was in the eye of a perfect storm that was about to engulf his company, destroy his reputation for the second time in his life and make enemies of the two most powerful families in the land,' Elliott wrote later. 'You would never have guessed.'

James, on the other hand, did not appear to be handling the pressure well. As soon as he got back from the south of France, he called Rich around to his apartment to tell him his fate was sealed. 'He told me I would have to go. He told me that's what Rupert and Lachlan wanted. And I told him I would do whatever was best for the company. And we put our arms round each other and cried. 'I'm not in control,' James told his friend, 'Dad's calling the shots.'

A week later, on 17 May 2001, the final deed was done at an emergency board meeting. It was quite obvious to staff that something was afoot because they could see James, Lachlan, Jodee, Brad and a crowd of stern-faced lawyers huddled in a glass-walled fishbowl office in the middle of the big open-plan floor at One.Tel's Sydney headquarters, but they could only guess at the seriousness of what was going on. The first item of business was to agree on a rights issue that would raise $132 million at 5 cents a share. James put it on record that PBL and News were 'surprised, disappointed and upset' to be asked to underwrite the rights issue but were prepared to do so. The second item of business was to get Rich and Keeling to fall on their swords. But here, as the official minutes of the meeting reveal, things did not go to plan.

RESIGNATIONS OF JODEE RICH AND BRADLEY KEELING

James Packer thanked Jodee Rich and Bradley Keeling for their enormous entrepreneurial vision and hard work which had taken the company from its small beginnings six years ago to the global organisation that it was today. He noted that today marks a new beginning for One.Tel.

> Lachlan Murdoch expressed News Ltd's gratitude for the passion and energy of Jodee Rich and Bradley Keeling. They had created remarkable value over the last six years. News Limited accepts their resignation with mixed emotion.

Then came the problem.

> Jodee Rich said that they had not offered to resign . . . and that they believed they should stay.
> . . . Lachlan Murdoch said that he took back everything that he had said. Jodee Rich said he hoped he was joking.

But Lachlan was not joking. Nor was James. Only then did Jodee finally realise he was going to lose control of his creation. For the next half-hour he dug in his heels and refused to budge. He was threatened with the sack, first by Yates and then by James, who told him he would be fired on the spot unless he went quietly. Finally, he agreed to go, but such was his ego that he regarded it as the only mistake he made in all his time at One.Tel. He should have stayed around longer to protect his shareholders, he said, the ones whose billions he had already lost.

What happened to One.Tel over the next two weeks would become the subject of dispute and legal argument, but essentially the $132 million rights issue was canned and One.Tel was handed over to the corporate undertakers. James and Lachlan's justification for killing the business they had invested so much in was that they had been 'profoundly misled as to the true financial state of the company'. Seven months later, ASIC took action against Rich and Keeling on precisely this basis, suing them for $93 million in damages allegedly suffered by creditors who had continued to deal with the company while it was insolvent. Keeling pleaded guilty to the charge, handed over all his assets to One.Tel's liquidator, and was banned as a company director until 2013. Rich on the other hand spent the next eight years fighting the charges and, astonishingly, in late 2009 was still waiting for Justice Austin in the New South Wales Supreme Court to reach a verdict.

Rich's defence, backed up by a meticulous 511-page affidavit, was that James and Lachlan had always been fully informed of the financial state of the company, which was never as bad as they (and ASIC) claimed. In his version of events, the two biggest shareholders had buckled to pressure from Kerry and simply changed their minds about investing more money. In doing so, Rich maintained, they had breached a legally binding commitment to rescue the company.

Whatever the final legal outcome there was probably truth on both sides, but some insiders remain convinced that crucial financial information *was* kept from James and Lachlan in the last few months of the company's life. For example, they were not told that One.Tel was losing money on local calls, or that the financial controller reckoned the company was going to fall $50 million short of its budget in the 2000 financial year. Nor were they told that major creditors remained unpaid. Worst of all, they were given no idea of the extent of the company's bad debts. Perhaps, as directors, they should have asked more questions.

When the Packers' investigating accountants went into the company in late May 2000 they quickly discovered that at least $50 million of the $160 million owed by One.Tel's customers would have to be written off. One-third of the debts were more than 330 days old and half were already with debt collection agencies.

Many of those who owed money could no longer be traced and others, like Barney Rubble, Fred Flintstone, Astro Boy and Yogi Bear, had never existed in the first place. Remarkably, these cartoon characters remained on the list of debtors who were expected to pay up for the simple reason that One.Tel would have been forced to notch up even bigger losses if it had admitted its debts were uncollectible.

One.Tel had fought a running battle with its auditors Ernst & Young over these bad debts, but somehow Jodee had managed to convince them the money could be collected. And battles inside the company had yielded the same result. 'The bad debts were the ones that Jodee *accepted* could not be collected,' a senior member of One.Tel's collection team revealed. 'The real figure was always higher. We might tell him that 95 per cent of a category was un-collectable but he would say he wanted us to collect half of it. So only half would be counted as bad.'

This was fairly typical of how One.Tel had been run from the beginning with its culture of optimism, exaggeration and deceit. The company's first auditor had been disciplined by the Institute of Chartered Accountants of Australia in 1999 for allowing an overstatement of profits. And the notorious $6.9 million bonuses paid to Rich and Keeling had been deliberately kept secret from shareholders and the public for fully eighteen months. There was also the manner in which One.Tel had reported its results for the 2000 financial year, when it had lost $295 million and chomped through $750 million in cash, yet failed to mention the word 'loss' in its glossy account of how the business was travelling. It had not been revealed in the Chairman's Letter to Shareholders nor in the Managing Director's Report nor even in the year's Key Finan-cial Highlights. The only place where the company's losses were recorded was in the dull, grey figures at the back of the annual report, where the law required they be reported.

One.Tel had regularly covered up key facts, hidden information or tried to dazzle investors with optimism. And if, as James and Lachlan maintained, they had finally been fooled by the smoke and mirrors, they were hardly in a position to complain. In fact, they were quite possibly lucky that ASIC was not asking them to pay the price.

And even if they had been deceived, Kerry had seen through the bullshit. It could be argued that the old man was always pessimistic and just happened to be right on this occasion, but he was hardly alone in his doubts. Brian Powers and Nick Falloon had been deeply suspicious of One.Tel and Rich from the start. And in the last nine months of the company's life, rivals, customers, headhunters, creditors, brokers and the financial press all knew it was in strife.

One.Tel had always consumed cash at an alarming rate, and it had always been an act of faith to believe it could outlast its deep-pocketed rivals like Telstra, Optus, Orange and Vodafone. It might have been argued that it was Kerry's fault the Packers and Murdochs lost their nerve after the new $1.1 billion mobile network had been built, but they should never have been playing the game in the first place. And it was undoubtedly James who had landed them in it. He was the one who had championed One.Tel and persuaded Kerry to invest. He was the one who brought in the Murdochs to help One.Tel conquer the world. And he was the one who had backed Jodee right to the end.

At the liquidator's hearing in May 2002, after a three-day grilling from Michael Slattery QC, James emerged from the courtroom with a face like thunder. Surrounded by his lawyers, mother, sister, wife and hangers-on, he spluttered: 'I may be a fuckwit but I'm not a liar. I was a believer.' It summed him up exactly. His faith had blinded him.

James's problem was that he had trusted too much. He had desperately wanted One.Tel to succeed so he could show his father how smart he was. And he had never really been able to stand up to Jodee Rich, whom he saw as a genius. Even after One.Tel crashed in flames—as Imagineering had done in the 1980s—Rich remained incredibly confident and convincing and hard to disagree with.

But it was not just Jodee's Olympic optimism and powerful personality that was to blame. James was as much at fault because he was so susceptible to these charms. He was ever ready to believe and prone to fall in love. Almost everyone who has worked alongside James, including Brian Powers, highlights this major weakness. 'He tends to be bedazzled by people he thinks can bring him a pot of gold,' says one who has known him for more than a decade. 'He's too credulous, he believes too easily,' says another who worked with him almost as long. 'James is binary in business and personal relationships,' says a third, who probably knows him as well as anyone. 'There are no shades of grey. Everything's either really great or really terrible.'

And of course it was now really terrible. He had gone from hero to zero in one mighty flash.

CHAPTER 13
THINGS FALL APART

It's fascinating that he has buckled emotionally over
One.Tel. Here's someone who can be quite brutal with
other people and he has just buckled.

James had staked almost everything on the success of One.Tel,
believing it would win him freedom and financial independence
and earn his father's respect. Now it was all in ruins and he was
back where he started, or worse. He had sniffed the air of freedom
and was back in the shackles.

Not only had he been forced to abandon his close friend Jodee,
he had let down Rupert Murdoch and made a fool of himself by
crying in Lachlan's kitchen on the day that it finally became clear
their investment was worthless. Worst of all he had lost out to his
father, who had been proved right yet again and who now came back
from his deathbed to resume complete control of the business.

Kerry was skipping into work as happy as a sandboy, pleased he
was needed again and that his view of the world had triumphed,

even if it had cost him $400 million. As one banker observed, the crisis had added five years to his life. A joke now went around the stock market that James had asked Kerry, 'What's my punishment?' The old man had replied, 'I won't die yet.'

Two weeks after the collapse, Kerry invited a group of analysts and fund managers to lunch in the Channel Nine boardroom. They arrived to find him sporting a hearing aid, but looking much better than he had at his brother Clyde's memorial service a few weeks earlier. He told them he had been in semi-retirement for a few years but was now back to run the company. As they tucked into smoked salmon and roast lamb, he said that One.Tel was a 'fuck up', and there would no more of those with him in charge. He chose to ignore the fact that he had happily invested the family's money in One.Tel in 1999 and had been hugely enthusiastic about the family's hi-tech adventure in India, which was proving to be a disaster of similar magnitude.

By now James had taken off to Europe with his wife Jodie to play polo, lounge around on the *Arctic P* and forget about it all. But this was easier said than done. Friends reported he was devastated, depressed and even suicidal. 'I was worried he was going to neck himself,' says one close friend. There were also rumours that he was in rehab, that the son of a wealthy Sydney Eastern Suburbs family had run into him at the Betty Ford clinic in Los Angeles. More plausibly, there were suggestions he had suffered a nervous breakdown.

One former adviser was amazed at how badly he was taking it all. 'James admires people who have made millions: players, movers and shakers,' he observed. 'His motto is, "Whoever dies with the most money wins". It's fascinating that he has buckled emotionally over One.Tel. Here's someone who can be quite brutal with other people and he has just buckled.'

On reflection it was hardly surprising that this is how James reacted. One.Tel had been the climax of his lifelong struggle to stand up to Kerry and prove his worth. And it had ended in humiliation. Perhaps it was just as his father always said: he couldn't be trusted, he couldn't be let off the leash, and he still wasn't up to doing the job on his own.

Kerry was certainly accepting none of the responsibility for the debacle. When PBL's annual results were published in August 2001, the old man was nowhere to be seen. It was left to James to announce the company's first-ever loss and assure investors that he and his father had never been closer. He looked pale and pudgy and confessed he had been suffering nightmares and sleepless nights. When the meeting was over he wandered out of the Hilton Hotel looking dazed and miserable. He waited a few moments for his colleagues to join him and then struck off up George Street on his own. It was almost two blocks before he stopped abruptly and turned on his heel, having apparently realised he was heading in the wrong direction. 'James was completely fucked,' a PBL executive told *Good Weekend*'s Richard Guilliatt. 'He went from one of the most confident executives in the world to a complete mess.'

According to Brian Powers, 'James was so shocked by the company's failure he became dysfunctional . . . He couldn't or wouldn't come out and defend himself in public.' At Foxtel board meetings, according to Ziggy Switkowski, he said little and appeared to be 'traumatised'. Others who know him well say he was 'catatonic'.

Many of his so-called friends deserted him. Almost all the people who had been hanging around because of his power and money melted away. Eighteen months earlier he had been a master of the universe, a business genius whose vision had added billions of dollars to the family fortune. Now he was in hock to the ANZ

Bank and his father for money he had borrowed to buy One.Tel shares. He was also potentially at risk of being prosecuted by ASIC for allowing the company to trade while insolvent, even though he was claiming he had been misled.

And Kerry's attitude didn't help. 'It was despicable the way Kerry treated James over One.Tel,' says one of the old man's most trusted former lieutenants. 'He left him hanging out to dry. It was as if he was jealous of him.' And perhaps this was the case. At the height of the boom, James had boasted that he had made more money than his father. And this had got back to Kerry, amplifying the rivalry that already existed between them.

In the aftermath of the collapse James took little or no part in running the business, even though he was still executive chairman. Shortly after the PBL annual general meeting in October, at which he was again forced to carry the can for losses on One.Tel and Himachal, James disappeared overseas again. One former Channel Nine executive remembers seeing him for the last time on election night, 10 November 2001, looking fat and depressed. 'He was in David Leckie's office at Nine watching the coverage. The kitchen had made three plates of shepherd's pies and I remember he ate nearly all of them.'

He was away for most of that southern summer, in England and Los Angeles, reappearing only briefly on a couple of occasions. When he did come back for a longer stint in April 2002, it was to prepare for the much anticipated liquidator's inquiry into the One.Tel collapse. He made his debut in the witness box in May in Court 20A of Sydney's Federal Court, which was packed to the rafters with some 200 journalists, lawyers, accountants and casual spectators. Oddly enough, Kerry was neither in the audience nor called to give evidence, but James's wife, sister and mother were all there to support him. Also in the melee was One.Tel's one-time visionary and James's former friend and guru Jodee Rich, who had installed himself in the courtroom directly behind Michael Slattery QC so the young tycoon would be forced to meet his gaze as he answered questions.

It promised to be an intriguing spectacle and the gallery was amply rewarded as it was given the rare chance to see a Packer perform in public. For the first few exchanges James did a passable impersonation of his father's unforgettable TV performance in the 1991 senate inquiry into the print media. He grimaced, looked scornful and was sometimes plain rude. When told by Michael Slattery to 'answer the questions' he smirked at his legal team and raised his eyebrows in mock alarm. This was his father's son, a chip off the old block.

Then, just as the court tensed for a fight, he became calm, polite and attentive. By mid-afternoon he was as mild as a schoolboy in the headmaster's study, even saying 'Sorry, Sir' to Michael Slattery's questions. The following day he seemed to be more sure of himself and how he should behave, but on day one he looked lost, as if he didn't know what role he should play.

And lost he was. Seven years on, no one is entirely clear on the exact chronology of his distress, but there were stories that he was taking anti-depressants and other drugs, that he had been helped out of a bar in tears and that his personal life was falling apart under the strain. And this last part was certainly true. One month after the hearings, after less than three years of marriage, he and his wife Jodhi (as she had now decided to call herself) announced they were going their separate ways.

According to the *Sun Herald*'s gossip columnist Annette Sharp, who had talked to some of Jodhi's friends, there had been precious little fun in the marriage for a long time. 'It took more than a year to finally summon up the courage,' she wrote, 'but after months of bitter tears and caustic blow-ups, it was Jodhi Packer who finally put an end to her marriage . . . turning her back on his empire and the family billions.'

Two weeks later James gave an extraordinarily frank interview to Jeni Cooper, editor of the *Sunday Telegraph*, in which he described Jodhi as his 'absolute soulmate' and 'the most-loved woman in his life'. He said his father's illness, the problems with One.Tel and (strangely enough) a 'downturn in advertising' had put their relationship under intolerable pressure. They remained the best of friends, he said, and he hoped one day they might reunite.

Certainly, it was Jodhi who had walked out. She had never shown much interest in the Packer billions, even though she had been happy for James to bankroll her swimwear business, and she had never wanted to be on the A-list or to spend her time at public functions. She had also struggled with the duties of being a Packer wife and had grown tired of Kerry ringing James in the middle of the night to abuse him. James had promised they would go away when his father died, sell out of the media and live on a boat in Europe for six months of the year, but Kerry was stubbornly still alive.

Sharp claimed James was furious that his wife had left him: 'He has always had a temper, and she has felt the full force of it. He is a very angry man.' She added that he was unhappy and putting on weight, and quoted a friend as saying, 'He hasn't been looking after himself. He's smoking too much, eating fast food, not exercising. He's plummeting into middle age and he knows it.'

There were also rumours that James was having an affair, as he had done in the latter days of his engagement to Kate

Fischer, and there was possibly some substance to this gossip. Two weeks after the break-up, and just as his sad confession was appearing in the *Sunday Telegraph*, he was photographed at Los Angeles airport with British glamour model Gabrielle Richens, whom he had met many years before. Richens, who was widely known in tabloid land as 'The Pleasure Machine', was boarding a flight to England, while he was going back to Australia, but they had been at Tom Cruise's fortieth birthday party together, had both been staying at the Peninsular Hotel in Beverly Hills and had spent the day sightseeing in each other's company.

It wasn't just bad luck that Richens and James had been sprung. *New Idea* had been tipped off that the couple would be in LA together and had hired well-known paparazzo Frank Griffin to stake them out. He had tried to get them at the hotel, then followed them across town to Fox Studios and finally managed to catch them at the airport. They had arrived in two separate limousines and kept well clear of each other but Griffin was adamant that they were together. And Richens later admitted as much to an English newspaper.

New Idea laid out the photographs as a two-page spread at the front of the magazine and advertised the story on the cover, then packed the issue off to the printer. A couple of hours later the magazine's editor, Jenny Gilbert, was at her doctor's surgery when she got a call from a friend at Park Street wanting to know whether *New Idea* was running pictures of James that week. She said it was.

The next morning, staff arrived at work to learn that management had stopped the presses the previous night, halfway through the print run, and ordered 100 000 copies of the magazine to be pulped. The instruction had come from Ian Meikle, managing director of Pacific Publications, but it appeared he had taken his orders from higher up. At the time the magazine group's proprietor, Kerry Stokes, was in the middle of negotiations with the Packers over control of their jointly owned magazine *TV Week*, and word was that Packer executives had hinted the deal might turn out better for Stokes if the photos didn't run.

As it transpired Stokes did not get what he wanted: the Packers exercised their option to buy Stokes out. One week after *New Idea* was pulped, Stokes suggested the magazine should have another shot at running the story.

This time, he was told it was too late.

CHAPTER 14
XENU CALLING

You find a religion that can take away the Packers'
money and I'm going to convert.

Shortly after James's marriage broke up, a Channel Nine producer
spotted him slouching along Sydney's Broadway. Dressed in a
T-shirt, shorts and thongs and eating a large tub of ice cream, he
looked like a broken man. Out of curiosity, the producer followed
James to see where he was going and was surprised to see him duck
into the Scientology Centre and disappear inside.

Scientology, for those who don't know, is the cosmological
'religion' devised in the 1950s by Lafayette Ron Hubbard, an
American pulp science fiction writer with dyed hair and extremely
bad teeth. Its followers claim it's a wonderful self-help system. Its
critics regard it as a crackpot cult. Over the years it has been ridi-
culed and condemned by judges, journalists, academics, churches
and governments, yet it still gains converts. And in 2002 it added
James Packer to the list.

The story of James's epiphany broke in late November that year when Sydney's *Sun Herald* reported he was taking courses at the church. He had been undergoing intense 'auditing sessions' a couple of hours a day, twice a week, the paper said, in an effort to get hold of his life again. Annette Sharp had been sitting on the story for months after a tip off from some bankers and PBL executives who were worried that James might give away the family fortune, but she had not been able to run the story until she had pictures. Freelance photographer Peter Barnes was hired to stake out the Broadway headquarters of the church, and he eventually managed to capture James parking his Mercedes CL600 coupe in the loading dock and having a quick cigarette out front.

It was also discovered that James had hired a Scientologist to run his Bondi apartment, and neighbours were reporting he liked to play a loud Scientology anthem, 'Brass in Pocket', before heading off to church. The chorus of this song by the Pretenders is a plea for attention, which might well have been a message to his father.

Five weeks later, on Boxing Day 2002, James was spotted boarding a Qantas flight in Sydney, apparently on his way to Los Angeles to see Tom Cruise, Scientology's most famous recruit. *Good Weekend*'s Richard Guilliatt reported that James was 'casually dressed in a jumper, T-shirt, long pants and loafers' and looked 'decidedly overweight'. He took a seat by himself in the first class cabin and started reading his Scientology books.

For much of the flight, Packer focused intently on a fat paperback copy of *Dianetics*, Hubbard's rambling philosophical manifesto. Occasionally he would peruse other pamphlets from the church, or put on a set of headphones to listen to a Scientology CD on a portable player. As the hours passed on that long trans Pacific flight, Packer's attention rarely shifted from his Scientology studies—although he did order a succession of Paddle Pops, which he sucked on ruminatively. For a man who stands to inherit several billion dollars, he cut a rather forlorn figure.

Six months earlier, James had flown to Los Angeles for the Hollywood star's fortieth birthday party. Two weeks after this latest trip he would be with him again in New Zealand, filming *The Last Samurai*, in which Cruise had found his friend a role in the cavalry charge even though, at two metres, James was hardly a typical Japanese warrior.

James had first met Cruise in the mid-1990s, then got to know him better through Lachlan and Sarah Murdoch. By all accounts he was dazzled by the world's biggest star, even though he felt they had much in common. Not only was Cruise dyslexic (and claimed Scientology had cured him), he also had a terrible relationship with his father, who had abandoned him as a boy, and by 2001 his marriage was breaking up. But best of all, Cruise had emerged from these heartbreaks more positive than ever, which was what James desperately wanted to do.

James told the *Sunday Telegraph*'s Jeni Cooper that Cruise had become one of his closest friends. 'I admire him enormously,' he enthused, 'the way he behaves, his humility, his values, his decency and the way he has managed to be the biggest star in the world and also be one of world's nicest guys.'

Cruise had been a Scientologist since the mid-1980s, and initially tried to keep his faith a secret. Latterly, he had become the church's poster boy and recruited others to the cause. James was the perfect catch. He was sad, vulnerable, credulous and desperately in need of help. He also had billions of dollars—which he might want to give to the church—and was famous enough to act as a beacon to others. Thanks to Cruise, James received star treatment and was taken into the C-org, or celebrity section, which gave him privacy and special attention. Consequently, he studied at the church's Celebrity Center in Beverly Hills, in a former luxury hotel that looks like a Disneyland castle, where courses start at US$376000 a pop.

The basic premise of Scientology, as James soon discovered, is that we are all spiritual beings who are prevented from being happy and reaching our true potential by things that have happened in our past or in previous existences. By submitting to a process of 'auditing' using an 'E-Meter', a primitive form of lie detector, Scientologists can get rid of these so-called 'engrams' and become 'Clear'. They can then cross the 'Bridge to Freedom' and rise through the levels of 'Operating Thetan', by which time they will be 'immortal spirits' who 'can control matter, energy, space, time, thought, and life . . . escape the cycle of birth and death . . . operate independently of the physical world and become one with God'.

It is not known how far James climbed the ladder, although it seems he crossed the Bridge to be Clear, but Tom Cruise has risen to the level of Operating Thetan VII, or OT 7, one rung below Scientology's great leader, L. Ron Hubbard, who naturally climbed as high as it was possible to go. Getting to these exalted levels takes an age and costs a fortune. Hollywood actor Jason Beghe, who is known for his roles in *The X-Files* and *CSI: NY*, spent twelve years and more than $1 million on Scientology courses to reach the level of OT 5. During that time he sang its praises: 'If life is a game, Scientology gives you the tools to play it with a stacked deck and win consistently . . . It is a rocket ride to spiritual freedom.' But in April 2008, he left the church and contacted a cult buster. His subsequent interview scored 400 000 hits on *YouTube* in two days.

'My experience personally is that . . . Scientology is destructive and a rip off,' said Beghe, 'and that it's very very dangerous for your spiritual, psychological, mental, emotional health and your evolution.' Branding it 'brainwashing', he continued: 'If Scientology is for real, then something is fucked up, because it ain't delivering what it's promised, that's for sure.' The incident that convinced the actor to turn against the organisation he thought so fabulous was a car crash. The Scientologists told him it shouldn't have happened—as an Operating Thetan he ought to have been able to control his own mortality and not run into other people. Hauled in for interrogation, it was suggested that a gay friend might be at the root of his problem. Beghe's broadside against the church came too late for James Packer, but he could have discovered any number of similar warnings had he spent five minutes on a Google search for 'L. Ron Hubbard' or 'Scientology'.

In 1965 Justice Kevin Anderson of the Supreme Court of Victoria published a famous report into Scientology that branded it 'a delusional belief system, based on fiction and fallacies and propagated by falsehood and deception'. 'Scientology is evil,' he wrote. '[I]ts techniques are evil; its practice is a serious threat to the community, medically, morally and socially; and its adherents are sadly deluded and often mentally ill.'

Two decades later, in 1984, in a landmark case in London's High Court, Justice Latey damned the 'cult' as 'immoral and socially obnoxious'. He also concluded that it was 'corrupt, sinister and dangerous . . . based on lies and deceit' and had as its real objective 'money and power for Mr Hubbard . . . and those close to him at the top'.

Kerry Packer wanted James to be a champion cricketer. He hired Test players to coach him and bought a baseball-training machine to chuck balls at 120 mph, faster than Jeff Thomson in his prime.

Private collection

'I want my children to know one thing, that I adore them,' Kerry Packer told Michael Parkinson. But while he made it easy for Gretel, because she was a girl, he was much tougher on James, whom he branded too soft, a mummy's boy and rarely praised.

Private collection

Rex Features/Austral

Rick Stevens/Fairfax

Caught between two powerful dominant males. In the early 1990s James's two mentors were his father and Al 'Chainsaw' Dunlap, who was even tougher than Kerry. James found it so hard he wanted to quit, says Dunlap. He also seemed more interested in his girlfriends, weather girl Tania Bryer (right, top) and model Jennifer Flavin (right, bottom).

Steve Christo/Fairfax

Roberta Parkin

Kate Fischer, James's first love, nearly became the first Mrs Packer. Fun, feisty and famous, she was hardly a typical Packer wife. They dated for three years before splitting up in October 1998, two months before the wedding. Two weeks later, James was snapped on the beach at Noosa with swimsuit model Jodie Meares.

Vedat Acikalin/Austral

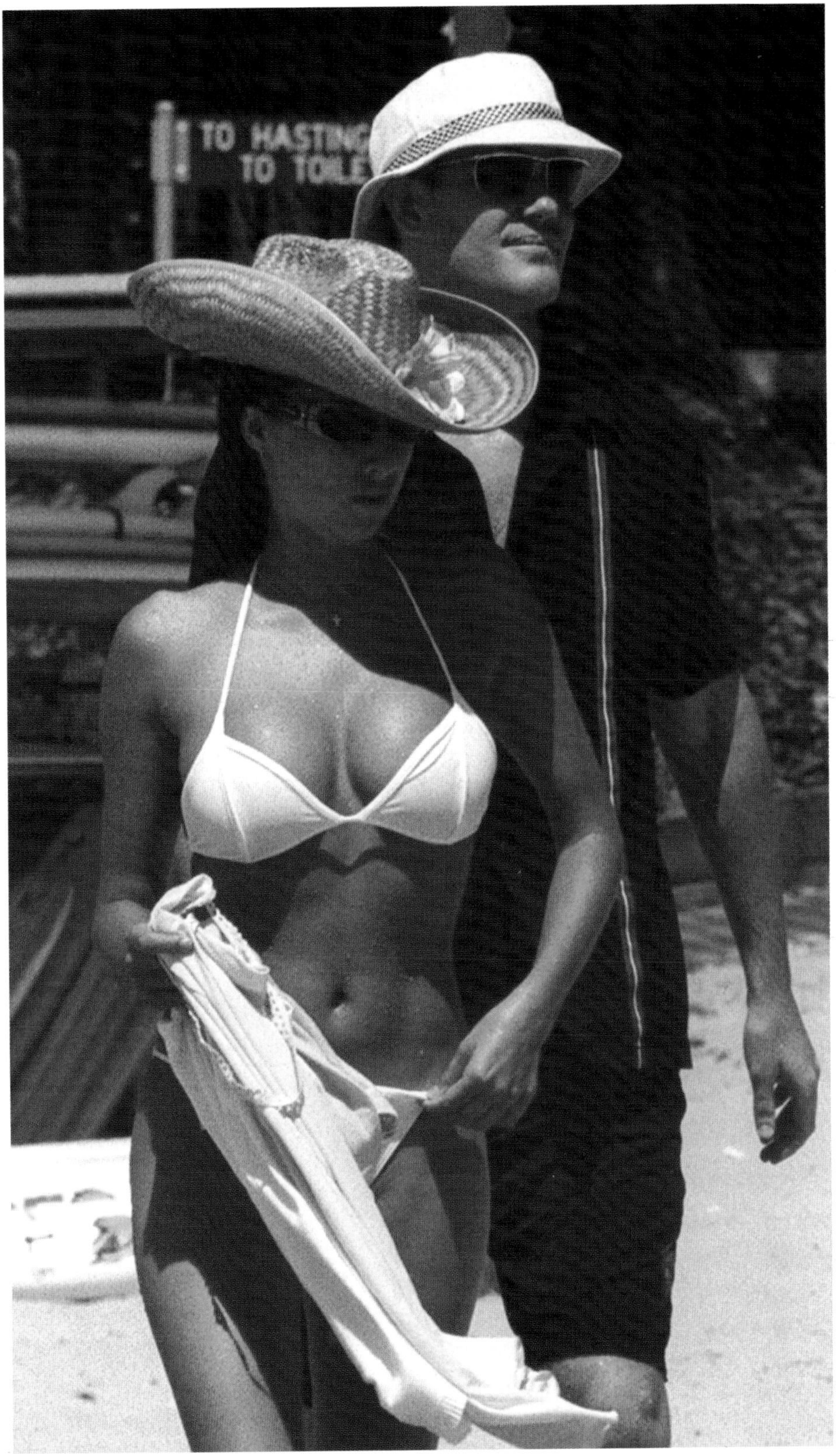

Angelo Soulas/Newspix

Julian Andrews/Fairfax

James and Jodhi were married in October 1999 in a $10 million wedding. But it lasted less than three years. James was stressed by his father's illness and losing millions in One.Tel. After they split in mid 2002 James dated Jodhi's best friend, model Erica Baxter (below left), seen with Jodhi (right) at the launch of her Tigerlily swimsuit range. He married Erica in France in June 2007.

Dallas Kilponen/Fairfax

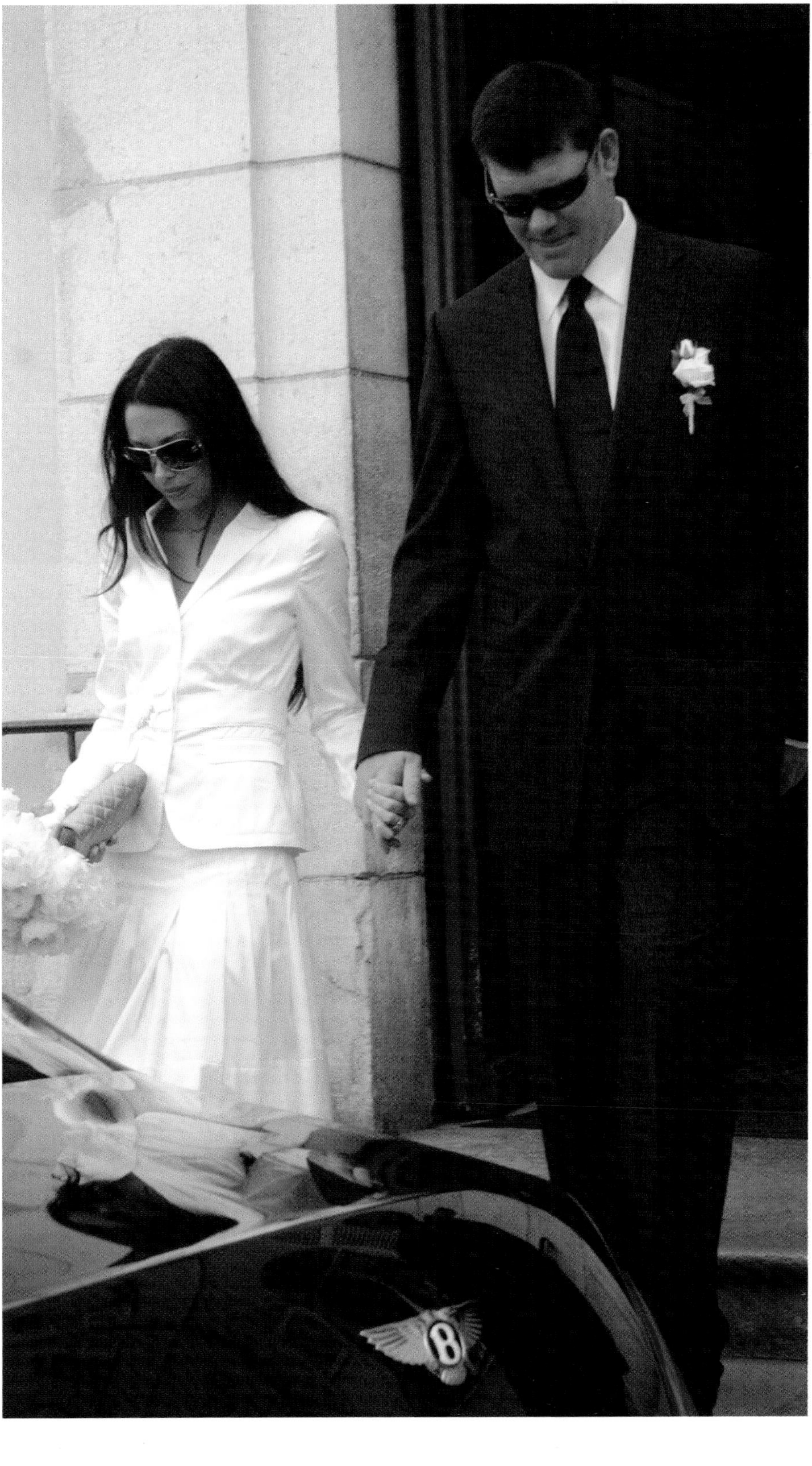

Megan Cullen

Wayne Taylor/Fairfax

The Packers' purchase of Melbourne's Crown Casino in 1999 was James's idea. So were the investments in One.Tel and ecorp. As the dot.com boom roared ahead, James even persuaded Kerry to tip $400 million into hi-tech projects in India. For a time James was Master of the Universe, telling people he had made more money than his dad.

Ken Myers

'There will be no more fuck-ups,' Kerry told brokers after One.Tel collapsed in May 2001. The Packers lost nearly $400 million in the phone company and $400 million in India. James (seen right with Peter Yates and far right with Renee Rivkin) was distraught. His marriage broke up, he put on weight and sought solace in Scientology (far right, standing outside its Glebe church, Sydney).

Mark Williams/Newspix

Kerry had a kidney transplant in November 2000. Despite being very sick for the next five years, he refused to let go of the reins. James (with John Howard and Peter Costello, below; John Alexander, top right; and Sam Chisholm, bottom right) was nominally in charge, but Kerry stayed in control, especially in TV, almost until the end.

Jon Feder/Newspix

Kitty Hill/Newcastle Herald

Kerry Packer's last journey to Ellerston in December 2005. 'My father was a legend,' James told mourners at the State Memorial Service two months later.

Stephen Cooper/Newspix

Six weeks after Kerry's death, James bought himself a new $60 million business jet that could fly non-stop to Macau or Las Vegas. His dream was to turn Crown into a global gaming brand.

Not content with his father's 86-metre converted ice-breaker, the *Arctic P,* with its cinema, swimming pool and helipad, James splashed out $50 million on a sleek Mangusta 165, seen here off Portofino, Italy. In June 2007 he married Erica Baxter in Antibes, in the south of France. His best man was David Gyngell; Tom Cruise and Katie Holmes were guests.

Where did my money go? James Packer invested $1.6 billion in Las Vegas (and Canada) and lost the lot. The half-built Fontainebleau project (right) cost him $333 million, the abandoned Crown Las Vegas nearly $50 million. James escaped from a deal to buy Cannery Casinos from Bill Wortman and Bill Paulos (far right, top) for US$1.8 billion that could have left his empire in real trouble. Then Harry Kakavas (far right, bottom) started creating problems for Crown in Melbourne.

Bobby Yip/Reuters

James Packer's partners in Macau were the notorious Dr Stanley Ho and his son Lawrence, until Ho Senior stepped aside. Their first casino, Crown Macau, has lost money since it opened in May 2007. Their US$ 2.1 billion City of Dreams was launched in June 2009, making James look happy at last. But it faces stiff competition from the fabulous Venetian Macao, and is surrounded by casualties of the global financial crisis.

Ricky Zafra

Paul Barry

Like father like son. James smokes, likes fast food and struggles with his weight. And money is how he measures his success.

L. Ron Hubbard told several people in 1948 that the best way to become a millionaire was to start a religion. Two years later he wrote Scientology's bible, *Dianetics: the Modern Science of Mental Health*, which has now been translated into twenty languages, sold 15 million copies and become a worldwide best seller. In 1951 Hubbard's wife filed for divorce, alleging he was 'hopelessly insane' and suffering from paranoid schizophrenia. She told the court he had subjected her to 'systematic torture' by beating and strangling her and denying her sleep. Hubbard fled the legal proceedings, as he did in the 1970s when he was convicted of fraud in France and in the 1980s when he was pursued by America's FBI.

At other times, however, he got himself out of trouble by lying. His life story portrayed him as a genius, a nuclear physicist and a war hero. But as Justice Latey pointed out in his High Court judgment, this was all made up.

To promote himself and the cult [Hubbard] has made these, among other false claims:

That he was a much decorated war hero. He was not.

That he commanded a corvette squadron. He did not.

That he was awarded the Purple Heart, a gallantry decoration for those wounded in action. He was not wounded and was not decorated.

That he was crippled and blinded in the war and cured himself with Dianetic techniques. He was not crippled and was not blinded.

That he was sent by U.S. Naval Intelligence to break up a black magic ring in California. He was not. He was himself a member of that occult group and practised ritual sexual magic in it.

That he was a graduate of George Washington University and an atomic physicist. The facts are that he completed only one year of

college and failed the one course on nuclear physics in which he
enrolled.

There is no dispute about any of this. The evidence is
unchallenged . . .

Mr. Hubbard is a charlatan and worse.

But Hubbard was not just a fantasist. He also held the bizarre
belief that our problems on Earth can be sheeted home to a galactic
warlord called Xenu. According to LRH, as Hubbard is commonly
known to Scientologists, Xenu brought billions of people to Earth
75 million years ago frozen in DC-8 like spaceships. He stacked
them around volcanoes on the island of Hawaii before destroying
them with hydrogen bombs. In doing this he released a vast army
of spirits, or thetans, who roam the earth attaching themselves to
humans and spoiling their lives.

There are various accounts of this story, but *Wikipedia*'s is as
good as any. Backed up by references to the relevant Hubbard documents, and quoting from a 1968 tape of Hubbard in which he tells
the Xenu story, the entry recounts how the Galactic Confederacy
had a population problem with 178 billion people (who, incidentally, wore 1950s and 1960s clothes and used cars, trains and boats
identical to those of that era) on each of its 26 planets.

Xenu summoned billions of his citizens together under the
pretense of tax inspections, then paralyzed them and froze
them in a mixture of alcohol and glycol to capture their souls.
The kidnapped populace was loaded into spacecraft for transport
to the site of extermination, the planet of Teegeeack (Earth). The
appearance of these spacecraft would later be subconsciously
expressed in the design of the Douglas DC-8, the only difference
being the DC-8's jet turbines. When they had reached Teegeeack/
Earth, the paralyzed citizens were unloaded around the bases of

volcanoes across the planet. Hydrogen bombs were then lowered into the volcanoes and detonated simultaneously. Only a few aliens' physical bodies survived.

The now-disembodied victims' souls, which Hubbard called thetans, were blown into the air by the blast. They were captured by Xenu's forces using an 'electronic ribbon' ('which also was a type of standing wave') and sucked into 'vacuum zones' around the world. The hundreds of billions of captured thetans were taken to a type of cinema, where they were forced to watch a 'three-D, super colossal motion picture' for thirty-six days. This implanted what Hubbard termed 'various misleading data'. . . into the memories of the hapless thetans . . . (including) all world religions, with Hubbard specifically attributing Roman Catholicism and the image of the Crucifixion to the influence of Xenu.

Not surprisingly, Scientologists try to keep this story secret and deny it has ever been part of their teachings. But Jason Beghe confirmed in a recent interview on Channel Seven's *Today Tonight* that he had been taught the Xenu story when he reached the level of Operating Thetan III. The program also played some of the Hubbard tape from 1968. Strangely enough, this did not shake Beghe's faith at the time. But as one wit points out, 'The fact that members of the church apparently believe in inter-galactic travel, reincarnation and the possibility of a more fulfilled existence through mind control probably isn't a big deal. Who in California doesn't?'

More than twenty years after Hubbard's death, Scientologists still keep an office for him in every church around the world. There's one in Sydney, complete with his naval Commodore's cap. (Hubbard spent many years at sea with a select band of followers, the Sea Org, trying to escape fraud and conspiracy charges brought by the French and US governments.) And as far as the church is concerned L. Ron did not really die. In 1986 the new man in charge, David Miscavige, told the faithful that their leader had taken the decision to *discard* his body because it had become a nuisance:

> The body he had used to facilitate his existence in this messed universe had ceased to be useful, and had in fact become an impediment to the work he now must do outside of its confines . . . the being we knew as L Ron Hubbard still exists, however the body he had could no longer serve his purposes . . . he has simply moved on to his next step.

And that next step was to continue his research into the higher OT levels, research he is presumably still conducting today.

David Miscavige, who is often known as COB or Chairman of the Board, is a good friend of Tom Cruise and is cut from the same perfect mould. With his smart Sea Org navy uniform and clean, youthful appearance he could easily pass for a Mormon, but there is something eerily robotic about him, a real-life version of Max Headroom.

In presenting Cruise with Scientology's first-ever Freedom Medal of Valor in October 2004, Miscavige described the Hollywood star as 'the most dedicated Scientologist' he knew. Cruise responded that he had never met 'a more competent, intelligent, tolerant, compassionate being' than Miscavige except, of course, for LRH.

James Packer was by Cruise's side that day at the church's UK headquarters, Saint Hill Manor, in Sussex, just down the road from

Kerry's old country retreat at Fyning Hill. The ceremony, held in a splendid theatre with golden arches, golden eagles and five-metre golden torches spouting faux red flames, was the church's version of the Oscars. A couple of hundred people in evening dress stood to applaud the unveiling of a huge new portrait of their leader, LRH. As the camera rolled along the front row, there, right next to the movement's biggest star, was James himself.

At around the time James joined the Scientologists he started dating Erica Baxter. She was with him at a dinner given by the Friends of Taronga Zoo in November 2002. By January 2003, she had moved into his Bondi apartment and was following him into the clutches of L. Ron Hubbard. In April 2003 she and James were sighted several times at the Scientologists' Sydney headquarters, and she was reported to be going through an intensive process of auditing.

The church's online 'completion register' lists an Erica Baxter as finishing two courses in 2004. The first was the Happiness Rundown, which one happy UK graduate described as allowing her to 'be what I like to be, think what I like to think, do what I want to do and experience what I want to experience without any feeling that I shouldn't'. Erica's second course was the Arc (Affinity, Reality, Communication) Straightwire, which comprises a series of auditing sessions that encourage participants to remember the good things in their lives.

Like James, Erica would have also been required to undergo the Purification Rundown to get rid of any traces of drugs, alcohol and toxins in her body. Undertaken over several weeks, the 'Purif', as it is often known, involves running on a treadmill in a sauna in temperatures of up to 60°C after drinking a cocktail containing cooking oil and mega doses of niacin and vitamins. The niacin dose is often high enough to produce a rash, which Scientologists say is sunburn leaving the body but which many toxicologists say is an indication of the damage being done. The aim of the 'Purif', according to L. Ron Hubbard, is to melt fatty tissues into the bloodstream, then sweat the toxins out through the pores. Scientologists believe it can increase your IQ by up to thirty points.

Hardly anyone except Scientologists take the process seriously. Toxicologists and doctors say it is ineffective at best and life threatening at worst, in that it can cause heat stress, dehydration and liver damage. Indeed, President Ronald Reagan's Surgeon General, C. Everett Koop, warned: 'Keep away from it . . . you don't need it . . . It's dangerous.'

But Scientologists swear it does them good. And in Sydney—where detox was all the rage—James's friends recommended Purif to others. Jodhi Meares even said it had helped get rid of her tan lines.

Others have been less impressed with the experience, however. One woman who went through the Purif and a preliminary audit at 'The Org' in Sydney recounts how she was told to put gel on her hands and hold what looked like handlebars on a machine—clearly the E-Meter. As she did so, she was asked if she was from the media or the FBI, and if any of her family or friends was against Scientology. Her American auditor was dressed in khaki and looked 'like a cross between the Hitler Youth and Steve Irwin'.

The auditing process, which is at the heart of Scientology, is the religion's answer to the Catholic confessional, but in some ways it is more like interrogation with its use of a lie detector. According to Hubbard, 'The E-Meter is never wrong. It sees all; it knows all. It tells everything.' Justice Anderson, who devoted an entire chapter to the E-Meter in his 1965 report, was a lot more blunt, concluding it was 'no more than a powerful gimmick for controlling pre-clears and developing in them a sense of awe and submission'.

But without the gimmick, auditing is like psychological counselling: participants get to sit down with someone who is prepared to listen to their problems and concerns about parents, childhood, relationships, drug taking, sexuality or whatever. For men in particular, and especially those unable to open up about such issues, it can be a therapeutic experience. People close to James say it did him some good.

One confidant believes that Scientology saved James. 'It gave him some stuff about relationships, about getting through bad times, about accepting his mistakes and dealing with his father. It also gave him a moral framework. After all, what had his father given him? Money is everything, and take what you want.' A former PBL executive has a similar view. 'It was good for James. It gave him a new value framework which wasn't just money, and it boosted his confidence. He came back stronger and sorted, determined to drive ahead again.' What his father thought about it all can only be guessed at, but Kerry certainly would never have swallowed Scientology himself, even before his brief trip to the other side on the polo field in 1991 to discover there was 'fucking nothing there'.

In late 2002, when James's conversion to Scientology became public, the tension between Kerry and his son was obvious, although this was not necessarily a result of James embracing Scientology. At a shareholder meeting in November the two men shared a platform but didn't exchange a word. James, who had come straight from an auditing session at the church, sat with his head down, sighing and biting his fingernails. He left as soon as the meeting finished. A couple of weeks earlier, at a similar function, several journalists had tried to get a comment from him and he had pushed past shaking his head and mouthing 'No, No'.

It is almost inconceivable that Kerry didn't talk with his mates Singo, Ben Tilley and Russell Crowe about James's belief in Scientology. He would doubtless also have asked James about it. According to a story in *Crikey*, he even hired a private investigator to look into Scientology, and was alarmed when he was told it made slaves of its followers and caused them to hand over their money to the church. According to *Crikey*, he then fireproofed the Packer fortune to ensure James didn't give it all away.

It is a fabulous story, of course, but there's no way of checking whether it's true, and insiders scoff at the suggestion. They say Kerry was never worried about James giving his money away because he knew his son was far too ambitious and far too acquisitive. Brian Powers also doubted Scientology's capacity to corrall the family wealth, commenting dryly: 'You find a religion that can take away the Packers' money and I'm going to convert.'

CHAPTER 15
THE BIG FELLA'S BACK

I know more about gambling than anyone in this fucking country.

Peter Yates liked to tell people that when he took over as managing director of PBL in 2001 it was like five fire hydrants going off at once and he didn't know which to shut down first. Nine was losing in the ratings for the first time in years; a ban on smoking at Crown was threatening the casino business; One.Tel was running out of cash; the PBL share price was down by almost 50 per cent; and to cap it all, the man who had hired him, James Packer, was on the brink of a nervous collapse.

Yates had been brought in as a deal maker but he was suddenly called upon to use all the skills he didn't have. With James out of action, he desperately needed Kerry to reassure the market that everything was under control. Hence the famous lunch with investment analysts at Channel Nine where the Big Fella had promised no more 'fuck-ups'. But he also needed Kerry to help him run the empire, so he instituted a weekly lunch in the boardroom to keep the old man briefed and put him in charge of the investment committee which had to give the green light to any new business ventures. Or, in Kerry's case, the red light, because he had decided he never wanted PBL to buy anything again.

Shortly after the One.Tel collapse in 2001, Kerry issued a categorical instruction that the company's debt had to be below $1 billion by the end of 2004, a reduction of some 40 per cent. He reckoned this would effectively earn 10 per cent a year after tax through the interest saved, and no other investment could do better. He told his chief financial officer, Jeff Kleemann, 'Just pay down debt. Don't let them spend my money.'

It occurred to some of his executives that the old man was now beginning to channel his father, Sir Frank Packer. At a board meeting six months earlier, he had lit upon the $25 000 allocated to move a magazine to a different floor in Park Street. After scream-ing for an hour at John Alexander, his magazine boss, about what a 'fucking waste of money' it was, Kerry decreed that no one was going to move a desk without his permission. It was a performance Sir Frank would have been proud of, but its absurdity prompted ecorp's founder, Daniel Petre, to burst out laughing. James shot him a horrified glance and dived into Petre's office fifteen minutes later to tell him, 'Dad's really angry.' A few months later Petre resigned from the board and quit the company, unable to tolerate an atmo-sphere where there was so much fear of Kerry's moods.

Whenever James was around, Kerry screamed at him as well. 'James would kiss his father when he arrived at board meetings, in front of everyone,' says Ian Johnson, who was a PBL director throughout 2002. 'And in return, Kerry would scream at him. James would bring up good business ideas and Kerry would just

reject them. James was always incredibly polite, always respectful and never hit back. But you could see how frustrated he was.'
Johnson particularly remembers James saying to his father at a
management meeting, 'You're in a good mood today, Dad.' Kerry's
response was to turn on one of the other executives in the room
and savage him, before turning to James, 'So you think you fucking
know, do you son?'

Another executive who observed James and Kerry's relationship a little bit later—after James came back from his Scientology
holiday—saw none of this bullying but was fascinated nevertheless.
'There was no affection between them; it was just so distant. You
could see that James had enormous respect for his father but he
was incredibly hurt by him. He kept on saying how unfair Kerry
had been to sin-bin him over One.Tel and how he had never been
forgiven for it, even though he had done so many good things, like
Crown, that Kerry didn't want to do.'

It was certainly true that Kerry had not been wild about buying
Crown, but he was proud of it now that he owned it and wanted to
get into the nitty-gritty detail, boasting to Ian Johnson, the casino's
chief executive from 2000 to 2002, 'I know more about gambling
than anyone in this fucking country.' Every day at 6 a.m., the fax
machine in Johnson's house would spit out the high-roller report
on how much the casino had won or lost the previous night. Kerry
would ring if there had been a big loss and would want to know
who the winner was, which game had been played and what the
odds of winning were. On one occasion he rang Crown's table
games expert, Andrew MacDonald, at 3 a.m. to ask about the odds
of getting a hand he had just played at another casino. MacDonald,
who was in bed, said he would have to go and get his calculator.
Kerry said, 'That's OK, I'll wait.'

On another occasion, Kerry decided to walk through the main gaming floor at 1.30 in the morning and found dirty glasses and full ashtrays. The next morning at Crown's board meeting, he started screaming at Johnson and abusing him. 'So do you understand?' Kerry finally asked.

'Yes, Kerry,' Johnson replied.

'Well, have you got anything to say?'

'When are you planning to wander round the casino at 1.30 a.m. again?'

'You'll never fucking know, son,' Packer shot back. 'But when I do I hope I bump into you.'

Kerry never gambled at Crown because his casino licence prohibited it, but he occasionally played at Star City in Sydney. In the late 1990s, he went there three or four times a year to win or lose up to $6 million at a time, signing himself in as Mr Smith to keep his visits private and playing in a high-roller room by himself or with his regular gambling buddy, Ben Tilley.

Tilley had been one of James's best friends after they left Cranbrook, but had moved on to Kerry in the late 1990s. Friends of James said that Tilley had been asked to choose between father and son and had decided to go with the money. For the last few years of Kerry's life, he was the old man's constant companion and probably closer to him than anyone.

By all accounts, Tilley was charming and funny. He was good at golf, which Kerry was now too sick to play, and even better at cards, winning large amounts of money. Kerry played poker with him regularly and took him on trips to Las Vegas and London. Back at Bellevue Hill, in Kerry's own special card room with its cashmere wall hangings, cashmere-upholstered chairs and cashmere-inlaid card table, they had a Friday night game which often lasted until morning. They also played on the *Arctic P* as it cruised around the Mediterranean in the northern summer. Naturally, they played for money, often in large amounts. 'Kerry did everything for money,' says his chopper pilot Nick Ross. 'He would bet on the footy with you while you were watching, or on go-kart racing: "Bet you $500 you can't get round the track in less than 55 seconds".' He also gambled at golf. It was nothing for him and his bookmaker mates to bet $10 000 on nine holes or $1000 a putt.

But his real fun was reserved for Las Vegas, where only the biggest casinos were prepared to take him on. And there he received a spectacular welcome because he was capable of leaving so much on the table. During the 1990s, the four casinos he favoured—the Hilton, Caesar's Palace, the MGM Grand and the Bellagio—all built super-luxury suites to attract high-rollers like him, leapfrogging each other in an effort to create the new 'ultimate' experience. The Hilton's huge Sky Villas with fantastic views over the Strip were reckoned to be unbeatable in 1995 when they were fitted out at a cost of US$45 million. But they were soon made to look modest by the Garden Suites at the Bellagio, with their private gardens and fountains. The Bellagio in turn was rapidly outdone by the US$200 million Mansion at the MGM Grand. Naturally, Kerry stayed in these suites free of charge, even though they could have been rented out for up to US$20 000 a night, which was a clue to how much the casinos wanted him there.

The super suites were massive—three to five times the size of the average house—and decorated regardless of expense with French furniture, Italian statues, Chinese earthenware horses and Matisse paintings on the walls. Some came with their own English-trained butler to iron the newspaper and put drinks on ice. Naturally, there was separate accommodation available for pilots, nannies, chauffeurs, bodyguards and assorted hangers-on if required.

The casinos also offered Kerry free jet travel, free limousines, free luxury dining, free alcohol and just about anything else he wanted for his entourage, including free sex. But in this regard, he normally made his own arrangements. One high-class call girl who gave evidence at the 1995 money laundering trial of Hollywood madam Heidi Fleiss testified that she and eight other prostitutes had been flown to Las Vegas in 1992 to service an Australian billionaire businessman, whom court papers identified as Kerry Packer. She swore on oath that she and at least three other girls had spent the week with him and his guests for a fee of US$10 000 apiece. Nor was this an isolated occurrence.

When Kerry's private jet touched down in Las Vegas, the VIP limos met him on the tarmac as if he were royalty or a foreign potentate come to town. On one occasion, as he and his party entered a hotel foyer with flunkies hanging on his every word, Kerry remarked on a car that was suspended from the ceiling as a prize for the keno jackpot. Before he had gone much further, the management was ordering it to be cut down so it could be presented to him.

Kerry was such a big gambler that despite this huge investment the big four casinos almost all came out ahead in their dealings with him, with Steve Wynn's Bellagio doing best. In September 2000 Kerry reportedly lost US$20 million in a single visit to the casino, which by this time had become his favourite haunt. Twelve months later, he appears to have lost even more. Stranded in Las Vegas after 9/11, he was at the Bellagio again, munching hotdogs between trips to the tables. On this occasion he supposedly dropped US$29 million, although he claimed the figure was a wild exaggeration.

Nor was it only in Las Vegas that Kerry lost heavily. In mid-1999 he shed a reported US$28 million in the course of a couple of weeks in London, including a US$16 million loss at Crockfords, which had famously turned him away in the 1980s for winning too much. As usual, Kerry played several hands of blackjack at a time, staking the maximum bet of £250 000 on each, a rate at which he quickly ploughed through the cash.

Back home newspapers occasionally picked up on these stories, and on one celebrated occasion Labor leader Mark Latham laid into Packer in federal Parliament, branding his behaviour 'morally offensive' and suggesting he did not pay his fair share of tax. For once, Kerry was so upset by the criticism that he called *The Australian* and offered it an exclusive interview. 'This is not someone else's money,' he told the paper, 'this is mine, and I am entitled to spend it in any way I choose.' He had given more money to Westmead Children's Hospital, he claimed, and it was his business how he spent the rest.

Prime Minister John Howard was quick to come to his defence, branding Latham's attack 'ludicrous' and assuring anyone who would listen that Packer was a good corporate citizen. It was nobody's business how he spent his fortune, Howard continued. 'I mean, he made the very legitimate point that he doesn't gamble with his company's money and I think if you look at his corporate record, that's right.'

Kerry had actually told *The Australian*, 'I take risks for recreation ... I don't take risks with the company,' and he had never said a truer word. He was still intent on paying down debt at PBL and selling anything if the price was right. In August 2002 he ditched the group's share in eBay for $120 million because he could record a profit of more than $110 million on the sale. He couldn't see, or didn't care, that it would be worth far more in the future, and no one was around to challenge him: James was deep in his Scientology studies, and Daniel Petre had left ten months earlier. Peter Yates managed to persuade Kerry to use some of the proceeds to buy back the 20 per cent of ecorp sold to the public in June 2000, but it was small compensation for missing out on the bonanza.

Three or four months after the eBay sale, James returned in a much better state than when he had departed and began concentrating on making money once more. He and Yates were keen for PBL to grow again, and resolved to expand the casino business. But the challenge was to get Kerry to agree. 'Kerry was increasingly irrational and irascible in the last few years,' says one top PBL executive. 'It was more and more about point scoring, trying to assert his authority.'

The old man now hated spending money. He was also wary about buying casinos, even though Crown had proven to be such a bargain. Every time he was presented with a deal, Kerry wanted to talk about high-rollers and how much had to be given away to get them to gamble. And since he always believed he could beat the house, it was hard to convince him he should own the casino instead. Especially if James was proposing it.

In December 2002 the opportunity arose to buy Jupiters, which owned a medium-sized casino on the Gold Coast and smaller ones in Brisbane and Townsville, plus a fast-growing betting business called Centrebet. But Kerry would not countenance borrowing the hundreds of millions of dollars needed to fund the purchase and the prize was snapped up by PBL's biggest rival, Tabcorp (which had gobbled up Star City in 1999).

Almost immediately, Burswood Casino in Perth also came onto the radar, and this time PBL managed to get a clear run. Kerry's initial opposition to the purchase was overcome by persuading him that Tabcorp had to be stopped from getting even bigger. Graham Richardson was despatched to see Geoff Gallop, Western Australia's premier, to ensure he had no intention of allowing gaming machines into pubs. With confirmation that this would not happen the deal was given the go-ahead, but only on Kerry's terms, which involved getting the casino at bargain price.

On AFL Grand Final weekend in September 2003, Peter Yates flew down to Melbourne to meet Bill Wylie, the Western Australian entrepreneur who owned a 15.7 per cent stake in the casino with his friend Jack Bendat. Yates was not expecting them to sell at the price Kerry had approved, but to his surprise they accepted his offer.

James had assumed he would now be allowed to make a full bid for the casino, but his father had other ideas. As far as Kerry was concerned, enough had been done to put the casino out of Tabcorp's reach. And while James was incredibly fired up about the deal he still wasn't game to take on his father, even with his new Scientology armour. 'He was in awe of Kerry and incredibly concerned about his power to stop decisions,' says one ex-PBL executive. 'Even at this stage, he never stood up to him in public and never went toe-to-toe. But it wasn't sensible to do that with Kerry, anyway, because he wouldn't have been able to handle it.'

Just as James had used Brian Powers in the mid-1990s to fight his battles, he now turned to Peter Yates. Between them they commissioned PBL's first-ever strategic plan, which showed that growth would continue until 2010 if they expanded the casino business, but would tail off if they didn't. They then lobbied the board. By March 2004, it was obvious to everyone except Kerry that the Burswood deal had to go through.

The night before the crunch meeting to approve the plan, Kerry hosted a dinner for the board at his home in Bellevue Hill. As the staff cleared away the entrées and PBL's directors savoured Kerry's expensive wines, Sir Laurence Muir chose to open the batting. As the old man's biggest ally in the drive to reduce debt, his new-found support for James and his plan was doubly significant. 'I think we should invest in Burswood,' he argued. 'Western Australia is growing, they're keen to have us and our team needs a challenge. They tell me we'll get our investment back in five years.' The gaming division's chief executive, Rowen Craigie, then explained how he intended to make this happen. And Kerry was left high and dry.

The next morning the old man was even grumpier than usual. Opening the board meeting, which looked certain to give Burswood the go-ahead, he said, 'You may think that was a very expensive dinner last night.' Then, looking straight at Yates, he continued, 'But not as expensive as it's going to be for you.'

There had already been tension between the Big Fella and Yates, centring on the efforts the young managing director had been making to turn PBL into a more transparent public company rather than a family fiefdom. But on a more basic level Kerry simply didn't like the man, so Yates's days were numbered.

The final showdown arrived three months later, again over Burswood, when the takeover was at risk of failing. Kerry had agreed to the bid on the basis that only one offer was to be made. Yates urged Kerry to allow the board to raise the price. Kerry dug in his heels. The two men then stepped out of the meeting to continue the argument in Packer's office, with James shuttling between the two groups in an effort to mediate.

The final outcome gave something to both sides. Yates and James got the Burswood bid through, and received board approval to pursue two other projects in the strategic plan: one being to establish an Australian version of the UK online betting site Betfair; the second to build casinos in Macau, where the market had recently opened up to foreign operators. Kerry got his way by ridding himself of Yates. The managing director was sacked three days after the board meeting, collecting a $6.5 million pay-off as he went out the door. Kerry also got to select the next chief executive, John Alexander, who would not be so dumb as to challenge him.

Burswood turned out to be a landmark deal. At a final price of $666 million, the casino was a bargain at nine times annual earnings, and four years later it would look even cheaper because it would be making twice as much money. More significantly, the purchase marked James's first big victory since One.Tel. Not only had he and Yates slipped the decision past Kerry, they had also overturned his dictum that debt must be reduced. And with Betfair and Macau they had set a new strategy for the company, which was to expand into gaming. In this area, at least, James was quite definitely running the show.

The same could not be said for television, however, where Kerry was still calling all the shots.

CHAPTER 16
KILLING NINE

Who killed Channel Nine? Kerry killed Channel Nine.
He hated the fact that Leckie was running *his* network.

Even if Kerry had been rolled on James's casino deals, he was still running the television network. Nine had always been his pride and passion and the perfect playground because there were no rules. In TV you didn't defer to a bunch of bean counters telling you about theoretical win rates; you listened to those with the most experience, instinct or flair, or who shouted loudest and had most power. And Kerry was all of these, which is why James had decided to steer well clear of Channel Nine when he came back from exile.

Nine had been number one for longer than anyone could remember, and Kerry was the main reason it was so good. He knew what worked, and he wasn't afraid to take risks. He had backed *60 Minutes* and *Sunday* through thick and thin and told his executives he wanted them to be the best. He also kept a stranglehold on cricket and rugby league, which were the sports he and many other Australian men loved to watch.

Despite the fact that he was a billionaire, Kerry was really an ordinary bloke with ordinary tastes. And this was where his strength lay. He knew what his audience wanted because he wanted it too, and he made it his business to tune in to their lives. Often in conversation he would point towards 'those blokes out west' and ask how they managed on the money they made.

'Kerry knew the price of everything and what everyone earned,' says one former adviser. 'Wherever you went he was asking people how much they were paid or how much things cost, and he remembered all of it. He knew what a schooner of beer cost in Liverpool, a ham sandwich in London, or a kilo of lamb chops in Parramatta. He could tell you exactly what someone on $40 000 a year spent and how much he had to spare for a mobile phone. James wouldn't have a fucking clue about any of that.'

That was the difference between father and son. Kerry had a grasp of all the detail needed to run a business. James was much more interested in making deals and then moving on, like a venture capital investor. The everyday tasks of TV, which involved tweaking programs, fiddling with schedules and massaging talent, were something for which he did not have the patience.

But Kerry also had good people running his network, like Sam Chisholm in the 1980s and David Leckie, who had been in charge since 1990, as well as the excellent programmer John Stephens, who was arguably almost as important in keeping Nine on top. Despite this, Kerry was rarely happy with the job they were doing and had an intense dislike for Leckie, whose ego and personality were almost as big as his master's. Leckie was loud, crude and irrepressible, especially when he had had a drink. And the people below him aped this behaviour, making Nine appear arrogant and untouchable with an unshakeable belief that it was the best.

Kerry hated the fact that Leckie was running *his* network and behaving like he owned it, says Steve Wood, executive producer of the *Today* show for many years. He also hated the fact that the Nine boss was prepared to go toe-to-toe with him, shout at him and tell him to fuck off. No one else dared to do that and survive.

In the late 1990s Kerry regularly asked Nick Falloon to sack Leckie, just as he had told Brian Powers to do many times before that. Powers would inquire whom they should hire in Leckie's place and Kerry would say, 'Anyone's better than that fuckwit.' Powers's response was, 'So there's someone out there who can control costs, keep hold of our stars and win one hundred weeks in a row, is there?' And Leckie would survive because things at Nine were always going so well.

But in early 2001 all that changed. At the beginning of the year, the TV ratings regime run by AC Nielsen was dumped for a new system run by Oztam. With a different sample of viewers Nine suddenly found it was running second to its arch rival Channel Seven, losing five of the first ten weeks of the year. Even worse, no one had bothered to warn Kerry of the change. Nine eventually recovered to win the year, but its air of invulnerability was gone, as was a good slice of its profit because each ratings point was reckoned to be worth around $25 million in advertising revenue.

Kerry had never been easy on Leckie, but he now started to slap him around unmercifully and treat him like the village idiot. One Channel Nine executive remembers having lunch with Leckie late that year and seeing him called out five times in the space of two hours to answer phone calls from Kerry. Life with the Big Fella at that time would involve Leckie being called in to Park Street every Wednesday. There would be no agenda, just what was in Kerry's head. It might be six things or it might be thirty-six—there was no way of knowing—and Leckie would not be allowed to say a word until Packer had gone through all of them. If he tried to interrupt or defend himself, Kerry would tell him to 'Shut the fuck up' or call him a 'fucking imbecile'. When Leckie eventually got to speak for himself Kerry would have lost interest, and Leckie would find himself talking to the elephants on the wall. 'I'm fifty years old,' he protested, 'and I'm still putting up with this shit.'

Leckie was also being undermined by Peter Yates and John Alexander, who were both in Kerry's ear. Neither of them liked Leckie's confidence or the brash, blokey culture at Nine. But, above all, they didn't like the fact that the television network was beyond PBL's control. They wanted to bring it back into their empire, but they could only do that over Leckie's dead body.

Typically, Leckie believed he was immortal. 'I'm bombproof,' he boasted in the week before Christmas 2001. 'It's been a bloody hard year, for sure, but that's behind us. We showed 'em.'

He had reckoned without Kerry, however. In late December the old man was rushed into hospital again, this time with lymphatic fluid around his kidney, and he lay there for three weeks apparently close to death. His TV network was also looking sick again: it had been thumped in the ratings in the last two weeks of the year, and its profits and revenue were down. According to one PBL insider, 'It was Kerry's dying wish to get rid of Leckie.' So, in early January 2002 James flew back from his long overseas lay-off and Yates was hauled away from his holiday to fire the bullet. Leckie had six months left to run on his contract, but he was told he would not be getting a payout. It was a strange way to get rid of someone who had delivered so much, and an expensive reminder that 'loyalty' only ever seemed to flow one way where the Packers were concerned.

After eleven and a half years as Nine's chief executive and twenty-five years with the network, Leckie's departure was slipped in at the end of a press release announcing the formation of PBL Media, a new division to run TV and magazines that would be headed by John Alexander. 'David Leckie will not be renewing his contract', it said baldly. Leckie had played a huge part in making Nine number one. He had also made millions, or perhaps hundreds of millions, of dollars for the Packers, but all they could find to say was that he had made 'a valuable contribution' and they wished him success in the future. Had they known he would end up running Channel Seven, they would not even have said that.

Kerry's farewell message was even more pointed. He was so thrilled by Leckie's demise that he issued his own statement to say he was 'delighted' by the changes. 'They have my absolute support and I believe they will be beneficial to the business and shareholders.' He could not have been more wrong. It was obvious to most people that it was an act of stupidity and petulance to get rid of the man who had made Nine such a success. But only those who knew John Alexander, the new man in charge, could have guessed how devastating the effect would be.

Small, slim and immaculately dressed, Alexander is a very talented executive and an even more accomplished political operator. Widely known as Lord Farquaad, after the tiny tyrant in *Shrek*, he is an intriguing character. Some suggest he sees himself as a latter-day Medici, and the Packers have certainly made him rich enough to fill that role. He lives in Del Rio, an Art Deco apartment block in Sydney's Elizabeth Bay with wonderful views of the harbour, and collects beautiful art, first-edition books and Cambodian artefacts. It is claimed he has an interior designer constantly at hand in case a sofa needs recovering, a piece falls out of favour or a new touch is needed.

According to one ex-Packer executive: 'He takes infinite care about his clothes, his shirt fabrics, and where he gets his anchovies. He can tell you where to buy the best pair of cashmere socks or the best cheese grater. He cares passionately about these things. He is totally unlike Kerry in that he knows nothing about the ordinary bloke and shares none of his tastes. He lives on a higher plane.'

But it had not always been so. 'He can't believe how far he has come,' says one colleague, who reports that Alexander had a tough childhood and started out stacking boxes in Woolworths. And perhaps these memories have stayed with him because he has been known to take his chauffeur-driven Jaguar down to feed the homeless, rolling up his sleeves and serving meals for Just Enough Faith, an organisation for which he has also raised money.

Whatever his complexities, even Alexander's enemies agree he was a brilliant editor of the *Australian Financial Review* and *Sydney Morning Herald* in the 1990s, which is where he worked until he was sacked in 1998, just as Kerry was contemplating a takeover. He joined Packer shortly afterwards as publisher of the *Bulletin*. It was no surprise to those who knew him that he became managing director of the magazine group six months later and joined the PBL board nine months after that.

Several PBL insiders say he ingratiated himself with Kerry to an extraordinary degree. 'He and Kerry were enormously close,' says one former editor. 'JA was great at massaging, at networking, at being a courtier. He would have lunch with Kerry every week in the boardroom, sometimes with James, often a politician and always a plate of Violet Crumbles [which Kerry demanded]. And he would just sit at Kerry's right hand and hardly ever say a word.'

But what the Packers also loved about Alexander was that he was ruthless and made them money. He had worked wonders in the magazine group, cutting costs and boosting profits, and was now being given the chance to work this magic at Nine, which he believed had become fat, bloated and complacent. The only problem was he knew nothing about TV or those who watched it, and seemed to have little desire to educate himself.

His people skills also left a lot to be desired. One fellow executive described him as 'borderline autistic' because he never looked people in the eye. He would fiddle with his watch, play with his cufflinks or look out the window to avoid making contact. It was a challenge to find anyone with a good word to say about him. As Mark Day reported in a profile for *The Australian* in 2006, he was variously described as 'Machiavellian, pretentious, iconoclastic, imperious, fastidious, humourless, meticulous and eclectic'. Not to mention 'cold, calculating and manipulative'. At Park Street he was famous for walking up and down Mahogany Row on the third floor, past the offices of his management team, not looking at people. Those he had ignored would later meet in the canteen and ask anxiously, 'When did JA last talk to you?'

'He is not feared for nothing,' says journalist David Marr, who worked for him at the *Herald*. 'He is cunning and ruthless,' adds a former PBL executive. 'I'm sure he has a list of people he's going to get. Yes, he'll cut you down,' says a former Packer magazine editor, 'but he's so smart, and he can be funny, charming and charismatic. The key is to stand up to him. Many don't dare.'

This was the man who was being let loose with a mission to civilise Channel Nine and take it up-market while cutting costs dramatically; the man who was about to confront a culture where every other word was 'fuck' and people addressed each other as 'mate', 'buddy' or whatever nickname they had been assigned.

Alexander's new managing director at Nine—a man who did not actually fit this template—was a genial, footy-mad, long-serving Packer employee, Ian Johnson, who had run the Melbourne station until 1999 before being put in charge of Crown Casino. But, as he soon found out, he was only nominally in charge of the network. He had to report to Park Street, where Alexander wanted to make all the decisions.

To make matters worse, Johnson also had Kerry on his case. The old man liked to ring every day and chat for hours about programs, just as he had always done. But losing ratings made him crankier than ever, and this was compounded by his anti-rejection medication which brought about mood swings. As a result, Johnson found himself on the sharp end of some shocking abuse. In twenty years working for the Packers, he could remember half a dozen times when Kerry had really gone off at him, but none was as bad as what he now had to put up with. 'I copped a call at one o'clock in the morning and he just abused me, yelling so much I couldn't get a word in. It really shook me,' says Johnson. 'I just didn't know what to say. And it was about something really stupid, really trivial. It was about the credits on a program that I had fixed up in a way he didn't like.'

The abuse upset Johnson so much he thought hard about leaving. Other demands pushed him closer to the edge. After months of nagging, Kerry finally ordered him to close 'Sam's Bar'—where Sam Chisholm and David Leckie had traditionally entertained stars and senior executives at Nine's Sydney headquarters—as a warning to all that the old regime had been purged and the glory days were over.

Johnson was also fighting with Alexander. 'JA was incredibly close to Kerry,' he says, 'and he was prepared to sit with him at all hours and talk shit. Kerry would say, "This bloke's no fucking good, get rid of him", and JA would take it at face value.' Johnson was being forced to spend a lot of time and energy defending the people that Packer took a set against, most of whom had many years' experience in TV. And this brought him into conflict with Alexander, who held very different views on what Nine should be trying to do with News and *A Current Affair* in particular.

On a personal level Johnson also missed his family, whom he left behind in Melbourne all week while he worked in Sydney. So in August 2002, after only eight months in the job, he quit. He was fed up with the politics and didn't need the aggravation.

With Johnson out of the way, Alexander took over the managing director's job himself, with James's best mate, David Gyngell, acting as his deputy, even though he had vowed seven years earlier not to work for the Packers because it might spoil his friendship with them. And before long more talented people were heading for the exits, with Nine's highly regarded programmer John Stephens first to go.

Like Johnson, Stephens got calls from Kerry, sometimes three times a day and again at night, to discuss the ratings. Every so often he would also be called over to Park Street, where he would wait outside Packer's office for half an hour and then be stuck until midnight. Kerry, who was bored and lonely and couldn't sleep, would often eat a sandwich and have a drink, but Stephens was never offered anything. Nor was he allowed to argue, because the boss didn't like that. Kerry might occasionally say sorry if his bullying went too far, but he would never, ever admit he was wrong so there was little point arguing with him anyway.

Stephens had been with Nine since 1990 and had played an important part in making Nine number one. Indeed, he and Leckie had been given gold Rolex watches by James as a reward for winning the ratings 100 weeks in a row. But Kerry was never happy unless the ratings were cracking forty every night, which was once in a blue moon.

By the end of 2002 Stephens was thinking of calling it a day. He had just negotiated a new one-year deal with Gyngell, which he hadn't signed, and figured he would quit when it expired. Before going on holiday, he was summoned to Park Street to discuss the schedule for the non-rating summer period. He told Kerry he was putting on new episodes of *The Sopranos*.

According to friends of Stephens, Packer went ballistic.

'You fucking what?' Packer yelled.

'I'm putting on the new series, as you suggested.'

'I never fucking told you that.'

'You said you wanted the strongest summer ever.'

Packer was a great fan of *The Sopranos* and demanded Stephens keep it back until February, when the ratings began again. Stephens explained the program had never rated well and would not bring in the numbers Nine was looking for. He also pointed out that the summer season was starting in just three days, telling Kerry, 'You can't take it off, we'll get slaughtered in the press.'

'Don't tell me what I can and can't fucking do, son,' Kerry replied. 'I want it off.'

After years of fights with his boss, this was one battle too many. Stephens went over the road to the pub, had a few beers and told colleagues he was thinking of leaving. The next day, the weekend papers hammered the decision to postpone *The Sopranos* at such short notice, just as he had known they would. A week or two later he ran into Posie Graeme-Evans, the independent film producer and creator of Nine's hit series *McLeod's Daughters*, at a Christmas party. He told her he had heard 'crazy rumours' she was coming to Nine. 'Surely that can't be true?' he asked.

'Yes,' she said. 'I'm the new head of drama.'

Now he was even angrier. It was normal practice to consult the head of programming about such an important appointment, but at the very least Stephens felt he should have been informed. He tried to phone Alexander and Gyngell, both of whom refused to take his calls.

The following Monday morning Nine's existing head of drama, Kris Noble, was told he had been replaced. Hours later, Stephens received an offer from Channel Seven to be its head of programming. The timing could hardly have been better. He signed a contract on 2 January 2003 and handed in his resignation at Nine. He was given ten minutes to clear his desk and frog-marched off the premises. He wasn't asked to return his gold watch.

The third high-profile desertion was even more directly linked to Alexander, whose desire to take Nine up-market and 'improve' its news coverage brought him into direct conflict with the network's head of news and current affairs, Peter Meakin, who had been just as important as Leckie and Stephens in Nine's success. The king of tabloid TV, Meakin had been responsible for introducing a string of infotainment and reality TV shows such as *Money, Sex* and the very successful *RPA*. He had also just been involved in commissioning *The Block*, which was set to be a huge ratings winner.

Alexander and Meakin could hardly have been more different. One was a blunt, blokey, beer-drinking ex-garbo who wore plaid shirts over old jeans. The other was like a maitre d' at an expensive restaurant: softly spoken and invariably clothed in an Italian suit. Meakin was no giant himself, but he couldn't resist a dig at Alexander's size, telling *Good Weekend* he found him 'extremely intelligent, meticulous, and very small. He looked like he'd spent the first half of his life on a charm bracelet.'

The two men had lunch a few times and sized up the considerable gulf between them. 'I'm not sure whether JA was channelling Kerry or vice versa,' says Meakin today, 'but he and Packer both made it clear that *A Current Affair* was horribly down market, and he said he couldn't get a handle on Nine's news. He didn't know whether it was trying to be the *Sydney Morning Herald* or the *Bankstown Torch*.'

For years Meakin had been allowed to do pretty much what he wanted at Nine because Packer and Leckie trusted his judgment. So he was not wild about taking orders from Alexander, even if there was some substance in his criticisms. He became even less keen to accept Alexander's authority when some key decisions in news and current affairs were taken without him being consulted.

The first was when Jana Wendt was hired at huge expense to host the *Sunday* program in place of Jim Waley. Meakin had heard the rumours and rang the papers with a denial. He found himself looking stupid when the rumours turned out to be true. Confronted by Meakin, Alexander apologised profusely, promising, '*Mea culpa, mea maxima culpa*. It won't happen again.' But six weeks later it did. This time Meakin was summoned to Alexander's office and told to sack Nine's veteran finance correspondent Michael Pascoe, on the grounds that he 'wasn't taken seriously round town'. Meakin disagreed, but Alexander had already hired Pascoe's replacement.

Meakin went back and fired Pascoe, then rang Kerry to tell him, 'I'm out of here. I'm not working with that 24-carat cunt.' Packer asked if they could talk about it. Meakin replied, 'I'm not one to play games, Kerry. It's him or me, so I'll make it easy for you. I'll go.' He walked out of the network that afternoon after a round of emotional farewells. Like Stephens he had already arranged to parachute into Channel Seven, where he was acknowledged as the best in the business.

Two months later, David Leckie completed Channel Seven's trifecta by joining Meakin and Stephens as the network's managing director. Thus, in the space of thirteen months, the Packers lost the three people who had brought Nine success in the 1990s. Worse still, they allowed them to join the arch rival, where they would prove to be just as effective as they had been at Nine. To add insult to injury, Ian Johnson later joined Seven as well.

James Packer did not play a central role in these events because he had ceded control of Nine to his father. But he clearly approved. At PBL's annual conference in Melbourne a year later he paid tribute to Alexander, whom he described as 'the most accomplished media executive in the world'.

'Fuck, how would you feel if you were Peter Yates?' one executive in the audience thought at the time. But Yates was already halfway out the door. One month later, in June 2004, after he was sacked over Burswood, Alexander took his place at the top of the pile as PBL's new managing director.

This left James's best mate, David Gyngell, 'running' Nine in the same limited fashion his predecessor, Ian Johnson, had been permitted two years earlier. Gyngell certainly had the right pedigree for the job—his father Bruce had been the first man on Australian television and had run Nine and Britain's TV-am for the Packers—and he showed signs of inheriting the family skills. He had lived and breathed TV since joining the network in 2002, was well liked and could rally the troops. But he was desperately short on experience, and Kerry felt he needed a helping hand.

That was his first problem.

The second was that Alexander had no intention of giving up control and now had an ally in Chris Anderson, who had been his boss at Fairfax before becoming chief executive at TVNZ in New Zealand. 'Poor David, he just got rocks rained on his head all the time,' says a sympathetic Nine executive.

Some of these rocks were being thrown by Kerry with his daily phone calls to dissect the ratings and offer ideas for shows. Kerry had seen the British TV series *Strictly Come Dancing* while he was cruising round the Mediterranean on the *Arctic P*, and told Gyngell to get it. Unfortunately it was produced by Granada TV, which had links to Seven, so Nine's rival snapped up the program instead. When the Australian version, *Dancing with the Stars*, made its hugely successful debut in October 2004, Packer rang Gyngell as soon as the ratings came out.

'Hi Kerry,' said Gyngell, 'I suppose you're ringing to give me a bollocking.'

'Well I'm not fucking ringing to congratulate you,' Packer replied and put down the phone.

Gyngell also had to trek into Park Street for his weekly interview with the boss, which followed a similar format to the one Kerry had enjoyed so much with Leckie. After a couple of hours, Gyngell would come out swaying and punchdrunk. But that's what it felt like to be called a fucking idiot by Kerry for hours on end.

This punishment might have been bearable if Kerry had actually trusted Gyngell enough to let him run the network. But he didn't. In September 2004, three months after Gyngell took over, the old man asked Sam Chisholm, Nine's boss from the 1980s, to come onto the PBL board and help look after the young managing director. The network's supposed supremo now had five different people in his ear telling him what to do: Kerry and Chisholm, James, Alexander and Anderson. Worse still, he was getting mixed messages about what strategy to pursue. Kerry still wanted Nine to be number one, and bugger the expense. 'I love Channel Nine,' he confessed months before his death. 'It's the only thing that ever made me proud.' James and Alexander, on the other hand, wanted to cut costs sharply and concentrate on making profits. James, it seems, had no interest in programming, but regularly rang the network's finance director and head of sales to ask about Nine's revenue share and projected profits.

'Gyngell told Kerry four or five times to call off the dogs or get some other cunt to deal with these clowns,' a friend says today. 'Kerry said he would, but then he did nothing.' Instead, in April 2005 he brought in another veteran Nine executive, Lynton Taylor, to help negotiate contracts and sports rights, and started talking to him and Chisholm directly, going straight over Gyngell's head. 'That was the last straw. He was trying to save money and here was another one million dollars on his payroll and another bloke doing his job for him.'

By this time Gyngell was being ordered to make big cuts in staff. One executive remembers Nine's chief operating officer, Mick Morris, coming back from Park Street white-faced and shaking to warn colleagues, 'the tsunami is about to begin'. Morris resigned shortly afterwards. Gyngell soon followed. He phoned James on the weekend of 7 to 8 May 2005 to tell him he was quitting, and refused to answer the door when Chisholm, Alexander and his old friend came to his house in an attempt to change his mind. The next day, he went to tell Kerry.

Gyngell told friends it was the hardest thing he'd ever done in his life. He was so nervous that he walked up and down in front of the mirror rehearsing his speech out loud. But when it came to the showdown, it was Kerry who was in tears. He was fond of David, whom he had known since he was a boy. In fact, he was quite possibly fonder of him than he was of his own son. And he thought it was his fault that Gyngell was leaving. Which it was.

As he walked out the door, Gyngell issued a statement saying he had not been allowed do the job properly. 'Unhelpful and multi-layered management systems . . . between Nine and PBL' had made his position 'untenable'.

It was rare for someone to have the guts to walk out on the Packers. But even fewer made their reasons for leaving so public. Putting his surfboard on the roof of his car, James's old friend headed off for Byron Bay, saying he was pleased to be out, that he had made the right decision and had never felt better.

But back at Nine, the fun was only just starting.

CHAPTER 17
WHAM BAM, THANK YOU SAM

He was an absolute fucking monster . . . I've never
encountered anyone like that in my entire life.

In May 2005 Sam Chisholm got to run Channel Nine for the second
time in his life. He said he was only doing it as a favour to Kerry,
that his old friend was in trouble and he had agreed to help out. But
he seemed to relish the chance to strut the stage again. And even
though his appointment was supposed to be a stop-gap measure
until the Packers found a replacement, he soon got into his stride.

Chisholm had made Nine a huge success in the 1980s and worked
wonders at BSkyB in the UK for Murdoch in the 1990s when he
got close to James, who had seen him as a father figure. But he had
changed a lot since those glory days. He had been struck down by
a hereditary lung disease that had killed his father at thirty-nine
and brother at forty, and had undergone a double lung transplant.
There were a couple of times when it looked like he might not
pull through, but he had. And, like Kerry, his trip to the other side
seemed to have brutalised rather than softened him.

A year after the operation, he told *The Australian*'s Christine Jackman, 'They transplanted my lungs, not my personality.' But others disagreed. 'He was completely different from the man he was in 1980s,' says one old friend. 'It's shocking the way he behaved after he came back to Australia.'

Like so many people in top TV management, Chisholm had always been brash, arrogant and full of himself. His head of sport at BSkyB, David Hill, used to drive to work listening to Wagner's 'Ride of the Valkyries' at full volume to get into the right mood to deal with him. But Chisholm's megalomania appeared to have reached new heights in Australia. 'Coming back to Nine', he told one executive producer, was 'like running Belgium after running the world'.

And it wasn't only his ego that was out of control. 'He was running wild, a free-range sociopath,' says one of his most senior executives at Nine. 'He was a funny, witty man, but dear god, he was drinking for Australia and taking anti-rejection medicine at the same time. He was like sweaty gelignite. You never knew when he would go off.'

'Anti-rejection drugs plus alcohol turned him into Captain Queeg. He was fucking ga-ga,' says another who worked closely with him at the network both in the 1980s and in 2005. And almost everyone who dealt with him on a daily basis reached the same conclusion.

But it wasn't just the cocktail of drink and drugs that made Chisholm offensive. He also had a talent for it. A couple of days after returning to Nine he held a lunch for his department heads. Having kept them all waiting for ten minutes, he then berated them for being a bunch of sycophants. 'Yes, a bunch of sycophants. Nothing I love more than a bunch of sycophants,' he chortled. The managing editor of *60 Minutes*, Mark Llewellyn, tried to bite his lip but couldn't help himself. 'I couldn't agree more, Sam, I couldn't agree more.' When the laughter died down, Chisholm, who was not amused, told them that Nine was now fat and lazy and it would be a different place with him in charge. It had become a business run by the staff for the staff, he said. With him in the chair it would be run by the management for the shareholders, chief of whom, of course, were the Packers.

Not that he had much greater regard for Kerry and James, whatever he may have said about them in public or to their faces. On several occasions he told his executives that Kerry had 'no fucking idea about TV', and described James as 'just a schoolboy in long pants', adding, 'What would he know about television? Look at the mess he made of One.Tel.'

Chisholm brought with him a certain manic energy, and he used it to terrify the people who worked for him. He inherited David Gyngell's personal assistant, who lasted a month. Then his old assistant from the 1980s was brought back, only to leave within weeks. The third woman to get the job lived in fear but survived. On one occasion she answered Chisholm's phone call from the canteen and was told, 'You shouldn't be there, you're too fat already.' On another occasion, Chisholm landed at Sydney airport to find his driver was not there to pick him up. In front of a crowd of shocked passers-by, he rang his assistant and abused her so viciously she was reduced to tears.

Nor did Chisholm's bullying stop there. He was forever marching round Nine's executive floor and walking into people's offices to ask, 'What the fuck are you doing?' Or, he would stand in the doorway simply staring and shaking his head. Like Kerry and Sir Frank Packer before him, he was constantly demanding people be sacked. Like them, too, he often forgot about these instructions if they were ignored.

But he presided over a huge exodus of talent all the same. A month after he arrived, sixty people were shown the door in a round of cuts Gyngell would have been expected to make had he stayed, saving $30 million. The head of news and current affairs, Max Uechtritz, who had been hired from the ABC fifteen months earlier, left before he could be fired. Steve Wood, the head of daytime television, was sacked. Others to jump or be pushed were head of light entertainment Glenn Pallister, head of reality and lifestyle Stuart Clark, and Jodie Leonard, the head of marketing. Shortly afterwards Posie Graeme-Evans, the head of drama, and Vance Lothringer, the head of sales, also quit. 'Chisholm's tired old joke was, "There are more people here than run the European Union in Brussels, and I don't know what they do,"' says one executive who survived the purges. 'Well, he found out when they left: they made programs, found new talent and kept Nine ahead of the game.'

It takes time for the loss of such a creative group of people to manifest in the decline of a network, but Nine's ratings fell steadily from 2003, the year after Leckie's sacking, and its tally of Australia's most popular programs dropped even faster. In 2003 Nine had eight shows in the top 10, led by *The Block*, *Channel Nine News* and *Who Wants to be a Millionaire?* In 2004 it had six, in 2005 four and in 2006 just one.

Chisholm's 'trump card' in arresting this slide was to bring back sixty-seven-year-old Bert Newton, who had been a big star at Nine during the 1980s before being exiled to Channel Ten's morning show. Newton was called in to host a revamped version of the 1970s game show *Family Feud*, to run as the lead-in to Nine's struggling six o'clock news. To no one's great surprise

Family Feud was comprehensively thumped by Seven's *Deal or No Deal*, presented by the much younger and funnier Andrew O'Keefe. Sam also backed *Magda's Funny Bits*, a sketch comedy program starring Magda Szubanski which was one of the biggest flops of 2006.

It was not entirely Chisholm's fault that he couldn't halt the decline, because Nine had lost its all-important dominance in news. This was partly due to the departure of Meakin, but also to the retirement in November 2002 of Nine's much-loved Sydney newsreader Brian Henderson, who had been in the chair for forty years. Hendo had delivered the network a ratings lead of 100 000 people every weeknight that had made it almost impossible for Nine's rivals to catch up.

Henderson had handed over to the veteran *Sunday* presenter Jim Waley, who had done a fine job in holding the ratings until late 2003, when David Leckie (now running Seven) decided to lure Nine's second-string newsreader, Ian Ross, out of semi-retirement to read Seven's revamped Sydney bulletin. Before long Ross was closing the gap, and by the end of 2004 he was pulling level.

Kerry's response was to replace Waley with the younger Mark Ferguson, who was impressive that December in linking Nine's coverage of the tsunami. There was good sense in making the switch. Waley's 'Q scores', which rate the popularity of presenters, were bad and falling, and some viewers admitted they had switched to Seven because they liked Ross better. But the change was handled badly. Waley—the man Nine had built up to the public as a wonderful journalist and all-round good bloke—was told he would have to take a big pay cut if he wanted to stay with the network. He was so angry he decided to leave. After thirty-seven years of loyal service and twenty-one years with *Sunday*, he was told he couldn't send a farewell email to his friends at Nine; nor was he allowed to clear his desk.

Amid a blaze of bad publicity, Waley promptly sued Nine for damages. Since his contract still had eighteen months to run he believed Nine should pay him out, but Park Street apparently believed that employment contracts could be torn up or ignored. Nine was eventually forced to settle, but it was now clear that the Packers' word meant nothing. Gone were the days when Kerry and James could be trusted to do deals on a handshake.

With Mark Ferguson in the chair the ratings fell further, headlines about life at Nine got worse, and Seven's Sydney bulletin cruised to an easy win, establishing a lead of around 50 000 viewers a night and taking thirty-nine out of the forty rating weeks in 2005 (Chisholm's year in command). Nine's Melbourne bulletin was also losing audience because experienced journalists were being replaced by raw recruits at half the price. By mid-2005 Nine was also on to its third head of news and current affairs since Meakin had left, with each bringing a new philosophy to the job and confusion to the viewers. Meanwhile, Seven had spent millions of dollars on new equipment and was looking sharper and better.

Chisholm was frustrated by the mess the network was in. According to one senior executive: 'He thought Nine had been run down badly.' And he was right: Kerry hadn't spent any money on the station to upgrade capital equipment, and James's only interest in the network was in cutting costs. It was increasingly hard for Nine to claim it was 'Still the One'.

Chisholm's other problem was he couldn't match the programs Seven was buying from the United States, where its long-term supplier, Disney, had undergone a sudden renaissance. This was made dramatically obvious at the beginning of 2005 when Seven unveiled and promoted *Lost* and *Desperate Housewives* during the Australian Tennis Open final to an audience of more than 4 million people. Together with *Dancing with the Stars*, these two programs topped the ratings by a distance in the first ten weeks of the year, leaving Nine trailing in their wake.

And unlike Seven, which had developed its own homegrown shows such as *Border Security*, *The Force*, *Medical Emergency* and *RSPCA Animal Rescue*, Nine had virtually nothing new to help it catch up. Nor was there any chance of Chisholm being given the money needed to turn this around. The best he could expect was to hold the line against further cuts.

While Kerry was alive and James was held at bay, this was still possible. Even though the old man was getting sicker and sicker, he was still calling the shots. The monthly TV management meetings in Park Street were '*his* meetings', according to a regular. 'Kerry said the same things every time. It was about content, news and current affairs, the competitive position of the business compared to Seven and Ten, and how to stay number one.'

James and John Alexander, who also attended the meetings, were known to have a radically different view, but never had the nerve to tackle the Big Fella. 'They were always looking to cut another fifty million dollars or sixty million dollars out of the business and saying it was profits that mattered, but they never pushed this to Kerry,' says one former PBL executive. 'I was astounded at the lack of courage shown by James and JA in these meetings. They spent an awful lot of time looking at their shoes.'

While the Mexican stand-off lasted, Chisholm was able to run Nine pretty much as he saw fit. But his days were numbered, not least because he managed to alienate just about everyone who worked for him. 'He was incredibly unpleasant to be around and he thought we were all stupid,' says one former senior Nine executive, whose views are echoed by at least half a dozen others. 'He was an absolute fucking monster,' says another of his most senior colleagues. 'I've dealt with a few people but I've never encountered anyone like that in my entire life. Excuse my language, but he was an absolute cunt. His ability to hurt people and destabilise people was incredible.'

One of Chisholm's greatest supporters concurs. 'I don't think you can deny he behaved like a monster. Everybody was uneasy. Everybody was wondering when they were going to get it. And everybody had to endure it at some point.'

When asked to comment on these views, Chisholm replied: 'Well, there you are. Everyone has an opinion. They can say what they like.' And asked if he abused and belittled people, he said: 'They probably deserved it. I have no regrets. It was a very difficult job, a very tough environment, but it was a better company when I left. Cash flow, profits and the balance sheet were all better. And the ratings didn't suffer. You might not like the way I did it. But I was in a hurry.'

It was the daily tyranny that people hated most. 'He was just a dictator,' says one survivor, 'who had all these rules,' one of which was that all male executives had to wear ties, and ties that met his approval. 'Call that a tie?' he asked one man. 'Go down to wardrobe and get a proper one.' On another occasion he caught the head of production, Andrew Backwell, tieless in his office at 8 a.m. Chisholm's response was to fly into a rage: 'Either you are a complete fucking idiot or you are totally defying me. Which is it?'

Women on the executive floor were told they had to wear high heels, and any who ignored this order risked being shouted at. But the strictest rule of all was that no one was allowed to eat at their desk. Chisholm defends this vigorously. 'When I arrived there were people wandering round the corridors eating,' he says, 'and blokes just sitting round chatting. I wasn't used to it. I said to them this is no way to operate, this isn't a holiday camp, it's a public company. I did exactly what needed to be done. I've seen a lot of businesses and I'm in a position to know.'

But others saw things differently. When Chisholm ran into Nine's political lobbyist, Creina Chapman, coming back from the staff kitchen with an apple, he stopped her and screamed, 'What the fuck are you doing with that apple? This isn't a fucking restaurant.' After a moment's hesitation Chapman turned around and yelled at Chisholm in return. For the next few minutes, the shouting match was witnessed by nearly everybody on Nine's executive floor. This was another of Chisholm's rules, that office doors had to be left open.

When word of the confrontation got back to James, he agreed that Chapman could work in Park Street to stay out of Sam's way but refused to get involved or challenge Chisholm directly. There is no question James knew Nine's boss was running riot, but he said his hands were tied while 'Dad' was still around, because it was 'Dad' who wanted Chisholm there. 'It's horrible how many people were hurt,' says one who lived through the period. 'It was such a destructive environment, yet James never intervened.'

So why didn't anyone tell Kerry what was happening? Well, in fact, they did. 'Kerry was aware of all this. I had the conversation with him,' says a senior Nine executive, 'but he was too sick to do anything about it. He said, "I'm too sick to fight this battle."'

A month later the old man was dead.

CHAPTER 18
A GREAT AUSTRALIAN

He wasn't Mother Teresa . . . he could be a really tough
bastard.

Kerry's kidney transplant in November 2000 had allowed him to
live another five years, but it was clear he was on borrowed time. He
could no longer play polo, race go-karts, fly his ultralight or do any
of the dangerous things he loved. He was even too sick to play golf
on the new championship course he had built at Ellerston. All he
had left was the business, where James wanted him out of the way.

It was amazing Kerry had lasted so long. He had suffered at
least four major heart attacks, and lost a kidney to cancer and
another to disease. He had also survived a heart by-pass, the kidney
transplant and countless episodes of invasive surgery to unblock
arteries, replace valves or implant defibrillators. Doctors had even
removed a malignant melanoma from his ear.

Since receiving his new kidney from Nick Ross, Kerry had also
been taking a daily cocktail of drugs in a vain effort to stop his body

rejecting the new organ. As well as the mood swings these had wreaked havoc with his immune system, making him vulnerable to every cold or virus going around. He kept on getting pneumonia—and occasionally pleurisy—which would cause him to stop chain-smoking for a bit. He tried all sorts of treatments to beat his nicotine addiction, which was a continuing cause of his ill health, but nothing ever worked. Ross and the doctors kept on at him, but he still never managed to kick the habit. Eventually they gave up bullying him.

In fact, Kerry no longer saw his helicopter pilot, anyway. Ross had stopped flying for him and the friendship had cooled. Many of the things they had enjoyed together, such as racing cars and chasing women, were now off limits, and perhaps the burden of receiving such an extraordinary gift was too much for Kerry to bear. 'I don't think he knew how to deal with it,' says Ross, sadly. 'I think he was embarrassed by the debt. To have someone giving to him without asking for reward was something he found hard to understand.'

Ross's recompense was to have a new $10 million transplant unit named after him at the Royal Prince Alfred Hospital. At the opening ceremony, the old man gave his benefactor a big hug and cried. 'It was the most emotional I've ever seen him,' says Ross. But after that the two men saw little of each other.

Strangely enough, Ros Packer was even less inclined to show gratitude to the man who had saved her husband's life. In the six weeks Ross spent at the Packers' compound in Bellevue Hill recuperating after the operation, she didn't once manage to take a trip across the courtyard to thank him.

In the last couple of years of his life, Kerry lost weight, suffered shortness of breath and became very frail. One of his magazine editors was struck by how ill he looked at a weekend gathering at Ellerston in 2004. Kerry made his appearance at the go-kart racing to give his executives some free advice about tackling the difficult track. 'Anyone who can't get under sixty seconds,' he told them, 'should be wearing a fucking skirt.' But he was too weak to show them the way, which was normally the second act of this performance. Wearing an old shirt and tracksuit that could have come from K-Mart, he looked awful, the editor recalls. 'His skin was like rice paper. It was so thin you could have stuck your finger through it.'

It was only physical and emotional fortitude that kept Kerry going, or so his doctors believed. Lesser men would have given up the fight, but he continued to drag himself into the office every day and spend hours on the phone to his managers at Nine. 'No one else I've ever seen could handle illness and work like he could,' says Dr Ian Bailey. 'He was super human.'

In the last few months of 2005, Kerry got even weaker. When Alan Jones visited him shortly before Christmas, he complained there was no joy left in his life: 'I can't eat what I want to eat. I can't do what I want to do and I can't go where I want to go. Son, what am I doing here?' Weeks earlier, he had complained to another friend that he was too old for sex, the activity that had kept him amused and aroused for so many years. There were only two things in life, he declared, 'fucking women and making money'. He could no longer manage the first and the second now seemed pointless.

By now, the kidney he received from Nick Ross was packing up because the artery supplying it was blocked, just as it had been in 1997 when he had been so close to death. His body was also winning the battle to reject the organ. And the combined effect of this and diabetes—caused by the anti-rejection drugs—was putting an intolerable strain on his heart.

Come December 2005, Kerry was desperate to fly to South America to watch his polo team, Ellerstina, play in the Argentine Open and say goodbye to the people who looked after his horses. His doctors were horrified at the prospect of him embarking on such an arduous trip, but they couldn't talk him out of it. He came back a week later in even worse shape than when he had departed.

About ten days before Christmas, Kerry underwent another round of tests. The prognosis was bad. When he got off the bed and started to walk out of the room, Dr Bailey asked if he was feeling nauseous. 'No, I'm hungry,' Kerry replied. 'I could eat two doctors on rye.' He was running out of petrol, he said. His time had come, and life would go on without him. 'I've been waiting for this. I'm going to die. That's the reality.'

Kerry wasn't going to hang around if he could no longer do things for himself. He could think of nothing worse than losing his dignity, and he had banned his doctors from mentioning dialysis, which would have had him bedridden and tied to a machine for eight or nine hours a day. Dr Bailey had already agreed to help him die peacefully when the time came, fearing that the old man would do it himself. There was no doubt he was determined enough, and he had plenty of staff to assist him.

Kerry was not at Bellevue Hill during this time. For much of the previous five years he and Ros had been living apart, with the old man dividing his time between Ellerston, his floating palace the *Arctic P* and the penthouse apartment in the Toft Monks building that he shared with Julie Trethowan. As well as the full-time chef, butler and housekeeper, he kept a nurse there to look after him. But in the weeks and months before his death Kerry was not at Toft Monks either because he was renovating the penthouse, spending $2 million to connect it with two other apartments he owned on the floor below.

Kerry and Julie had met in the early 1980s, when she was in her mid-twenties. She had been with him ever since, running the Hyde Park Club, where Kerry had a private bunker with a bedroom and lounge he could enter from his own personal lift. Nearby was a steam room that produced rain, sun and snow, which Kerry liked to surprise his mates with when they were naked. Unfortunately, it sometimes started to snow without warning. More than once, Kerry rang the installer in the middle of the night and 'abused the shit' out of him, complaining he had paid 'thousands of fucking dollars' and expected it all to work. Eventually, it was discovered that a signal in the building was making the electronic equipment malfunction.

Kerry's relationship with Julie was an open secret among his executives, who encountered her at business dinners and Toft Monks. 'She was friendly but never looked you in the eye,' says one former employee. 'And she was ferociously worried about her appearance.' Naturally, she kept in shape while running the gym, and Kerry could pay for the occasional nip and tuck.

'Kerry was very discreet about it, but Ros certainly knew,' says Nick Ross, who spent more time with Julie than most. 'Ros simply chose not to acknowledge it. They lived separate lives in the last five years, anyway. She had her artistic friends and he had his rough mates.'

The marriage had not always been so distant, despite Kerry's constant philandering. A visitor to the Packers' English country house, Fyning Hill, in the late 1990s remembers him and Ros being very affectionate towards each other and talking 'in a delightful way'. But in the old man's final years the relationship had become increasingly difficult.

Right until the end, Kerry kept going into the office. Three days before Christmas, he hauled himself into Park Street to sign off on a massive $780 million bid for television rights to the AFL he had been working on with Sam Chisholm. If he couldn't win the prize for Nine, he wanted to force Seven to pay so much it could never make a profit. He was also hoping to spend Christmas in Las Vegas, and had his jet and its crew on standby. But he was obviously so close to death that it was finally decided he was too sick to go. On Christmas Day 2005 he was loaded into an ambulance and taken back to the family home at Bellevue Hill, where Ros was having Christmas lunch in his absence.

James was holidaying in the Maldives on the *Arctic P*, taking a break with his girlfriend, Erica Baxter, and John Alexander. He had talked to Kerry in the middle of the week and all had seemed fine. Now he was told to fly back as quickly as possible. He spent the next twenty-four hours jumping planes to Singapore and then to Sydney, where he finally arrived at about 9 p.m. on Boxing Day. Kerry had been sedated by his doctors and kept alive for this last goodbye. He was roused for long enough to see his son, then allowed to slip back into a morphine-assisted sleep. He died in Ros's arms an hour and a half later. His wife was the only person in the room.

Kerry Packer's death was announced on Channel Nine's *Today* show the next morning, and 24 hours later newspapers around the country pulled out all stops to laud the great man. There had been ample time to polish the tributes because Kerry had been at death's door for a decade or more. Yet, somehow, the obituary writers could find only good things to say about him. Here was a man who had bullied everyone who stood in his way, who had done all he could to avoid paying tax, who had contempt for politicians and journalists and little sense of civic duty. And suddenly he was a saint, a philanthropist, a Great Australian.

Typically, it was politicians who led the chorus, with Prime Minister John Howard singing loudest of all. Describing the death as 'a very big loss' and Packer as 'a generous philanthropist who was passionately committed to the interests of the Australian people', Howard claimed the media mogul was a personal friend. Australia's Treasurer Peter Costello and Communications Minister Helen Coonan joined the conga line, extolling Kerry as a 'giant of Australian business' and 'a generous philanthropist'. And on the other side of politics the praise was almost as lavish, with New South Wales Premier Morris Iemma claiming that Kerry would be forever remembered for his generous support of the state's public health system. It was true, of course, that he had helped put 'Packer-whackers' in every ambulance in New South Wales and had made his jet available for transplant teams to fly across the country to collect organs for needy recipients.

Journalists and business leaders also joined the Packer glee club, with Fairfax chairman Ron Walker describing the man who had abused his newspapers and its writers for so long as a 'Great Australian' and 'a very caring individual'. There were countless stories written about how generous Packer had been in helping the sick and needy, yet none mentioned the fact that, unlike so many rich Americans, he had never set up a charitable foundation. Nor were we reminded that Kerry had managed to pay a lower rate of tax than his gardener.

Packer's former right-hand man Trevor Kennedy could hardly believe what he was reading. 'He wasn't Mother Teresa. And while he could be a very generous bloke, he could be a really tough bastard and a difficult fellow . . . and I'm surprised at some of the senior journalists I had terrible fights with during the Costigan Inquiry . . . now writing these extraordinary things, saying what a wonderful fellow he was.'

Some of this media amnesia no doubt stemmed from a reluctance to speak ill of the dead. But it surely had as much to do with the fact that James still owned Australia's leading television network and biggest magazine group, with all the political power and patronage that entailed.

Four days after his death, with salvos of praise still ringing through the air, Kerry Francis Bullmore Packer was laid to rest at Ellerston in a private burial officiated by the Anglican Archbishop of Sydney, Peter Jensen, even though the old man had famously scoffed at the existence of an afterlife. Ros, James and Gretel, with their partners Erica Baxter and Shane Murray, flew up from Sydney in Kerry's big blue-and-white Sikorsky helicopter, while the hearse made its way up the back roads to the Hunter Valley with four TV-news helicopters in hot pursuit, apparently unable to find it.

About 50 kilometres out of Ellerston the big black Mercedes flashed past Kitty Hill, a young photographer from the *Newcastle Herald* who had just been taking shots of drovers moving cattle up the Gundy road to that little town's annual rodeo and was running late for her next assignment at the Scone races, the biggest meeting of the year. As it happened, Hill had just been talking to her passenger—an old drover named Treath—about Kerry's death when she spotted the hearse speeding in the opposite direction. Being a local, she knew Ellerston was close by and there were no cemeteries further up the line, so she swung the car round and gave chase.

'It had gotten quite a headstart on us and we sped along at around 130 kilometres an hour to catch it,' Hill recalls, with Treath yelling, 'We're not going to catch the bugger!' 'After about ten minutes, we still hadn't caught the hearse and I was cursing that it must have turned off somewhere, when we rounded a bend and there it was, moving quickly through the cattle on the road. I had no time to stop the car, so Treath held the wheel, with my foot still on the accelerator, and I took four shots through the windscreen which, luckily, was clean. Then it was gone, disappearing round a bend. When I got back into mobile reception, I rang my picture desk and they told me I'd been the only one to catch it on the 400-kilometre drive from Sydney.'

Hill was apprehensive about how the Packers might feel about the photos, but she got an answer of sorts when the *Women's Weekly* bought the rights to the images and ran a shot in its 24-page tribute. Not surprisingly, the *Weekly* did a good job of gilding the old man's memory, collecting a series of happy snaps that made Kerry, Ros and the kids look like the perfect family and telling its readers that Kerry had 'adored' them. The *Bulletin* also published a special tribute edition, and Channel Nine broadcast a one-hour documentary entitled *The Big Fella*.

The producers of the documentary discovered that Kerry's friends were suddenly prepared to talk frankly, as they had never dared to do when he was alive. Off camera, one or two of his closest mates were wildly indiscreet, telling tales of Kerry's sexual exploits and recounting shocking stories of how he had bullied Ros and James. But even on camera, their anecdotes occasionally sailed too close to the truth for comfort.

Hearing some of these stories, Sam Chisholm tried to have the reporter Graham Davis taken off the project. 'What's he fucking doing?' he asked one of the program's producers. 'No one wants to know about that shit. I want him out straight away. I want Jana [Wendt] in there.'

Davis survived and the filmmakers did their level best to avoid a hagiography. Nevertheless, on Ros Packer's decree they had no choice but to leave out a long and fascinating interview with Ian Bailey because the doctor had talked to the media the day Kerry died. Trevor Kennedy's observation that the old man wasn't Mother Teresa also failed to make the final cut, as did a small and poignant part of James's interview, during which Davis asked: 'I gather he died in your mother's arms.'

'Mmm, yeah, he did.'

'Peacefully?'

'I think relatively peacefully. Yeah, I mean I think it's, you know and I'm sure it's never perfect.'

Then came the two lines that were cut at Ros Packer's request after a family viewing.

'How important was she to him?' Davis asked.

James, somewhat lost, replied, 'You know she was his wife for forty years.'

It was clearly the only thing he could find to say.

The program was broadcast on 16 February 2006, commercial-free and in prime time on the eve of a state-funded memorial service. Monitors set up all over Kerry's Bellevue Hill mansion were watched by 300 people, several of whom were in tears. Chisholm rang the filmmakers afterwards to congratulate them. It was a fabulous documentary, he said, a triumph, the best there had been on Channel Nine. But there was no call of thanks or congratulation from the Packer family.

The next day, Kerry was given his final send-off at the Sydney Opera House. One thousand hand-written invitations had been sent out on the Packers' behalf, and the public had been invited as well, provided they registered first. In the event, there were several hundred seats to spare in the 2600-seat auditorium.

It had been the federal government's idea to give Kerry a state funeral, and the Packers had thought it impolite to say 'No'. But God knows what the Big Fella would have thought of it all. He would hardly have approved of taxpayers' money being wasted in this way, given his famous pronouncements on the subject. And what had he ever done for Australia, many asked? Had he ever been a taxpayer himself? Why wasn't the Bahamian government footing the bill, given that Kerry's empire—or the trusts controlling it—had long been domiciled there?

But Packer would surely have loved the tone of it all. Choreographed by the director of *Crocodile Dundee*, Peter Faiman, its star performer was that other tough-talking, cigarette-smoking, sports-mad, Great Australian, Russell Crowe, reading Kipling's famous poem 'If'. In the front row sat a small army of the old man's sporting mates, including former cricket captains Richie Benaud, Ian Chappell and Tony Greig, spin legend Shane Warne, champion golfer Greg Norman, Kangaroo and Manly coach Bob Fulton and the entire Australian cricket team, not to mention assorted jockeys, punters and boxers with whom the old man had so liked to mix. There was also a scattering of billionaires and the world's most famous Scientologist, Tom Cruise, dressed all in black with his very pregnant wife, Katie Holmes, and their minders.

A pack of politicians was also in attendance. Three decades earlier, prime ministers and premiers had queued up at Sir Frank Packer's funeral, and their successors now followed suit for Kerry, with John Howard and Kim Beazley in the vanguard and Bob Hawke, Neville Wran, Graham Richardson, Morris Iemma,

Bob Carr, Nick Greiner and others hard behind. But there were a few notable gaps in the ranks. No Paul Keating, who had turned from friend to foe after financial details of his involvement in a piggery were featured on *60 Minutes*, and no Gough Whitlam or Malcolm Fraser, who had united in horror at the prospect of Kerry winning control of *The Age* and *Sydney Morning Herald.*

James's cousin, Francis Packer, was also missing, having broken Kerry's cardinal rule of never talking to the media. Shortly after the old man's death, Francis suggested to a journalist that Kerry had contemplated turning his back on Australia in the mid-1980s after the Costigan Royal Commission accused him of involvement in organised crime. Francis hadn't been told not to come, but had realised he would not be welcome.

The most obvious absentee, however, was the unvarnished truth. For a man whose own view of the world was so brutally honest, there was a lamentable lack of plain speaking in the tributes, just as there had been in the media coverage. Almost the only speaker who did not set out to sanctify Kerry was James, whose goodbye was by far the most moving because it seemed both truthful and warm. The others seemed too scared, too awed, too sycophantic or too interested in buffing the legend to give the man the light and shade he deserved.

Watching from Heaven, which is where James and the master of ceremonies Alan Jones hoped he would be, Kerry would have been proud of his boy as he walked the fine line between eulogy and truth. 'My father used to think the word legend was tossed around far too often,' James began. 'I want to say today that in the opinion of his family, my father was a legend.'

'My most precious memories are of course not about the legend, but about my dad,' he continued. 'I have a million small memories that will sustain me through my life . . . Dad was my mentor and my teacher but above all he was my father, and that was my greatest fortune.' Even this, of course, was James putting the best possible gloss on what had been a painful and difficult relationship. But it was better than the other saccharin-coated eulogies on offer.

And Kerry would definitely have loved the final act—a seemingly interminable chorus of the World Series Cricket anthem 'C'mon Aussie, C'mon', filling the Opera House from floor to ceiling. In Packer's last hurrah sport beat art hands down, which was exactly the way he would have wanted it.

After the finale, mourners crowded into the Opera House foyer and tucked into party pies and sandwiches, while a select 150 repaired to the Opera House's three-hat restaurant, Guillaume at Bennelong, to be served tempura prawns and Peking Duck rolls washed down with French champagne. Tom Cruise and Katie Holmes mingled there for twenty minutes before being ferried to the middle of the harbour and James's outsize tinny, *Carpe Diem*. James and his girlfriend, Erica, joined them twenty minutes later. One of Kerry's close friends was horrified to see the host depart so quickly. 'It showed a lack of respect. People had come from all the way across the world and they were left standing there.'

Others were sad that two of Kerry's closest companions from the last few years had not been invited. It was no surprise that Julie Trethowan had been left off the guest list. This was not France, after all, where it is accepted that presidents and billionaires have mistresses. But Ben Tilley's absence was less easily explained. Friends reported that James had resolved to have no more to do with his old schoolmate and had told Tilley, 'You've had too much out of this family already.' James was also said to be angry because Kerry had taunted him that he was 'jealous' because Tilley preferred the old man to him. Whatever the truth, Tilley flew out to Hawaii shortly after the service, having thrown a party for Trethowan at his house the night before.

By this time, Kerry's long-running affair with his gym mistress had been laid bare by the *Sydney Morning Herald*'s Kate Mc-Clymont, who revealed the tycoon had signed over a series of properties to her in the weeks before his death. These included the penthouse and four apartments in the Toft Monks tower, a holiday house at Whale Beach, an apartment in Edgecliff and a commercial property in Bondi Junction with a combined value of more than $15 million. The article had been spiked for a few days because it used the word 'mistress'. The lawyers had been comfortable with this plain speaking, but Fairfax management had not. After a week of wringing of hands, the story finally made it into print with Trethowan being described as 'a close friend'.

The *Sun Herald* also ran a story on Trethowan. Annette Sharp highlighted Julie's absence from the wake, claiming she was distraught at Kerry's death and he had been the love of her life. This provoked a fierce complaint from the Packer camp and pressure to have Sharp removed from the job. But Sharp kept her column and the caravan moved on, just as Kerry had anticipated it would.

CHAPTER 19
THE SON ALSO RISES

Kerry died a lonely man and he deserved to. He treated
James like shit, and James hated him because of it.

Kerry Packer once confessed that the day his father died was the
happiest day of his life. Sir Frank had bullied him relentlessly, ridi-
culed him in public and refused to hand over control of the empire
as he got sicker and sicker. And some believe James now felt the
same. 'A huge burden had been lifted off his shoulders. He had
been hanging in there, with survival his only aim,' says a man who
knows him intimately. 'He had been in a war, and it had stopped
at last.'

But if this was what James really felt, it was not the story
he chose to tell the media. Three months after Kerry's death he
assured the *West Australian*'s Mark Drummond that he and his
father had parted on their best-ever terms and it was a source of
joy to him that they had made peace at last. Nine months later, he
was telling the *Australian Financial Review*'s Pam Williams that

he was 'terribly grateful' for everything Kerry had done and that he had 'nothing but great feelings towards him'.

'Relationships are complicated,' James went on, 'but I genuinely have made the decision—and it's been a very easy decision to make—that when I think of my dad I'm going to think great thoughts of a great man who's been incredibly generous to me.'

Kerry's incredible generosity was not what had struck James's friends while the old man was alive. Nor had it been widely noticed by those who had observed the family at close quarters. 'Kerry died a lonely man and he deserved to', said one, who was particularly savage in his comments. 'He treated James like shit, and James hated him because of it.' Another friend of James's recounted how Kerry would often call his son 'a loser' to his face, which was a description James would sometimes echo, lamenting, 'I'm a loser, I'm a loser.'

But whether or not Kerry's death made James happy, there's no doubt it gave him an enormous sense of release. At the age of thirty-eight he was at last going to be allowed to run the Packer empire and live his life as he thought fit, even if his father's ghost might still be looking over his shoulder.

Kerry's will was in the grand tradition of the Packer patriarchy. Read to the family by executors David Gonski and Lloyd Williams the day before the burial, it granted annuities to Gretel and Ros to keep them comfortable for life, but handed absolute control of the business empire to James, as expected. James dismissed any suggestion that the old man had tied up the money to prevent him passing the family fortune on to the Scientologists, telling Pam Williams: 'I don't want to go into it, other than to say that my father put me into his shoes in every sense. I've got no restrictions on me.'

And he soon set about enjoying this new freedom. His oft-repeated motto to friends, girlfriends and fellow executives was,

'Whoever dies with the most toys wins'. Almost as soon as Kerry was out of the way, he started putting this philosophy into practice. After all, what was the point of inheriting $6 billion if you didn't spend some of the money?

The first treat he allowed himself was a brand new boat. Not satisfied with the *Arctic P* and its cinema, swimming pool, helipad and fourteen-strong crew, he went shopping for something sleeker and smarter and settled on a new, 50-metre Mangusta 165 at a cost of around $50 million. Taking two years to build and christened the *Z Ellerston*, it would not actually roll down the slipway in Viareggio, Italy, until mid-2008.

James's new super-yacht was to be powered by three 16-cylinder German MTU diesels—which drive Britain's high-speed trains—teamed with Rolls Royce waterjets that can move enough water to empty an Olympic swimming pool in one minute. At its cruising speed of 65 kilometres an hour, this new runabout would burn 400 litres of fuel every 10 kilometres, or roughly what a Toyota Prius might use in a year. Filling the 40000-litre tank would cost around $100000. Clearly, running costs and carbon emissions were not one of James's big concerns.

Quite why a man who spent most of his time in Australia needed two huge yachts in the Mediterranean was not entirely clear. But the *Arctic P* was too big to pull up alongside the dock in some of the trendiest ports on the Cote d'Azur, and James's 25-metre day boat, *Carpe Diem*, in which he buzzed round Sydney Harbour, was too small to act as a northern hemisphere base. Besides, Gretel and Ros liked to use Kerry's tug from time to time.

And perhaps he intended to bring it back home anyway. By December 2006 the boat builders had lent him a smaller, 30-metre Mangusta 105, just as a stopgap, and this turned heads as it roared through the Sydney-to-Hobart fleet at the start of the Boxing Day race.

James wasn't only revamping the Packer navy; he was also re-equipping the air force. For years Kerry had made do with a secondhand DC-8 bought on the cheap in Amsterdam, which he eventually swapped for a smaller Falcon 200. This was unkindly known as the Toyota Corolla of air travel and was clearly inadequate for any self-respecting young billionaire. So, six weeks after Kerry's death, James put the Falcon up for sale and bought a $60 million Bombardier Global Express instead.

This was an ultra long-range, high-speed jet seating up to eighteen passengers, which could cruise at 900 kilometres an hour and hop over to Las Vegas without refuelling. Almost as big as a Boeing 737, it was described by its manufacturer as 'the most luxurious, most accomplished business jet' ever built. 'No other aircraft in its class,' the sales pitch continued, 'flies you faster, further. The BBG places you at the top of your game and the world in the palm of your hand.'

James had his refurbished in cream leather and birdseye maple with deep-pile ivory-coloured carpets. To the rear of the main cabin, with its eight deep swivel chairs and kitchen-cum-bar, was a private retreat for his use featuring a king-sized double bed that converted into a couch.

The new toys were the responsibility of James's best mate Matthew Csidei, or Ched, who had moved into the Bondi apartment in 2002 when James split up with Jodhi and stayed for several years. Commonly known as The Butler because of his habit of following James around, or as the Minister of Fun because it was his job to keep James happy, Csidei had flown to Europe to buy *Carpe Diem* for his friend 'because he knew about boats'.

James liked Ched. He was unchallenging and available. He was also happy to play second fiddle and to come when called. And, unlike so many of the others who hung around, he never wanted James to back him in business. Along with James's other friends who rode on what was commonly known as 'the gravy train' he was also well rewarded, except that James actually paid him a salary. As Ched apparently told the story, he thought of a figure to ask for but found James offering three times as much.

As with most of his friends, James had known Ched since schooldays at Cranbrook where they had been in the same year. According to one master who remembered him, Csidei had been 'a very naughty boy, who was always in trouble, always in detention, always in the headmaster's bad books'. But he had not turned into a crook like his father, Bela, who had been pursued on several charges of corporate fraud in the 1970s and was jailed for cultivating marijuana in the Northern Territory in 1978.

In his heyday, Bela Csidei had been a runner for Sir Peter Abeles and a front man for the notorious Sydney organised crime boss Abe Saffron, otherwise known as Mr Sin. As Csidei admitted in his autobiography—published by James Packer's Park Street Press—in the 1960s he had held the licence for a Kings Cross night club as a front for Saffron, and had paid police to turn a blind eye to Abe's highly lucrative sly grog business.

Ched had not been tempted by a life of crime. Instead, he had gone into stockbroking and made far more money. But he had inherited Bela's love of the high life. One man who knew him summed him up as 'a lovely, charming boy', then added: 'He is very interested in money and accoutrements, and very impressed by wealth, stature and possessions. He's the sort of fellow who'd be sitting in a high-powered meeting and all he'd be thinking is "Gee, that's a nice shirt that guy's wearing, or wow, I wonder where he bought those shoes".'

Ched was also famous for his parties, at which his wilder playboy friends snorted coke and had fun. One man who went to several remembers James appearing at one of them and complaining he was cold. Someone immediately rushed upstairs to fetch him a jumper.

Such sycophants and hangers-on made life difficult for the new controller of the Packer billions. As one of his senior executives at Nine observed, 'James is so isolated, he never knows who his friends are, and people are always trying to touch him for something.' Another concluded: 'If you've got all that money and you've spent your life like James has, you never learn to be a good judge of character. How does he ever know whether anyone wants to be his friend or take his money? That's why he relies on his schoolmates and people he's inherited from Kerry. He doesn't know who to trust.'

So what was this new master of the Packer fortune really like, and what were his ambitions?

Not surprisingly, in view of the difficult relationship with his father and his constant feeling of isolation, James said he wanted a happy life, telling Pam Williams: 'I want to be able to look at myself in the mirror at the end of the day, the month, the year and say I did my best, I didn't fritter away my life, I tried my hardest at whatever I was doing . . . I think if you do that you can probably have a higher chance of feeling good about yourself and therefore being happy and contented and all of those things.'

But in this modest endeavour the sad old Packer genes were always going to be a handicap. Both Kerry and Sir Frank had been prone to black moods and bouts of depression and had often felt cut off from their fellow men, and James suffered in a similar fashion. He seemed uncomfortable in his own skin and a man who didn't much like himself.

People close to the family described him as a loner with few real friends and no talent for intimacy. He would invite guests up to Ellerston for the weekend and then abandon them to their own devices. 'James liked getting away from people,' said someone who knew him well.

It had not always been thus. 'He was the friendliest of youngsters as a little boy,' according to Bob Darke, his headmaster at Tudor House. But by the late 1990s when Darke caught up with him again, he seemed to have become 'a loner, with no close friends, or none from the school'.

Many of those working at Park Street gave similar reports. One long-serving personal assistant says James was 'stony-faced', treated the staff 'like furniture', and made no attempt to be friendly, using her name only twice in all the years she was there. Another woman who worked on the executive floor for years was equally damning, declaring she found him 'humourless' and that she neither liked nor respected him. Both women preferred Kerry, despite his capacity to behave appallingly. There were many who actually adored the Big Fella.

Friends and fellow executives were much more complimentary about James than those who worked beneath him. He was a 'nice man' and a 'decent man' according to two colleagues. 'I hope he gets to enjoy his life,' said a third, 'because he deserves to.'

But having Kerry as a father was not the surest foundation for enjoyment or happiness, even though it had bequeathed him a $6 billion fortune, for James had also inherited the old man's addictive personality. As he approached his forties, he dieted constantly but seemed incapable of controlling his weight. He would blow out then shrink, blow out and shrink again, bingeing on exercise with his personal trainer, just as Kerry had done. Then he would give up running or going to the gym and get fat again.

He also shared his father's appetite for junk food. After sitting through a slap-up business lunch playing with his food, he would get his driver to stop on the way back to the office so he could grab a couple of cheeseburgers. Like Kerry, he smoked, though not heavily, and was forever trying to give up. He also drank in moderation.

One friend suggested brutally that James should go into therapy to sort himself out. He was more vulnerable than Kerry, this man observed, with no protective shell, and he was less strong-willed. Others simply branded him soft. But he was more complex than that. He was polite and respectful and had resolved not to bully people as Kerry had done. He also hated confrontation after years of having experienced so much of it himself. Yet he was quite capable of taking tough decisions.

In some ways he was like his old man in reverse, observed one Sydney businessman who knew both men. 'Kerry was tough on the outside and soft on the inside; James is soft on the outside and tough on the inside.' This assessment was echoed by Ashok Jacob, who told one new recruit to Consolidated Press Holdings that James seemed friendly but was harder and colder than his father. 'You never know where you are with him,' said Jacob. He would have his arm around you one minute, then cut you off the next.

Happiness aside, James's goal in life was to increase the Packer family fortune. It was no secret that he admired players, movers and shakers and that money was hugely important to him, if only as a benchmark of his success. 'He is so ambitious,' his friend Damian

Aspinall told an English newspaper. 'He wants to make twenty billion pounds or fifty billion pounds. It's the ambition, the wanting to prove himself.'

James tried to discourage any comparisons with Kerry. 'I'll probably be less successful,' he told the *West Australian*'s Mark Drummond modestly. 'My father is an iconic figure and I just think it's totally inappropriate to compare myself with him. My father was a legendary Australian.' But after a lifetime of being slapped down and told he was an idiot, and after four or five years of frustration at Kerry's refusal to let him take the reins, it was only natural that James was bursting to show what he could do.

And he was already planning to take more risks than his father had ever done. Despite being one of the biggest gamblers in history, Kerry was always tight-fisted and conservative in business. James, by comparison, was prepared to back his judgment and bet the farm. Many who worked with him reckoned he was as smart as his dad, and not just because of his extraordinary capacity to work out discounted rates of return in his head. 'He's very quick and not only with numbers,' said one senior Nine executive. 'He's a really bright guy strategically, as good as any I've seen.'

But a well-known Sydney entrepreneur who had watched him closely over the years was not convinced. 'The greatest strength James has is that he is a nice guy, which is something he's gradually losing,' he said. 'You go into a room and you meet some people you immediately know are going to make money. James isn't one of those people.'

Certainly, James Packer had his weaknesses. As those who did business with him soon discovered, one of the biggest differences between him and his father was the speed at which things got done. With James, there was no preamble. You got straight to the deal and were in and out of his office in twenty minutes. 'Kerry would have you in there all night if he could,' says Peter Ivany, who was put through the mill when the Packers bought Hoyts in the late 1990s. 'Kerry put his size 14 feet on the table, in his fluorescent green socks and no shoes, and fired questions at me for four hours. It was like being cross-examined by a QC. He knew as much about the business as I did. I staggered out of there at 8 p.m. and have never been so exhausted in my life. We moved seamlessly from cinema goers in Australia, to Hoyts's assets in Argentina, to the price of copper. He had this relentless curiosity and a view on everything, and even if he knew the answer he still wanted to hear what you thought so he could size you up.'

And here was the rub. James had no interest in this level of detail and not much curiosity. As a result, he lacked Kerry's fine judgment and understanding of the world. 'James falls in love with people and takes them into his inner circle because he thinks they can make him rich,' says a former top PBL executive, echoing the views of others. 'There's no divide between business and friendship. One moment they're geniuses, then they disappoint him and he cuts them off. He also has an unrealistic view of business because it's usually about plugging away, getting things right, and he's just not interested in the grind.'

Kerry loved the grind and was a master of wearing down people to expose the weakness in their arguments. 'He was very good at making you take the decision you needed to take, but didn't want to take,' says one former top executive. 'He was very good at making you walk away.' He was also famous for his warning that doing deals was easier than undoing them, reminding James and his generals that: 'Investment bankers get you in. You've got to fucking get yourself out.'

James not only surrounded himself with investment bankers, he also thought like them. And, because he lacked the deep vein of suspicion that had served his father so well, he was always keen to believe in the schemes that would earn them million-dollar fees. He was desperate to do well, to make more of the business than Kerry had ever done, to conquer the world like Rupert Murdoch. But he was also blinded by this desire. 'He was so intent on being the biggest and brightest and an unqualified success,' says one former top executive, 'that I don't think he could see the dangers.'

It was to James's credit, however, that he had plenty of experienced people to advise him and keep him out of trouble. There was Ashok Jacob, whom many people (including Ashok himself) thought brilliant, plus John Alexander, whom James and Kerry believed to be the best media executive in the world, and Rowen Craigie, the ex-Victorian Treasury official who was in charge of the casinos. In addition, James had greatly strengthened PBL's board by including two of Australia's toughest businessmen, Chris Corrigan (who famously took on the unions on the waterfront) and Geoff Dixon (whose attitude to cost control had allowed Qantas to punch well above its international weight).

But the world had changed radically since his father had inherited the Packer empire three decades earlier, and business was much tougher. Kerry had enjoyed government monopolies in television and his Australian casinos, where the biggest risk was that government would take his toys away. James wanted to compete overseas, expose himself to market forces and challenge some of the world's most powerful corporations on their home turf. Even more dangerously, he wanted to move into countries whose culture he didn't understand and do business with some of the toughest people on the planet—in China, Russia and the United States.

James was also going to make far bigger bets than his father had ever done, spending billions of dollars building new casinos in Macau and Las Vegas. Years of watching Kerry lose millions at the gaming tables had taught James that gamblers never win. It had also convinced him that the house could never lose.

He had done the sums, he knew the maths. He was already making hundreds of millions of dollars at Crown and Burswood. Now he was set to go one further and show his father what winning was about. The future of the Packer business would be in gaming and not in the media. It was a licence to print money, and everyone knew it was recession proof. What could possibly go wrong?

The answer was just about everything.

CHAPTER 20
JAMES'S BIG GAMBLE

It's a horrendous mass-market destination . . . I reckon
they'll end up gutting it.

Ten minutes by helicopter or one hour by hydrofoil from Hong
Kong, the colourful old trading post of Macau is crammed onto a
couple of tiny islands and a peninsula jutting out from the Chinese
mainland. Squashed into an area 1/200th the size of Melbourne,
it would sink into Sydney Harbour with room to spare. Yet by the
end of 2005 it was on its way to becoming the gaming capital of the
world, the only place where 1.2 billion Chinese could legally gamble.
And James was joining the rush to do business there in the belief that
this was an Asian El Dorado whose streets were paved with gold.

For decades Macau had been a dirty little backwater full of
hookers, loan sharks and warring Triad gangs. But in 1999 it was
handed back to China after 442 years of Portuguese rule, and the
new government immediately set about transforming it into an
oriental Las Vegas. It cleaned up the crime, cracked down on the

gangs and invited the world's biggest casino operators to come and help run the gaming industry. In mid-2001 China's vice premier, Qian Qichen, summoned American casino mogul Sheldon Adelson to a private meeting in Beijing and suggested his Las Vegas Sands company bid for one of three new licences to be awarded. Soon afterwards, the competition was opened up to all comers and twenty-one international operators threw their hats into the ring.

Even though James had long wanted to expand Crown's casino business into Asia, the Packers were not among the bidders. It was only just after the One.Tel collapse; James was still shell-shocked, Peter Yates had been overwhelmed by the resulting turmoil, and Kerry was insisting the two of them never be allowed to spend another cent. So the Packers lost their chance of striking it rich in this first round of claims, as the lucky winners soon did.

When Adelson's Sands Macao opened for business in May 2004, a 15 000-strong crowd massed outside and ripped off the casino doors in the stampede to get inside. The police were forced to shut down the huge escalators ferrying gamblers to the gaming floors in case lives were lost. Eight months later, the Sands had made so much money that its entire US$265 million investment had been paid back and Adelson was tripling its size to make it the biggest casino in the world, with five times as many gaming tables as the largest in Las Vegas.

With the lifting of travel restrictions by the Beijing government, hordes of Chinese gamblers were now pouring across the border from the mainland. In 1995, only half a million tourists had been able to visit the colony; in 2004, the year the Sands Macao opened, 17 million made the trip to try their luck. And experts predicted the territory would rapidly overtake Las Vegas as the world's biggest gaming centre.

With such fortunes to be made James was understandably desperate to stake his claim, and by this time he was in a position to do so. He had returned from his Scientology sabbatical, Kerry was pre-occupied with the troubles at Channel Nine and the strategic plan had been prepared for PBL, with Macau on top of the list of places to conquer.

In mid-2004 James got his chance to join the action when he was approached by Lawrence Ho—the twenty-six-year-old son of the powerful Hong Kong tycoon Dr Stanley Ho—who was looking for a foreign partner. The Packers had known Dr Ho for many years as he often played at Crown in Melbourne and was a friend of the casino's founder, Lloyd Williams. And he was undoubtedly the man to know if you wanted to do business in Macau. In 1962, Ho had been awarded the exclusive right to operate the colony's casinos in exchange for running a ferry service to Hong Kong and funding Macau's public works. He had used this monopoly to amass a US$7 billion fortune. Now he had secured one of Macau's new licences and was keen to let family members share the spoils. His favourite daughter, Pansy, had already teamed up with the big American casino operator MGM, and his American-educated son, Lawrence, who had lived most of his life in Canada, was keen to do something similar.

In November 2004 James and Lawrence agreed to form a joint venture between PBL and a Ho family company, Melco International, to build a new hotel and casino on Macau's Taipa Island. Two other casinos would follow, at a total cost of around US$2 billion. On the face of it, the deal was exactly what James had been dreaming of. But on closer examination, there were a number of serious concerns.

The first was that Melco-PBL didn't actually have a casino

licence, so it would be forced to hand over the lion's share of its winnings to someone who did. The second was that this licence holder would inevitably be Lawrence's father, Stanley Ho, who was believed by authorities in numerous jurisdictions to be an organised crime figure with links to loan-sharking, money-laundering and the Triads. Such a close relationship with Ho was bound to cause James Packer problems with the Australian regulators who looked after Crown Casino.

In 1986 Dr Ho had been given the thumbs-down by the New South Wales police and banned from bidding for Sydney's first legal casino (which did not get built). Two years later, he had tried to buy a stake in the Cairns Reef Casino only to be knocked back by the Queensland government. And three years after that, he had again been barred from bidding for the Sydney Casino (which became Star City) because of his alleged criminal connections. Over the years he had also been rebuffed by casino regulators in the United States, Canada, Singapore, the Philippines and Western Australia. In fact, he had been blacklisted by every jurisdiction in which he had ever applied for a casino licence, except Macau.

This was a worry for James because the Victorian Commission for Gambling Regulation (VCGR) was required to assess any partnerships Crown formed (anywhere in the world) and might revoke Crown's Melbourne casino licence if it found the allegations against Dr Ho to be well-founded. For sixteen months, Packer waited nervously for an all-clear. Then he decided to save the VCGR (and himself) further trouble by cutting his ties with the tainted tycoon.

In March 2006, three months after Kerry's death, PBL forked out US$900 million to buy its own sub-concession from another of the winning bidders, American casino owner Steve Wynn, which would allow Melco-PBL to run casinos in Macau without having to rely on Dr Ho's licence. Two weeks later, Stanley Ho severed all remaining links with the joint venture by resigning from the board of Melco International and selling his shares in the company. And five months after that the Victorian authorities finally gave Packer's Macau operation a clean bill of health.

The opportunity to buy a sub-concession was a happy accident for James because this had never been part of Macau's original plans. Back in 2001 the government had awarded three new casino licences: to Stanley Ho, Steve Wynn and a consortium comprising Sheldon Adelson and a Hong Kong construction company, Galaxy International. It had been forced to split this last licence in two when Adelson's consortium fell apart, whereupon Ho and Wynn had pushed to receive the same privilege and had each been granted a sub-concession. Dr Ho had already offloaded his to his daughter Pansy and MGM, and Wynn was selling his to James.

With his Hollywood tan and much-coiffed hair, Steve Wynn was one of the brightest stars of the casino business. Starting as a boy in his father's bingo parlours on the east coast of the United States, he had become famous for 'reinventing' Las Vegas by building bigger, flashier and increasingly expensive resorts. Beginning with the Mirage in 1989, with its volcano and artificial lake, he moved on to create the fabulous fountains of the Bellagio, where his friend Kerry Packer loved to gamble, before selling out to MGM for US$6 billion and using the proceeds to build the casino company that bears his name.

Eight months before his death, Kerry had taken Wynn to breakfast in Sydney to ask if James was doing the right thing by gambling on Macau. Wynn had assured him the boy was in the right place at the right time and would do just fine. But others felt the American was taking advantage of him.

Wynn says he only agreed to sell the sub-concession after being badgered by James for months on end, telling him the price was US$900 million and he wasn't prepared to negotiate. According to Wynn, it was a great deal for James as he would get his money back in five years, but it looked like an even better deal for the American, who was getting much more than most analysts thought the licence was worth. In the opinion of one Sydney investment banker, it was 'an absolutely eye-popping price'. A former Packer executive described it as a 'ridiculously stupid decision to pay so·much'. James was paying US$700 million more than MGM and Pansy Ho had paid Stanley Ho for his sub-concession, US$900 million more than Adelson was paying to Galaxy and roughly US$150 million more than Wynn had spent on his new casino in Macau, which he was now effectively getting for free.

But ridiculous or not, the purchase gave Packer and Lawrence Ho the licence they desperately needed and James rid himself of any difficulty with the Australian regulators. And with these major problems solved, James and Lawrence were able to take Melco-PBL to market in December 2006 and raise more than enough money to pay for it. They found American investors so excited by the lure of Macanese gold that they were able to relieve them of US$1.14 billion in exchange for just 15 per cent of the company. And a 'ridiculously stupid decision' suddenly became a triumph.

The launch of Melco-PBL on New York's NASDAQ was one of the biggest fund-raising successes of the year, and James could not have received a better Christmas present. His joint venture with Ho was now valued at almost US$8 billion, with PBL's 42 per cent share worth around US$3.5 billion, even though they had only invested a few hundred million dollars each and their first casino had not yet hung out its shingle. Such was the madness of the time.

And such was the enthusiasm of stock analysts that hardly anyone warned the odds were stacked against the company. Packer and Ho were coming into the market three years later than most of their rivals and were paying far more to get into the game, so they were at a huge disadvantage. They were also going head-to-head with the toughest guys in the gaming world.

At the age of eighty-four, Stanley Ho knew more about running casinos in Macau than anyone else on the planet and had political connections in China that none could match. He was starting the race with thirteen casinos in Macau, plus another five on the drawing board, and around 40 per cent of the market. He also had a ready-made network of contacts to bring in high-rollers from the mainland.

His biggest rival, the seventy-two-year-old Sheldon Adelson, was almost as formidable. The son of a poor Lithuanian Jew who had sought refuge in the USA, young Sheldon had grown up in the tenements of Boston and started work at the age of twelve selling bagels and filling vending machines. After spells as an advertising salesman, real estate agent and publisher, he made money in the 1980s by introducing trade shows to Las Vegas. He then turned this into billions by rebuilding the Las Vegas Sands casino and floating his company on the stock market. A man of tireless energy, talent, vision and nerve, Adelson was hard on the heels of Dr Ho with his Sands Macao already making massive profits and another, much bigger casino, the Venetian Macao, on the way.

And last but not least—if you discounted MGM and Galaxy, who were also formidable opponents—was the remarkable Mr Wynn, who had earned a reputation as the king of style, a perfectionist and a man who never put a foot wrong. He had already opened Wynn Macau and had another big casino on the drawing board.

But the competition was just the start of Packer and Ho's difficulties. Their first property, the new '6-Star' Crown Macau, was already having problems. Supposed to be up and running by late 2006, the casino was behind schedule and over budget. And when it finally did open its doors in May 2007, at a cost of US$580 million or roughly three times the initial estimates, things got off to a shocking start. The hotel wasn't finished, the restaurants and VIP areas weren't ready and valet parking was not working. Nor had the water supply been certified by the authorities.

Almost as bad, the launch was a public relations disaster. Guests had to walk several hundred metres to the reception on a hot and steamy night, and several important local dignitaries were left off the invitation list. Luckily, it remained a well-kept secret that Packer and Ho were forced to stay at Steve Wynn's nearby hotel because none of the VIP suites at Crown were ready.

Six weeks after it opened I went to Macau to take a look at Crown Macau for myself, catching one of the jetfoils that stream across the water from Hong Kong like trucks down a freeway. I found cranes crowding the skyline, hundreds of day-trippers queuing at immigration and scores of buses lined up at the border with China.

The big new casinos along the waterfront, close to the ferry terminal, were all doing a roaring trade. The Sands Macao, which is designed like a large gold chocolate box with two Daleks on top, was packed with around 2000 middle-class Chinese gambling their heads off on four floors. Outside, buses spewed out hundreds more onto the footpath.

Two hundred metres down the street, the new Galaxy Star World was also pumping. Decorated in garish whorls of gold, purple and red—the Chinese answer to Las Vegas bad taste—it was bursting with mainland Chinese. At several of the baccarat tables gamblers were standing five deep, pushing, shouting and leaning in to watch the progress of the game. Yet another 200 metres away, the magnificent Wynn Macau—with its Versace meets Vegas meets China style—was also humming with punters queuing at the check-in desks and the casino floor busy with wealthy-looking gamblers.

But a ten-minute taxi ride away over the road bridge to Taipa Island, Packer's gleaming new concrete and glass tower was as still as a morgue. The gamblers were outnumbered by dealers, waiters and other hotel staff, and the uppermost of five casino floors was almost deserted with only one of the thirty tables in the public area in play. It was always like this, the barman told me. The poker machines were no busier. There were supposed to be 479 in the building and that afternoon at least 90 per cent appeared to be idle.

Crown Macau's problem was quite obvious even then: it was built in the wrong place, in the midst of run-down apartment blocks and shabby old casinos miles away from the main drag. It was like being in Redfern when the action is in Darling Harbour, or in Broadmeadows when the racing is at Flemington. Why Packer and Ho had decided to build their casino here is a mystery, although it was presumably because they couldn't get land anywhere else. And because of its small land size, the casino was built in the wrong shape for a mass-market venue. As gamblers hate going up stairs and will only go as far as they can see, there is a rule that casinos do best if they're all on one level. But Crown Macau with its 220-odd tables broke this law four times over with its gaming area split into five small floors stacked on top of each other and connected by closed-in escalators.

'It's a horrendous mass-market destination,' one Hong Kong gaming analyst observed bluntly. 'Crown said they were going to concentrate on VIP gamblers, then they open five floors of mass-market tables and, surprise, surprise, they're all empty.' When asked whether the mass-market section would get busier in time, his answer was, 'No, I reckon they'll end up gutting it.'

And that is just about what happened. Three months after Crown Macau opened, Packer and Ho announced they were reconfiguring the casino to cater for VIPs and high-rollers. They ripped out half the poker machines and most of the mass-market tables and started again.

After its refit, Crown Macau certainly did better. It was always an attractive destination for high-rollers because the hotel was fabulous, with a breathtaking reception area on the 38th floor and superb views from every room. But it still failed to do well. Melco-PBL had begun losing money long before the casino opened and it continued to do so throughout 2007 and 2008, accumulating losses of US$258 million in its first eighteen months of operation, which was quite an achievement in the context of a gold rush where everyone was expected to strike it rich.

To say James must have been disappointed by its performance is an understatement. With two-thirds of the number of tables at Crown in Melbourne and one-third of the building cost, Crown Macau had been expected to make at least as much money as its Australian namesake, yet it wasn't even breaking even after interest payments and depreciation. By comparison, Sheldon Adelson's Sands Macao had earned more than US$1 billion profit in three years. And it wasn't just that Packer had come late into the game:

Galaxy Star World and Wynn Macau, which opened a few months earlier, made money from day one because they were on the main strip and got the product right.

The good news for Packer and Ho was that Crown Macau was only the warm-up for their main act, the City of Dreams, which they planned to open in mid-2008. This new casino would be on the Cotai Strip, a big patch of reclaimed land linking Taipa and Coloanne islands, which was even further from the centre of Macau but close to the airport and in the heart of a new gaming hub. Originally billed as an 'underwater casino' then as just 'underwater-themed', it would be twice the size of Sydney's Star City, with 550 gaming tables, 1500 poker machines, 2200 hotel rooms and its own 1700-seat 'wet theatre'. But like everything else in Macau, it was a year behind schedule and US$1 billion over budget.

Most analysts believed the City of Dreams would make James the fortune he was hoping for. As one rival operator put it, 'Crown Macau will make money; the City of Dreams will make money; we will all make money; the only question is how much.' But in 2007, almost everyone was optimistic because the market was expanding like crazy. Visitor numbers were growing at 30 per cent a year and casino revenues were rising even faster, roaring past the Las Vegas Strip in mid-2006 to hit US$10.6 billion in 2007. As a result, Las Vegas Sands shares were selling on the NASDAQ at 100 times earnings and Adelson had become the world's third-richest man.

But not all were convinced that endless blue sky lay ahead. The number of casinos was growing even faster than visitors, and competition was getting much tougher. In the four years since foreign casino operators had been ushered in the number of gaming tables in Macau had increased tenfold, but casino revenues had only risen threefold. Putting it even more graphically, twelve new casinos the size of Crown in Melbourne had been built in an area less than half the size of Parramatta, so it was no wonder some were struggling to make a profit.

Nor was it likely to get any easier because the territory's casinos were becoming more and more extravagant. In August 2007 Adelson opened his amazing Venetian Macao just across the road from the City of Dreams construction site. Dominated by a huge hotel tower that could be seen 20 kilometres offshore, it appeared to have recreated half the Renaissance city, complete with canals and gondoliers. The Bridge of Sighs was there, along with the Grand Canal, St Mark's Square and its famous bell tower, Campanile di San Marco. There were also blocks and blocks of replica 16th century houses.

Adelson's Venetian boasted 3400 poker machines and 800 gaming tables—or more than twice as many as Crown in Melbourne—on a casino floor two-and-a-half times the size of the Melbourne Cricket Ground. But this was just for starters. When its shopping malls and conference centre were included, it was the fourth-largest building in the world. And more was on the way—Adelson intended to clone half the Las Vegas Strip, adding another 11 500 hotel rooms in ten new hotels with five casinos, 2150 tables, 12 000 poker machines and nearly 280 000 square metres of shops, three times the area of Westfield's biggest Australian shopping centres.

It was going to take a massive influx of Chinese tourists to keep all these hotels, casinos and shopping malls busy. Yet Adelson had no concerns. 'Forget about dating services,' he joked to Bloomberg in January 2007. 'You can't make a better match than bringing casinos to Asians. It's just like a person in the desert needs water, these people need entertainment. There's no question in my mind we're going to achieve the level of success we're shooting for.'

Others were not so sure. At the very least, it seemed certain that the huge supply of new casinos would make life tougher for existing operators. Credit Suisse's Hong Kong gaming analyst, Gabriel Chan, predicted in late 2007 that it was likely to lead to 'destructive competition'. And this is what happened almost immediately: a price war was set off by James Packer and Lawrence Ho, who were desperate to attract more big gamblers to Crown Macau.

Unlike Las Vegas, where the profits come mainly from ordinary punters, Macau relied on high-rollers for 70 per cent of its revenue. Most came from mainland China and gambled on credit because they did not have overseas bank accounts and could not smuggle enough cash into Macau to cover their gaming. And since the casinos refused to lend them money because they couldn't collect debts on the mainland, someone else had to do it. This is where the junket operators came in: they found the high-rollers, gave them credit and brought them to Macau in return for roughly two-thirds of the casino's winnings.

Like every other casino, Crown Macau was forced to depend on these powerful junket operators. But what Packer and Ho did in November 2007 was help unleash an even more potent force in the form of junket consolidator A-Max International, which scooped up eight existing junket operators, raised a large amount of money on the Hong Kong Stock Exchange—to increase its lending power—and granted its services exclusively to Crown.

The pay-off was dramatic and immediate. In the first three months of 2008 no less than US$20 billion was wagered in Packer and Ho's casino, more than in any other casino in the world. Crown's share of Macau's high-roller market tripled to 27 per cent, as did its winnings. Naturally, its rivals suffered in equal measure, with Adelson's Venetian particularly hard hit.

But this change of fortune came at a price. Crown Macau was forced to pay A-Max a commission of between 1.2 per cent and 1.35 per cent of turnover, compared to the 1.1 per cent that was previously the norm, effectively cutting the casino's slender profit margin in half. This was fine if Crown could hold on to market share, but as Packer and Ho soon discovered it could not. Their rivals raised commission rates to win back the junkets, and by early 2009 Crown Macau's turnover had halved and its profit fallen by two-thirds. In other words, it was back to where it started, or even worse. Melco–PBL was going to have to rely on City of Dreams to come to the rescue.

While Packer and Ho were placing bets in Macau, they had also been trying to set up casinos outside China with the aim of making Melco–PBL 'the largest Asian-focused gaming company in the whole world'. But in this they enjoyed no better luck. In January 2006, they pulled out of a competition for Singapore's first casino-resort in Marina Bay for cost reasons. In September that year they bid for a second Singapore casino, on Sentosa Island, which was set to cost even more, but lost out to the Malaysian operator Genting International. Thereafter, there was talk of making bids in Vietnam, Japan, Thailand and the Philippines should these countries relax their casino laws. But there was nothing remotely bankable in any of these markets.

James was also striking out on his own. Shortly after Kerry's death he made a bid for PBL to become Russia's first foreign casino operator, signing a deal with Aras Agalarov, Moscow's answer to Donald Trump, to run a huge new casino on the outskirts of the capital. Amid luxury shopping malls, entertainment complexes, exhibition centres and hotels, Agalarov's Crocus City was intended to be Russia's answer to Las Vegas. But Packer needed the laws to change for the casino to go ahead, and in December 2006 his dreams were dashed when the Russian Federal Assembly limited casino gaming to four remote regions in the country's Far East. Simultaneously, Prime Minister Vladimir Putin declared gambling an addiction like nicotine or alcohol, so James's plans had to be shelved after millions of dollars had been spent.

Britain looked more promising, at least for a while. Here, James and his private company teamed up with Damian Aspinall, whose gorilla-loving father had owned the famous London casino that bore his name. When his father died Damian had been unable to hang on to Aspinalls as the old man left his fortune to his private zoo, and the Packers had helped him buy back the casino. As a result—or so it appeared—James and Damian now each had half shares in Aspers, which owned not only Aspinalls but a small casino-cum-nightclub in Newcastle Upon Tyne and two similar venues under construction. More significantly, the company had also won a contract to build a new 'super casino' in Cardiff.

The Blair government was expected to give the green light to eight such casinos in regional centres around Britain, each of which would be about half the size of Crown in Melbourne. And in anticipation of this bonanza, James sold his shares in Aspers to PBL in October 2006 for $92 million. Shortly afterwards, it all went pear shaped. Because of concerns about problem gambling, only one super casino was licensed. Then the prize went to Manchester, not Cardiff. The net effect of all this was that PBL was forced to write off half its $92 million investment. In August 2009 it would write off the rest.

But if none of James's casino bets was hitting the jackpot, he did have one spectacular win which made up for these disappointments, a win that came from a most unexpected quarter.

CHAPTER 21
JAMES GETS HIS ALAN BOND

You only get one Alan Bond in your lifetime and I've
had mine.

Within six months of Kerry's death and James's accession to the
Packer throne, almost all the people who made Channel Nine's
valedictory, *The Big Fella*, had either been sacked or had left the
network. The man who choreographed the memorial service, the
distinguished director Peter Faiman, had also been given his pink slip.

An old friend of Kerry's from the 1970s, Faiman had been hired
on a handshake in June 2004 to improve the station's image and
look after David Gyngell, but late in 2005 he received a call from
Nine's chief hatchet man, Ian Audsley, who told him his services
were no longer required. Faiman asked Audsley what he should do
with the deals he was negotiating for Sam Chisholm. 'Give them
to me,' was the reply. He then got a call from Chisholm: 'Profuse
apologies, terrible mistake. Ha, ha, ha, you can put this in your
memoirs, the day you got sacked by Channel Nine.'

For the next six weeks Faiman continued to turn up for work until his business manager noticed Nine's cheque had not arrived. Told by the accounts department that a Post-It note on his file said, 'Not to be paid', Faiman rang Chisholm, who said, 'We don't employ consultants any more, so you're no longer working for us.' Asked why he hadn't been paid, Sam shot back, 'Well, you're not doing anything, are you?'

Despite having already been sacked Faiman directed Kerry's farewell service at Ros Packer's request, and by the time he finished the job Chisholm was also heading for the exit, to the immense relief of everyone at Nine. By his own account, Sam had done the job he set out to do and had told James he wanted to leave. But with Kerry no longer alive to protect him, it was clear the old warrior had no future at the network.

In Chisholm's place came James's mate Eddie McGuire, the fast-talking host of *The Footy Show* and *Who Wants to be a Millionaire?* He had never run a TV network in his life but was still going to pull down his $5 million salary, five times what David Gyngell had earned for doing the job. By all accounts the idea to appoint Eddie was James's, and one he had first raised in mid-2005 when Gyngell walked out. McGuire, who had acted as master of ceremonies at James's wedding in 1999, was a star whose motto was 'Winning isn't everything. It's the only thing.' This made him just the sort of person James loved.

It seemed a crazy idea to put McGuire in charge of a multi-billion-dollar business, but Kerry had signed off on the appointment before his death and there hadn't been many other options. PBL had hired two sets of head hunters—in June and November 2005—and neither had come up with a decent candidate prepared to take the job. According to Chisholm, three suitable names had been put forward, but none would work with John Alexander. In these circumstances, McGuire was arguably the best they would get. He would be good with advertisers. He was a great salesman. And he had signed up sponsors at Collingwood Football Club, where he was chairman. He was also a believer who would bring a bit of excitement to the network.

And if it appeared to be a problem that he had no experience in programming, cost control or running a TV station, it probably didn't matter because others could do that for him. Eddie would be just a figurehead, while the hard men in Park Street, led by John Alexander and Chris Anderson, would make all the key decisions. Which is presumably why no one at Packer HQ fought too hard against James's decision.

McGuire was told he could develop the business, and claimed to have plans to do so, but if James ever wanted him to do such a thing he soon changed his mind. 'As soon as he got in there, Eddie found he was managing decline,' says someone close to him. 'He was expected to cut costs and sack people and then defend it all. None of this was his forté, but he turned round and did their bidding, because he was in love with those blokes. He desperately wanted to be a big player.'

McGuire's arrival at the network was heralded by a reception at the North Bondi Italian, a hip new restaurant 50 metres from the crashing surf at Bondi Beach. Naturally, James was there and so was Nine's former head of drama, Posie Graeme-Evans, in her reclaimed role as an independent producer. Steeling herself for something she felt needed to be done, she planted herself in front of the towering young Packer and told him passionately: 'Nine is dying. I don't know whether you know this already, but there are so many frightened creative people and they won't work for you if they're frightened.' James gave her a tolerant smile and said nothing. By this time, according to two of Nine's most senior executives, he had already decided the free-to-air TV business had no future.

Soon after the Bondi launch, PBL's Chief Operating officer Pat O'Sullivan was installed at Nine and told to cut costs. 'He came in and just cut the shit out of the joint,' says one executive bitterly. It was great for the shareholders and great for James, but it was terrible for Nine. 'The new people at Park Street didn't give a fuck about content or creative people,' says one disillusioned producer. 'They were only interested in money.'

The new regime made life at the network even worse than before. 'Kerry had accepted everyone would need to tighten their belts,' says Peter Faiman, 'but he believed you could still produce quality stuff in news and sport. James and JA reckoned you were pushing shit uphill and the only answer was to hack away at costs and make TV much cheaper. They thought Kerry had spent huge amounts of money on a business that was dying and a waste of management time. And maybe they were right, but they still went about it incredibly badly. TV relies on creative people and you have to motivate them, give them the right atmosphere, not treat them like shit.'

And treating them 'like shit' was exactly what Nine was doing. Even Eddie McGuire was showing flashes of talent in this area, where his first major achievement was to alienate the extremely able producers of *The Block*, Nine's top-rating show of 2003 and 2004, which had become the most successful series on Australian television. Nine's one major home-grown success, it had been backed by David Gyngell and Peter Meakin against opposition from Kerry, who couldn't believe anyone would want to watch a show about renovating. It was also cheap to make, at only one-quarter the cost of home-grown drama, because companies were happy to pay to have their products placed in the show. The second series had taken more than $13 million in sponsorships and Nine had then made more money by selling the format to seventeen different countries, including the Unites States and the United Kingdom. As far as the network was concerned, TV didn't get much better than this.

At the end of 2005, the two people behind the show—Julian Cress, an ex-*60 Minutes* producer, and David Barbour, the former executive producer of *Changing Rooms*—shook hands with Sam Chisholm on a three-year deal that gave them an increased share of overseas sales revenue. Then Cress went off on his honeymoon and Barbour on holiday. Arriving back at Sydney in early February, on the day Chisholm announced he was leaving the network, Cress asked if their agreement was safe, given that no one had put pen to paper. 'Don't worry,' Chisholm told him, 'I gave my word and it's solid. I'm still on the board of this company.'

By this time series three of *The Block* was almost ready to go into production: the cast had been chosen, sponsors signed, and the producers were talking to architects. New seasons of Barbour's high-rating *Celebrity Overhaul* and *Celebrity Circus* were also planned, so he and Cress were excited and looking forward to meeting McGuire, whom they expected to be sympathetic and supportive.

Their new boss was still trying to find his way around, so it took them an age to arrange a meeting. 'I've only been here two weeks,' McGuire told them. 'I haven't even found the dunny yet.' By the time they walked into his office six weeks later, they were a little more apprehensive about their reception, although they had no inkling of how bad it would be. Eddie turned his back to them, placed his palms on the desk and offered them his rear end. 'I suppose I'd better assume the position,' he said. Moments later, he was telling them Nine would not be honouring their deal: 'I've heard good things about you and I want you to stay with the network, but we're just going to have to start over.'

Cress and Barbour were devastated. But instead of demanding that their deal with Chisholm be honoured, they agreed to wait a few weeks and talk to Jeff Browne, an AFL lawyer who was about to join the network to handle contracts and whom McGuire described as 'a really tough negotiator'. This time they were accompanied by a lawyer, who witnessed Browne's threat that if Cress and Barbour walked away from Nine, they would lose the money they were owed.

This was an extraordinary way for the network to be treating two of its most valuable program makers, but it was clearly McGuire's idea of how big boys did business. It was also pretty much how Chisholm, Alexander and the Packers had treated everyone at Nine.

Cress and Barbour had their lawyer tell Nine they were quitting. They were immediately snapped up by David Gyngell, who was in self-imposed exile in Los Angeles running the American arm of Britain's Granada TV. The third series of *The Block* was never made.

Losing *The Block* was not McGuire's only achievement. He also managed to get rid of Mark Llewellyn, Nine's head of news and current affairs, who had overseen the TV tribute to Kerry a couple of months earlier. And, with Llewellyn's help, he added a colourful new expression to the lexicon, 'to bone'.

Llewellyn was a Sam Chisholm appointee, and therefore was unlikely to live long in a regime run by John Alexander. He had also been the hit man in a failed execution in January 2006 of

Sunday's executive producer, John Lyons, who was regarded as one of Alexander's favourites. Consequently, it was even more certain that he would eventually catch a bullet. In the aftermath of this unsuccessful ambush, Alexander had warned Llewellyn: 'You need to be careful here, very careful. Think about your answers. Think very carefully about what you do and say because I tell you Sam is not going to be around for long. I'm telling you that now. James likes him but Sam's time is over. You need to protect your own backside.'

A month later Chisholm had indeed left the network and added his own warning to Llewellyn as he departed: 'Your life is going to be a nightmare. You are going to have to watch your back. They will want to bump you off and put Lyons in.'

And the putsch was not long in coming, even though Chisholm had incorrectly identified Llewellyn's replacement. In May, Alexander offered his job to the *Bulletin's* editor, Garry Linnell, a very accomplished print journalist with no experience in TV. Linnell was told by Alexander that he would become head of news and current affairs, while Llewellyn concentrated on TV specials. He was also told that Llewellyn was more than happy with this arrangement. This, however, was untrue. Llewellyn loved his job, liked being paid $750 000 a year, and had no intention of parting with either his power or money unless he had to.

On 31 May, three months after Chisholm departed, Llewellyn was called to McGuire's office for a chat with him and Jeff Browne. The first item on the agenda was Jessica Rowe, the ex-Channel Ten newsreader who had been brought in by Chisholm to save the struggling *Today* show and was not doing well. According to the affidavit Llewellyn tendered in the NSW Supreme Court in subsequent legal proceedings, and which would later become one of the hottest documents in the media, McGuire opened the batting by asking:

> 'What are we gonna do about Jessica? When should we bone her? I reckon it should be next week.'
> [Llewellyn] said: 'Are you sure you want to get rid of her?'
> Mr Browne said: 'She's a laughing stock and if we keep her on air we will be the laughing stock.'

In this context boning obviously means to sack, but in its established usage in the United States it means to fuck, perhaps forcibly. McGuire denies using the expression.

Having dealt with one of his network's stars, McGuire moved on to his news and current affairs boss, telling him, 'Now, let's talk about you.' Llewellyn's sworn version of what followed has not been seriously disputed.

> Mr Browne said: 'We've got big plans for you at the network and Eddie and I think you are one of the real talents at Nine. This is therefore a difficult chat, because there is a shit sandwich you're going to be asked to swallow. We want to cut your pay to $400000 and we want you to consider taking on one of two new positions.'
> [Llewellyn] said: 'That's some shit sandwich.'
> Mr Browne said: 'We are being squeezed by Park Street and this is the best deal we can offer. If we pay you more it means someone else is losing a job.'

There was no mention of McGuire taking a bite of the shit sandwich himself or of surrendering any of his $5 million salary, which could have saved a great many more jobs than this.

Llewellyn was also told that along with the pay cut he would be replaced by Garry Linnell as head of news and current affairs and that his new job would be producing TV specials.

> Mr McGuire said: 'I want the two of you to work hand in glove, and together you can turn the network around.'

Llewellyn was no more enthusiastic about being demoted than he was about having his pay slashed, so he asked straight out whether they thought Linnell would do a better job. McGuire dug deep into his kitbag and unleashed a storm of sporting metaphors to persuade Llewellyn to take one for the team. He had already suggested Llewellyn's new role would allow him to play to his 'forehand'. Now he told him:

> Look me in the eye, because I'm going to give it to you straight. I don't know whether Linnell will be better or worse but I think you are being played out of position. I regard you as a mate and hopefully a friend and I want you to be part of my team.

Browne eventually summed up the discussion:

> There are three ways you can play this. You can tell us to fuck off which is not a helpful answer or you can say yes and be part of our team going forward, or you can say you'll think about it, which isn't the greatest answer for us either.
> [Llewellyn] said: 'I will have to think about it.'

In fact, Llewellyn took no longer than Cress and Barbour to decide on his next move, which was to call his lawyer and make detailed notes of the conversation. A week later, with nothing settled and Nine still offering no more than a demotion and a pay cut, McGuire told Llewellyn he was going ahead with the announcement that Linnell would be the new head of news and current affairs. It was a fait accompli.

When Linnell came across to Nine's headquarters at Willoughby for the press conference, he found a war room had been set up next to the boardroom. He was handed a press release, with the grandiose heading 'Nine Unveils Vision for Future of News and Current Affairs', that was full of guff about change, challenges, leadership, innovation and invigoration, plus news of his appointment. At the bottom of the document, almost as an afterthought, came the revelation that this new 'vision' would involve 100 job losses, or one-in-five people in news and current affairs. Even though Linnell was now in charge of this area, it was the first he knew of it.

Not surprisingly, there was a hue and cry over this latest round of job cuts, especially since it involved the emasculation of Kerry's favourite program, *Sunday*, and the sacking of a number of senior producers, including Peter Hiscock, who had made *The Big Fella*. But the row soon got much worse. Two weeks after the launch of Nine's new vision, Llewellyn discovered that someone else had been moved into his office while he was out to lunch. Almost immediately he also found his salary had been cut, even though his old contract was still in force.

By this stage Llewellyn was talking to Peter Meakin, Nine's old news and current affairs boss, who wanted him to join Channel Seven. And not even a last pep talk from McGuire could stop him from leaving. 'I really want you to stay,' Eddie assured him. 'It's like a footy team. If you're on the team, you'll be looked after for life. We'll be blood brothers.' Using whose blood he did not say.

McGuire's entreaties were in vain. Llewellyn told Nine it had broken his contract, and he proceeded to sign with Seven. McGuire, Browne, Alexander, Anderson and whoever else was running the network while James thought about more interesting matters immediately decided to seek an injunction to prevent this from happening. Predictably, this shot backfired in spectacular fashion. It allowed Llewellyn to tell his inside story about life at Nine, complete with all the swearing, boning and bullying. Better still, it allowed him to do it with complete legal protection. He could say what he liked—and the media could report it once his evidence was read into court—without any risk of being sued.

As the two sides faced each other at an emergency hearing in the New South Wales Supreme Court on Friday 23 June 2006, Llewellyn's legal team produced his affidavit revealing all the explosive details of conversations with McGuire, Browne and Alexander. The room was packed with journalists who had come to watch the fun, and they couldn't help but notice how this document was being digested by Nine's lawyers, whose faces registered increasing shock and dismay as they turned the pages.

Within an hour, the hearing had been adjourned. By late afternoon, Nine had thrown in the towel. But this merely served as a signal to Llewellyn to sue the network for breach of contract. He filed his statement of claim that evening, and by this time everyone who had been in court knew that sensational revelations would be a part of the case.

The Packer camp now moved as fast as it could to settle. Llewellyn and his lawyers were called to a meeting on Sunday afternoon and were offered the seven-figure sum they were demanding for the eighteen months left on the contract. But this came too late to squash the affidavit, which was leaked to the online news site

Crikey.com.au, where it was published in full on Monday morning.

If this weren't already bad enough, Nine then managed to make things worse by returning to court and getting an injunction stopping anyone else from publishing the contents of the affidavit. This must have seemed like a good idea at the time, but it was a terrible decision for a number of reasons: first, because *Crikey*'s 30 000 subscribers (and all their friends) had already seen it; second, because the injunction didn't apply outside New South Wales so *The Age* and *The Australian* were able to publish its contents to at least half of Australia; and third, because the stories detailed in the affidavit were bound to surface in the Sydney papers sooner or later anyway.

The sum total of all this was sufficient to make James Packer and his advisers a laughing stock. But they weren't even smart enough to stop there. Their next trick was to issue subpoenas to *The Australian*, *The Age* and the *Sydney Morning Herald* demanding they surrender documents and reveal their sources. One of the nation's biggest media organisations was now trying to muzzle the country's major newspaper groups. As Fairfax's Bruce Wolpe told ABC-Radio's *AM*:

> The implications are breathtaking. I mean, by demanding that we disclose our sources, the Nine Network is seeking to eviscerate a principle that is indispensable to the operation of a free press in a democracy. That a leading media company, such as Nine, would wilfully undercut a fundamental tenet of broadcast and print journalism that you protect your sources is a disgrace.

Or, as the ABC's *Media Watch* noted, it was 'hard to imagine a more hypocritical attack on press freedom'. But aside from the ethics, it was also so unutterably stupid. Even Kerry, who hated the media and Fairfax so passionately, would surely have never been as angry or as dumb as James and his subordinates had been.

As McGuire tried desperately to field the flak, John Alexander was watching tennis at Wimbledon and tucking into strawberries and cream. His close mate James—the man who had put him in the job—was busy playing polo down the road at Cowdray Park. God knows what must have gone through McGuire's mind at this time or what private support, if any, he may have received from James. But to most observers it appeared that Packer and Alexander weren't too bothered about the mess they had left behind. Summing up the mood perfectly, Murdoch's Sydney tabloid, the *Daily Telegraph*, ran a front page picture of James on his polo pony with a banner headline, 'Home James'. The story read:

> Facing his biggest crisis since taking over his father's multi-billion-dollar empire and sacking 100 staff, James Packer has flown to Europe to enjoy playing polo, watch the Wimbledon tennis and buy a $100 million mega-yacht.
>
> As the once-impregnable Nine Network publicly unravels, the media mogul plans to spend the next few weeks schmoozing with clients after touching down in his newly refurbished $50 million jet.
>
> Insiders at Publishing and Broadcasting Limited, the Nine Network owner, are questioning their chairman's judgment, saying his trip and corporate spending are tasteless after embarking on brutal cost-cutting and removing 100 staff.
>
> They say he should really be in Australia to help new Nine CEO Eddie McGuire restore order and morale at the network.

'He's the invisible man at the moment. He's gone from Jamie to James and back to Jamie and his short pants again,' one ex-senior PBL manager, who maintains close contacts with former colleagues, told the *Daily Telegraph*.

The 'short pants' reference was a dead giveaway to a number of people. It was the expression Sam Chisholm had often used to disparage the boss's son. But perhaps others at PBL had reached the same conclusion. Typically, one of James's acolytes was deputed to ring News Limited's boss, John Hartigan, and complain about the article in the strongest possible terms.

As far as the public was concerned, the most damaging revelations in Llewellyn's affidavit were to do with the 'boning' of Jessica Rowe and the exposure of Nine's appalling corporate culture. But the men who ran Nine for the Packers had always talked in this sort of language. 'I have never worked in a place where the words "fuck" and "cunt" were so much a part of the lexicon,' says one ex-head of news and current affairs at Nine. And the brutality of McGuire's regime was no worse than it had been under Chisholm, who had been equally determined to destroy all traces of the Gyngell regime. Indeed, bloodletting at Nine had been a common event since the execution of Leckie in 2002.

It was like watching the French or Russian revolutions unfold, where each coup was accompanied by a purge of the previous regime's supporters. And it was one key reason why the Packers managed to virtually destroy the once-proud TV network as a creative force. Between 2002 and the end of 2006, Kerry and James and their executives had hacked their way through no less than five managing directors, five heads of news and five heads of news and current affairs. It was hardly surprising that Nine was in such a mess.

In terms of performance it was just hanging on to a ratings lead (which it would lose in 2007), but Seven had already overtaken it in advertising revenue. In the words of one senior executive: 'Nine was stuffed. They had cut so much out of it that revenue was falling because they no longer had the programs.' Worse still, morale was at an all-time low because no one felt safe in their jobs, and the station's broadcast equipment was hopelessly out of date. Technologically, and in almost every other way, Channel Seven was killing Nine. Which made what happened next even more of a miracle.

Suddenly, from out of the sky, a saviour appeared.

In October 2006, after ten years of trying, John Howard's Coalition government finally succeeded in scrapping the cross-media laws that Kerry and James had fought so hard to get rid of. Simultaneously, it put Australia's media assets into play by abolishing all limits on foreign ownership. Within ninety minutes of the new law being passed Packer's public company, PBL, announced it was moving Channel Nine and its stable of magazines into a joint venture with a foreign private equity firm, CVC Asia Pacific.

Essentially, PBL was selling half the Packers' old media assets for $2.75 billion. But it was also pocketing a staggering $4.6 billion in cash from the deal because the new joint venture planned to load up the television and magazine group with billions of dollars of debt, just like a 1980s-style leveraged buy-out. Better still, James was keeping hold of his stake in Foxtel (which had a much brighter future than free-to-air TV) and in Seek.com.au, the online job-search site (which he would sell in late 2009 for another $500 million).

There had been six weeks of frantic negotiations behind the scenes—which McGuire had known nothing about—with CVC beating off two other private equity titans, Kohlberg, Kravis,

Roberts and Newbridge Capital, to win the prize. It would soon be sorry that it had.

Almost exactly twenty years earlier, Kerry had persuaded Alan Bond to buy the Nine Network for $1 billion. Now James was getting his own Alan Bond five times over. Both windfalls had been produced by changes in the media laws made with one eye to pleasing Australia's powerful press barons.

CVC's strategy was to cut costs, boost revenue and sell the network again at a profit in five years' time. But it must have been dreaming. How anyone could have thought the Packers' traditional media assets were worth $5.5 billion beggared belief. And how CVC thought it was going to make a profit out of buying them at that price and making further cuts in costs was an even greater mystery. These were supposedly intelligent people, yet they seemed to have no understanding of the shape Channel Nine was in, nor any inkling that its proprietor and his right-hand man believed the business to be in terminal decline.

It was a brilliant deal for James to have pulled off, however. And who was he to argue if these fools chose to throw money at him? Soon, he would be heading to the casino again, to make even bigger bets than he had in Macau and turn Crown into a global brand. But first he planned to spend more money on himself.

Two months after the sale to CVC, word leaked out that he was buying a $38 million home in one of the ritziest parts of London —despite a four-page confidentiality agreement designed to keep the purchase a secret. James's new pied-à-terre was a huge five-bedroom apartment (roughly four times the size of the average Australian home) in Park Street, Mayfair. Behind its classic, heritage-listed Portland stone façade, it boasted a grand white marble entrance hall and sweeping staircase that led to the huge first-floor ballroom used by Sir Winston Churchill for meetings of his War Cabinet in the Second World War.

Originally built as an ambassador's residence at the turn of the twentieth century, it had been used as offices for more than sixty years until it was converted back into luxury housing for the world's super rich flocking to that part of London. And luxury was the word. Lavishly furnished in the style of Louis XVI, it had carved columns and cornices, crystal chandeliers, floor-to-ceiling antique mirrors, white marble fireplaces and carved, pale oak panelling. There was also a huge curtained four-poster bed. The only concession to modernity was a dazzling stainless-steel kitchen and a Japanese bathroom with a free-standing, lotus flower-shaped bath.

Situated five minutes from the Ritz, where Kerry once lost millions at blackjack, and two minutes from Hyde Park, it was close enough for James to pop out to listen to Kate Fischer's father Alistair—who had nearly become his father-in-law in the 1990s and was now a university lecturer in England—standing on his soapbox at Speakers' Corner. But it seemed James preferred to exercise indoors because he was also buying a small studio apartment for $2 million to turn into his private gym.

Not that he needed to worry too much about being recognised if he did go outside. Unlike Sydney, London was full of billionaires, and one of the great attractions for James was that he could blend into the background. As his uncle Clyde had discovered so many years before, it was impossible to do this in Australia, which was why he had fled the country in the 1970s to live in exile in California. Indeed, there were rumours that James might now do the same and live permanently in Mayfair, especially since he had announced he was planning to marry his long-time girlfriend Erica Baxter.

Like almost all of his consorts, Erica was several years younger than James and a model. She had been 'discovered' on a train station in 1992 at the age of fifteen while still a boarder at Sydney's Abbotsleigh School. A scout from Priscilla's, James's favourite model agency, had asked her if she had done any modelling. Soon afterwards, she was on her way to Milan.

Erica and James first appeared in public together in late 2002 five months after the break up of his marriage to Jodhi Meares, for whom she had modelled Tigerlily swimwear. Within two months she had moved into James's Bondi apartment, was going through the purification rundown and taking courses in Scientology.

'She is the best of his women,' one friend reported.

'It is impossible not to like her,' a journalist writing her profile enthused.

But others were not so convinced. Her ex-best friend, Jodhi Meares, was not thrilled that Erica was moving in on her ex-husband. And another woman who knew her well claimed she was 'a star chaser' who was 'obsessed with her own reflection'.

In the early 1990s, Erica had lived in London for two years with Jason Donovan, who was in the grip of a powerful addiction to cocaine. Some years later, she had a six-month affair with Russell Crowe after meeting him in the first-class cabin of a flight from Los Angeles to London. Shortly after that she was photographed topless on a beach in Thailand with Prince Andrew, with whom she claimed not to be having an affair. And in between, she was on the arm of Damian Aspinall at James's first wedding in 1999.

She and James stayed together for three-and-a-half years from the end of 2002, during which time she commuted to Los Angeles for singing lessons and acting courses to conquer her anxiety about performing. And eventually there was talk of marriage. She was in court for James when he was cross-examined at Jodee Rich's civil trial in December 2005 and by his side at Kerry's private funeral at Ellerston. In between, she holidayed with him in the Maldives on the *Arctic P*. But her beau was apparently unsure whether it was safe to commit to matrimony again. 'He didn't want to be a philanderer, because he had seen the damage Kerry did to Ros,' says a friend, 'but he was surrounded by men who screwed anything that moved, and he had women throwing themselves at him. He wasn't sure he could be faithful.'

In April 2006 they split. James handed over the keys to a $4 million house in Vaucluse as settlement and Erica returned to Los Angeles for more singing lessons in preparation for making an album. While she was away, James rang her constantly. 'Mate, how's the girl? How's she coping?' he would ask one of the men looking after her, who would be hauled out of meetings to give an update. On Erica's return to Sydney he showered her with attention, sending truckloads of flowers to her new home in Vaucluse to mark her birthday. Consequently, it was no surprise when they got back together again in October 2006, just after the launch of her first single, *I Spy*, and in time for Tom Cruise's wedding to Katie Holmes in Italy. Two months later, on Christmas Day, James proposed. He told friends at a lunch next day at the Boxing Day Test and the secret was out.

Erica completed her album, which was a compilation of covers called *Through My Eyes*, and told *New Idea*'s Phillip Koch she wanted to write songs for the rest of her life. But the album was not a success, and a few weeks later she announced she was giving it all up to be Mrs Packer and have babies.

They married in June 2007 in Antibes in the south of France, hiring the entire Hotel du Cap Eden Roc for a four-day party. The

Arctic P was moored offshore. Among the guests were Tom Cruise and Katie Holmes, Rupert and Lachlan Murdoch, Shane Warne, Eddie McGuire, Alan Jones and model agent Priscilla Leighton Clarke, as well as assorted bankers, deal makers, and captains of world finance.

The Australian media turned out in force to cover the event, hiring boats to stake out the hotel from the water and toting camera lenses the size of rocket launchers to compensate for being so far from the action. Channel Nine, which was still half-owned by PBL, also had a crew there, which was forced to film from the water or perch on the rocks like everybody else.

There was much speculation that it would be a Scientology wedding and that James would be treated to one of L. Ron Hubbard's homilies, such as 'Girls need clothes and food and tender happiness and frills, a pan, a comb, perhaps a cat'. But in the end they had two services, which were both straight down the line. The first was a quick civil ceremony in the town hall attended by half a dozen friends and family with David Gyngell as best man, for which the bride and groom managed to lose the media pack by parking the bridal car at the front of the hotel and slipping out the back.

Later in the day they had another, more public celebration in the gardens of the nearby Hotel Cap Ferrat, officiated by a female celebrant. According to the press reports, 'Baxter looked beautiful in a strapless, tiered, floor-length white gown—reportedly worth $100 000 and designed by John Galliano of Paris fashion house Christian Dior'. Wearing a long veil, and on her father's arm, she walked down a long, white aisle lined with decorative lanterns to a white silken pagoda whose pillars were laced with fresh white flowers. Overhead, three media helicopters tried to film the ceremony but with little success as the bride, groom and celebrant were hidden by the canopy. Several of the wedding guests also used umbrellas to ward off the afternoon sun.

Four decades earlier, Kerry and Ros had posed happily for photographers on the steps of St Mark's Church in Darlinghurst, smiling at the cameras. But this time the Packer magazines did no better than their competitors. For weeks editors at ACP Magazines had tried to persuade James to give them an official wedding photo, but he didn't even return their calls. Tom Cruise and Katie Holmes had provided a photograph of their nuptials to the media, as had Lachlan and Sarah Murdoch, but James would tolerate no such invasion of his privacy.

It was no wonder he had been so keen to sell his media assets, and not just because he got such a fabulous price. How could he continue to make money out of TV and magazines when he appeared to hate the industry so much? From that point of view, at least, it was just as well that he now saw the future in gaming.

CHAPTER 22
BILLION-DOLLAR BETS

He's got the scent of a guy who has just been let off the
leash. It looks to me like he's overpaying for everything.

The Las Vegas Strip is still the capital of the casino world even if
its annual winnings have been overtaken by Macau. And it is still
the place you have to come to if you want to be considered one of
the world's biggest players.

So it was to Vegas that James headed in early 2007, hoping to
turn Crown into a global brand. He had tried to build new mega-
casinos in Singapore, Russia and the United Kingdom to match his
expansion in Macau, and had been frustrated each time. But there
were still opportunities in the United States to satisfy his ambition
and he still had $4.5 billion burning a hole in his pocket.

Six kilometres long, with casinos and hotels packing either side,
the Las Vegas Strip is hard to imagine if you've never been there,
but chances are it's bigger, brasher and crasser than anything you've
ever seen. A huge Disney castle sits next to a life-size replica of

the Sphinx, a scaled-down version of the Empire State Building rises alongside a shrunken Statue of Liberty, and Roman columns sprout from the top of a huge hotel block in a feeble attempt to replicate the palace of a Roman caesar. It's all fake, of course, but so is everything in Vegas, which is desperately trying to transport you to Rio, Monte Carlo, New York, ancient Rome or anywhere else other than the middle of Nevada.

Of course, Las Vegas relies on fantasy in more ways than one: people come here with a dream of striking it rich but inevitably go away a great deal poorer. And the casinos and hotels are built on their losses. Most of the US$7 billion left by gamblers in the Strip's casinos each year is gobbled up by poker machines, or slots as Americans call them, which can be found all over the city. There are a quarter of a million in the state of Nevada—ten times as many as in Victoria—and they're everywhere: in gas stations on the highways, in casinos in the suburbs and even at the airport. Indeed, the first thing that strikes when you step off the plane is the incessant chink, chink, ching of hundreds of machines with their non-stop flashing lights. There are so many in the airport lounges that waiting passengers are forced to sit on the floor or prop against the walls to make way for gamblers. It's the city's last desperate effort to relieve travellers of their spare change before they leave.

Las Vegas is in the middle of the Mojave Desert, so when summer comes around daytime temperatures shoot up above 40°C, car tyres start melting and the pavements are hot enough to cook your feet. Yet Americans love coming here on holiday, and in recent years they have been flocking here to live as well, making it the fastest-growing city in the United States. Since the mid-1980s the population has grown tenfold, from 200 000 to more than 2 million, putting a huge strain on the city's water supply. This hasn't stopped locals watering the golf courses and building more resorts to hasten the day when the water runs out—currently forecast to be in 2021. Space is at a premium, too. Built in a bowl surrounded by mountains, the urban area now stretches almost as far as the flat land extends. Just about the only ground not covered with houses, hotels, casinos or shopping malls is owned by the government or protected by national park.

When James landed here in April 2007 with a jet full of cash, he was arriving on the end of a building boom that had been raging for nearly two decades. And, just as in Macau, he was forced to pay top dollar to get into the game. Typically, he didn't have the patience or caution to do what Kerry would have done, which was to sit on his hands and wait for bargains to appear. He wanted to play for high stakes and he wanted to start immediately.

Six months after selling his media assets, James slapped down $333 million of PBL's money to buy a 19.6 per cent stake in Fontainebleau Resorts, which was building a US$2.9 billion casino at the north end of the Strip. This was the shabby end of town, miles from the main action, in an area development had pretty much passed by, but the people behind the project were among the best in the business. One of Fontainebleau's founders, Glen Schaeffer, had built the fabulous Mandalay Bay Resort at the south end of the Strip in the late 1990s and sold it to MGM for a huge profit. His partner Jeffrey Soffer had made a fortune as one of the first builders of luxury high-rise condominiums in Las Vegas.

Just before James arrived Soffer and Schaeffer had bought the famous Fontainebleau Hotel in Miami, which had been the height of glamour in the 1950s. A favourite haunt of the Rat Pack—Frank Sinatra, Dean Martin and Sammy Davis Jnr—it had featured in several classic movies before going bankrupt in the 1970s and falling on hard times once more in the 1990s. Its new owners were planning to give this old Miami icon a US$500 million make-over—which Packer's money would help finance—and launch Fontainebleau as a new world luxury brand. This was something James was already trying to do with Palazzo Versace hotels. Three months after Kerry's death he spent $70 million buying shares in the Australian property development group Sunland, which had built one super-luxury Versace hotel on the Gold Coast and was busy building a second in Dubai, complete with fan-cooled beach and refrigerated sand.

Fontainebleau's Las Vegas resort also planned to set bench-marks for style and extravagance, although not on the scale used to measure such things in Dubai. It would have 3800 hotel suites and apartments, 27 restaurants and lounges, a 3200-seat performing arts theatre and a 5000-square-foot chocolate factory. It would also feature a seven-acre pool deck floating above the Strip, called Cloud Nine, that would be the 'ultimate adult playground' with a night-club, open-air casino and a huge spa with 10-metre high cathedral ceilings and artificial rain to cool its customers. The Fontainebleau's hotel suites would come with marble bathrooms, flat-panel TVs, modern artwork and 20-inch iMac computers.

Schaeffer and Soffer were delighted by James's involvement. 'We are extremely pleased to have such a renowned industry leader as James Packer's PBL as our cornerstone investor,' Jeffrey Soffer told the press. And James responded just as enthusiastically: 'This transaction provides PBL Gaming with a first-class entrance into the US casino resort market, in particular, the renowned Las Vegas Strip.'

Two months after the marriage, PBL paid $36 million for a 38 per cent share in an even more ambitious development next door, on the site of the old Wet 'n' Wild water park. Billed as the world's second-tallest building—roughly twice as high as Sydney's Centrepoint Tower—the new 142-storey Crown Las Vegas would be a scaled-down version of Dubai's famous six-star Burj Al Arab hotel. A rocket-shaped spire 1888 feet (575 metres) high, it would offer 4700 luxury apartments, 300 hotel rooms and a huge casino, and be a magnificent way for James to trumpet his arrival in town. But it would also cost US$5.5 billion to build, which Packer and his partner, Texan developer Chris Milam, would have to find. And even as James stumped up the cash, many were predicting the project would never get off the ground. Plenty of developers had looked at the site, which had been vacant for three years, and rejected it. Worse still, Milam had been struggling to get finance and none of the locals took him or his plans seriously, which is why Packer had been able to buy in so cheaply.

A few weeks after buying into this US$5.5 billion dream, James dipped into his pocket again and pulled out $242 million for a 5 per cent share in Las Vegas's leading suburban casino operator, Station Casinos, which owned eighteen properties in the Las Vegas valley. This purchase also had problems. Although Station was a good business, it had just been sold off to a private equity firm which had saddled the company with US$9 billion in debt. So even though PBL was paying cash for its shares, James was punting on a horse that was already carrying too much weight and could easily break down.

To add insult to injury—as far as Packer's shareholders were concerned—PBL did not even bother to tell the Australian Stock Exchange it was making the bet until six months after it had done so. The first anyone knew was in February 2008 when the company confessed it had also forked out $175 million for a 2.5 per cent share in the world's largest gaming operator, Harrah's, which owned Caesar's Palace and fifty other casinos in the United States. Here again, James was backing a high-risk private equity deal in which a staggering US$27 billion had just been borrowed to take over the company in the largest buy-out in gaming history.

Not surprisingly, some shareholders and investment analysts were as disturbed by the lack of disclosure as they were by the deals themselves, which were thought to have been James's idea. There seemed to be no point in spending hundreds of millions to buy into companies where Packer and his shareholders would have no management control and no share of the profits unless these were paid out in dividends.

By early 2008 James had also put PBL into its own debt-fuelled deal, in partnership with Macquarie Bank, paying $1.44 billion for one of the biggest casino chains in Canada. Gateway Casinos operated four casinos in Vancouver, two in Edmonton and four smaller ones in the backblocks of British Columbia, all of which had been put up for auction to the highest bidder. PBL and Macquarie Bank had been prepared to pay more than anybody else in the world and were staking $223 million apiece in addition to the $1 billion they were borrowing to fund the purchase. When this was added to the pile, Packer's public company had splashed out the best part of $1 billion in cash in just seven months. And this was by no means the end of it.

In December 2007, as world stock markets reached their peak, James made an even bigger bet on yet another Vegas casino business. With prices at dizzying heights, his now renamed Crown Limited (which had just been separated from the remaining media assets and floated as a stand-alone casino company) agreed to pay US$1.8 billion for Cannery Casino Resorts (CCR), which owned three suburban casinos in Las Vegas and a racino (or racetrack casino) in Pennsylvania.

According to Australian media reports, these casinos were glorified leagues clubs, running poker machines for the local market. This was selling them short, however. The biggest of Cannery's four casinos would soon have 3900 machines, or more than four times as many as the Penrith Panthers in New South Wales—the largest licensed club in the southern hemisphere—and the group would be running more than 9000 machines in total.

CCR did not publish its profit figures, so only Packer knew for sure whether he had dealt himself a good hand, but in early 2008 word from Las Vegas was that James had paid too much. 'I saw that number and went, "Wow",' commented Anthony Curtis, publisher of the *Las Vegas Advisor*. 'Maybe that's the price of getting into this town but he's got the scent of a guy who has just been let off the leash. It looks to me like he's overpaying for everything.' It was an oft-repeated verdict on Packer's American deals: the locals had seen him coming, as had the owners of CCR.

Bill Paulos, one of the two entrepreneurs who built the Cannery empire, was a silver-haired Greek from New Jersey who had started work at the age of thirteen, washing dishes, before getting his break as a lift boy at Manhattan's Waldorf Astoria Hotel. In the 1990s he worked as chief operating officer at Crown Casino in Melbourne, launching the enterprise for Lloyd Williams, and then ran several US casinos for Circus Circus. In January 2003 he built the first Cannery Casino in a rundown industrial area of North Las Vegas to cater for the residents who would be moving into the new housing that was about to be built there. And despite predictions of disaster, it was an overnight success.

Paulos and his partner Bill Wortman, who had left school at

fifteen to fill vending machines in Las Vegas and also worked his way up through the industry, were two of the smartest guys around, according to Curtis, and would not have sold out without getting 'a real premium on value'. They would later confess to the *Las Vegas Sun* that Packer's offer was 'too good to refuse', with Paulos adding cheerfully, 'Probably ninety per cent of life is being at the right place at the right time,' which presumably included the moment James and his wallet had walked through their door.

But if these two smart entrepreneurs made a decent killing, the investors who backed them had done even better. In August 2005, when CCR needed cash for new projects, a Los Angeles venture capital outfit called Oaktree Capital had snapped up 42 per cent of the company for just US$125 million. By selling out to James Packer, Oaktree appeared to have quadrupled its investment in little more than a year. At the very least, this suggested they had a better nose for a bargain than James did. Most likely, it also meant Packer had paid far too much.

The original Cannery Casino is a $40 taxi ride from the centre of Las Vegas—or an hour in the afternoon gridlock—in an area that was desert until a few years ago. The freshly built housing estates and their shopping malls have names like Fox Hollow, Springdale and Horizon Place, but there's not a fox or a spring in sight. The houses are huddled together behind walls bordering the freeway that stretch for mile upon mile. It's so new out there that there's still a big pig farm in the middle of all this development. In summer, they say, the stench is awful.

The casino itself is a replica of a 1940s canning factory, with steel girders, skylights and slow-turning ceiling fans above the fruit-patterned carpet. In the middle of the gaming floor is a raised area with Art Deco red leather armchairs, lamps on Betty Grable legs and an old-fashioned bar. High on the walls are outsized posters of 1940s and 1950s pin-ups.

Like everything in Las Vegas it's fake, but good fake, or good enough. And it seems to pull in the punters. When I arrived at 6 p.m. on a midweek winter evening the huge car park was already full. Inside, a third of the 1000 slot machines were occupied and another hundred people were lined up for the buffet. You can eat at the Cannery on a weekday for US$6 and walk away with change. The idea is that those who eat will also gamble, but my cab driver told me he brings his ninety-one-year-old mother twice a month and she never goes near the machines. The Cannery also has daily give-aways to get visitors to play the slots. On Mondays and Wednesdays it's a free pearl necklace for those who feed enough money into the machines. On Tuesdays and Thursdays it's salt and pepper grinders. Friday it's the buffet. And on weekends, it's a hand-held mixer.

Most of the customers were African American or Hispanic and many were couples with kids in tow, but few looked old or poor. One or two were leaning on walking frames, but there was little sign of the grey-faced, grey-haired army that chows down in some of the other local casinos. Out among the slots there was the oc-casional motorised wheelchair and oxygen cylinder, but the average gambler at the Cannery looked younger, leaner, healthier and less desperate than in most suburban Las Vegas venues.

Another of CCR's Las Vegas casinos is the new Cannery Eastside, which opened in late 2008. Twice the size of the original, with 2000 slot machines and 300 hotel rooms, it's the best of the group's three Las Vegas properties according to Paulos. Yet it cost only US$250 million to build, which begs the question, why would James Packer agree to pay almost US$2 billion—or eight times as much—to acquire four of the same?

The answer, if there is one, was CCR's new casino in Pennsylvania, The Meadows, which opened in June 2007. Built on an old harness-racing track half an hour south-west of Pittsburgh, it is the only casino within a hundred miles. It also has 2 million people living within a 50-mile radius, guaranteeing it will always do a roaring trade. Close to the border with West Virginia, one of the poorest states in the United States, and with a name that conjures up lush green grass and lazy rivers, the reality is sadly different. The site is surrounded by thin, scrubby trees and steep rocky hills scarred by slag heaps from old coal mines. In the nearest township there are several small brick churches and a collection of grimy weatherboard houses.

The trotting track was run down and broke when Paulos and Wortman bought it in 2006: the paint was peeling off the grandstand, the walls were stained with water, the floors were covered in old linoleum, and big nails stuck through the corrugated iron roof. But two years earlier Pennsylvania had decided to legalise slot machines, and Paulos and Wortman intended to be the first to get a casino up and running.

The day The Meadows opened for business in its temporary home—two huge tents in the middle of a vast car park—1000 people were waiting in line. Over the next twenty-four hours, ten times that number of eager punters pumped US$8 million into the slot machines. They have been stuffing cash into them ever since.

When I visited the temporary casino (since replaced with a bigger permanent structure) one snowy Saturday, there were long queues of people waiting to park. Even with 2000 spaces in the car park and acres of brand new asphalt, drivers were being forced to leave their cars on the road verges. Two shuttle buses cruised the car park and nipped down to two nearby hotels to ferry more gamblers to the front door, where a queue of minibuses was also waiting to disgorge passengers.

It was hard to be sure how many people were inside on the gaming floor, which was the size of a football field, but at least 90 per cent of the 1800 machines were being played, and almost as many people were watching or waiting for their favourite machine to become free. None of the gamblers appeared to be under thirty, more than half were over forty and the vast majority were white.

Almost all had white-cabled plastic loyalty cards that were clipped onto their handbags or belt loops at one end and plugged into the slot machines at the other. This ensured they clicked up reward points every time they made a bet and spun the wheel. Like the rewards program at Crown Casino in Melbourne, the more players gambled the more reward points they earned, and the more gifts they would be able to redeem. These aren't worth much—1000 points earns a free $1 slot play and 8000 points gets a $10 voucher to spend at Wal Mart, Target or Lowe's—but it still makes players feel they're winning.

When I asked a woman on the rewards desk how much it took to earn a point she refused to tell me, saying it was 'confidential', but it appeared that one point was earned for every dollar played. I saw one man feeding US$100 bills into a machine that had notched up 10 000 points, suggesting he had gambled US$10 000 (and probably lost at least a tenth of his money) in a sitting.

Remarkably, the machines at The Meadows also display how much a cardholder has gambled since joining the rewards program. One well-dressed woman in her late fifties, wrists and hands dripping with gold, played a machine that dealt her three hands of poker at once. The display declared she had earned 650 000 reward points since the casino opened eight months earlier, which suggested she had wagered US$650 000 in that time. In ten minutes she lost US$100 and then dipped into her handbag to feed another $100 bill into the slot. Next to her a man who was probably her husband appeared to be winning, but he needed to. His reward tally was just shy of one million points, meaning he had probably wagered US$1 million and lost around US$100 000 gambling there.

I watched another woman on a video-poker machine. Nearing sixty with blue-rinsed hair, she lost US$50 in five minutes. She pulled out US$20 from her purse and lost that instantly, then another US$20 and another US$20, before she eventaully won US$100. But within ten minutes she put that back too. Every time the credit ran out she dipped into her bag and pulled out more cash.

Perhaps these gamblers could afford to lose in this fashion, but the speed with which they were prepared to part with their cash was frightening, as was their manner. There was neither passion nor panic. They were in the zone, lines and lines of them, eyes fixed on the screens, fingers pecking away like battery chickens. There was no laughter, not much smiling and precious little chat, just the ever-present ringing of the slots and the flashing of the lights, 24 hours a day, seven days a week, 365 days a year.

This would have been music to CCR's ears, for the more people gamble the more they lose. That's how the mathematics works, and that's why James Packer likes the casino business as much as he does. Strategy saves nobody, nor does skill. The best anyone can do is slow down the rate at which they hand over their money to the house. The casino always wins, especially with poker machines.

Casino owners defend their business by saying gamblers are simply paying to be entertained and it's all harmless fun. And for many of their customers it is just that: a night out, a few drinks and a chance to try their luck. But there's a much grubbier side to the casino business. James Packer and his fellow operators are fully aware that they make a significant proportion of their profits by taking money from people who can't stop themselves, people who are hooked on gambling. It's this preying on the weak, the sick and the addicted that makes the casino business morally repugnant. And it's the same all over the world, whether you're in Pittsburgh, Las Vegas or Macau. Or, indeed, back at Crown in Melbourne, where James's love affair with casinos first began and where a number of recent cases have illustrated what James Packer is prepared to do to make his money.

CHAPTER 23
ILL-GOTTEN GAINS

A river of stolen money flows into the pockets of the
owners of Crown Casino and the amazing thing is that
no one ever says, 'Give it back.'

Kate Jamieson has never met James Packer, but she's the sort of
person his Crown Casino relies on. She's from Melbourne's working-
class western suburbs, the mother of two young children and a poker
machine addict. And until the police caught up with her in 2004
she was losing $20000 on the pokies every time she visited the city's
casino. Today she's serving a seven-year sentence in a Victorian
prison because she funded her habit by stealing $7 million from the
Bendigo Bank where she worked as a loans officer.

Crown Casino knew all about Kate Jamieson's losses because
she had a loyalty card that she slotted into the machine every
time she gambled. In seven years playing the pokies she racked up
10 million points and earned a truckload of freebies designed to
bring her back whenever she strayed. She scored free tickets to the

Melbourne Cup and a limousine ride to the course at Flemington, as well as similar outings to the tennis and Grand Prix, plus free accommodation at the luxurious Crown Towers Hotel and a chauffeur to take her home after she finished gambling late at night. She was also ushered into the casino's inner sanctums, the Mahogany Room and VIP Slots lounge, where she was given free food and drink and encouraged to lose her money a great deal faster than the average punter.

Crown tracked every single dollar Kate Jamieson lost. It knew she was glued to her machine for eight hours at a time, so its managers had plenty of evidence that she was addicted. But all they did was suck her in even deeper. And not once did they inquire what she did for a living or where the millions of dollars she was gambling might be coming from. 'There's one question they don't ask,' her lawyer Duncan Allen SC told the Victorian County Court in 2006, 'and that is, "What is your job?" Why would they turn a blind eye to that?' he asked incredulously. Was it that they didn't want to know?

By contrast, the people at Crown Casino knew full well that Frank De Stefano was an accountant. But they still didn't ask the former mayor of Geelong where he got the $7 million he lost in its high-roller rooms between 1994 and 2000. And they weren't any more contrite when De Stefano confessed to the police that he had embezzled the money from his clients.

For half a dozen years or more, the dapper De Stefano was a regular in Crown's Mahogany Room and VIP Slots lounge, where he was well known to fellow gamblers as a big punter. And for years Crown Casino treated him like a superstar. When he arrived at the desk staff would greet him by name, defer to him and escort him to his favourite poker machine. They would usher away anybody who disturbed him while playing, and lay on whatever he wanted for free: meals, drinks, hotel rooms, theatre tickets and limousines. As his lawyer Philip Dunn QC told the Victorian Supreme Court, it was like an 'Aladdin's Cave' luring him into crime. 'If you need to demonstrate the evil of gambling,' said Dunn, 'it is the ruination, the fall and jailing of Frank De Stefano.'

De Stefano played the pokies three days a week, sometimes for eighteen hours on end. He would get up in the middle of the night to gamble, lose all his money, drive back to Geelong at 4 a.m., then get back in the car an hour later and come into the casino again at 6 a.m. Crown knew everything about his habits: how often he gambled, how much he bet, what he drank, which machines he played and how much he lost. It had easily enough information to know he was an addict. Yet the casino's managers never offered a helping hand, nor did they ask where the millions of dollars were coming from, even though they knew De Stefano was using his firm's trust funds to settle his gambling debts.

In 2003, Frank De Stefano was sentenced to ten years in jail for theft. And that might have been the end of it. Apart from a bit of bad publicity, Crown and the Packers appeared to have gotten away scot free. And not for the first time, as Terry Lane noted acerbically in *The Sunday Age*:

> A river of stolen money flows into the pockets of the owners of Crown Casino and the amazing thing is that no one ever says, 'Give it back. You do not have good title to this money.'

But De Stefano's most tragic victim, a young quadriplegic named Tom Papic, wanted his money back. He sued the casino and his bank to recover the stolen funds and was soon joined by another five people whom the high-profile accountant had robbed.

Papic was an architecture student who had contracted Hodgkin's disease in the early 1990s and had become paralysed from the neck down by a chemotherapy injection wrongly inserted into his spine. In 1995 he was awarded $6 million in damages by the Victorian Supreme Court. This was put into an ANZ Bank trust account managed by De Stefano, who then forged instructions to the bank so he could withdraw Papic's money without the need for a countersignature.

The ANZ Bank was certainly to blame for the ensuing disaster, but Crown was equally at fault because it let De Stefano settle his multi-million-dollar gambling losses with cheques drawn on the 'Frank De Stefano & Associates Trust Account' which, as its name suggested, held money on trust for his clients. And the casino did not just do this a couple of times as a favour. It let De Stefano use these trust account cheques on 230 separate occasions.

It was no great surprise that Crown and the ANZ Bank eventually chose to settle the case just before it came to court. They also agreed to settle a second lawsuit—paying out five more of De Stefano's victims just before a ten-week trial was due to begin in April 2006—and a third suit two years later. These victories were never recorded on the public court files, and the bank and casino warned De Stefano's victims they would lose their compensation if they breached the confidentiality clauses of the agreement, which remained secret for more than two years. Nor, on a human level, was there any hint of an apology from the ANZ Bank, Crown or James Packer. Not a letter or a phone call or a statement in court. 'Who am I for them?' asks Tom Papic's father, Ivan, today. 'I'm nothing. These people don't care about the ordinary guy.'

As far as we know, the De Stefano case is the only one in which Crown has been forced to return stolen money won by the casino. But it would be nice to think that James Packer considered doing this of his own volition in the case of Sally Grossi, who is currently serving three-and-a-half years in a Victorian jail for stealing $1.7 million from her employers and gambling it away at Crown.

Like many addicts, Sally Grossi started playing the pokies to escape depression and an unhappy marriage. Like many addicts she ruined her life and is full of remorse. A parade of witnesses at her trial in Melbourne in December 2006 testified that she was an excellent person and a high achiever before her addiction took hold. But what makes Grossi's story stand out from half a dozen other cases involving Crown is that she worked as a secretary for Marilyn and Gordon Darling, the well-known Melbourne society couple who have been friends of the Packer family for more than fifty years.

The Darlings had an office on St Kilda Road just round the corner from Crown Casino, and every day Grossi would slip out to play the pokies. She gambled so much that before long she was being given the usual VIP treatment. But she was also pushing her credit cards beyond their limits and re-mortgaging the family home. And then she started stealing. Gordon Darling, who at eighty-two years of age was legally blind and deaf, trusted Grossi so much he would leave her blank cheques when he was away from Melbourne. She paid 127 of them into three different bank accounts in her name, making up fictitious invoices to hide her tracks, then lost it all at Crown.

As ever, the casino didn't know where Grossi's millions were coming from and didn't bother to inquire. But for once, this insatiable lack of curiosity was criticised by Victorian County Court trial judge Justice Dyett, who sentenced Grossi to six years in jail for theft. 'In my view,' said Dyett, 'cases of this sort, which are increasing in number, call for a consideration of legislation which would put the onus on Crown Casino and other gambling venues, to make reasonable inquiries to ensure that large sums of money continually being lost by regular customers, as in this instance, are emanating from a legitimate source. And in default of such inquiries, a civil liability should be imposed upon these venues to reimburse the victims of crimes of this nature.' In other words, if a casino receives stolen money without asking proper questions, it should be made to pay it back. To date no Australian government has taken up Justice Dyett's suggestion.

The head of New Zealand's Problem Gambling Foundation, John Stansfield, made a similar observation about the inadequacy of the law in 2006 after an almost identical prosecution in Dunedin saw pokie addict Christine Keenan jailed for three years: 'This woman stole almost half a million dollars, and the casino got that money. So they profited from the proceeds of crime. The woman herself was punished and went to jail. Her family and workmates were punished, her employer was punished: he lost a bunch of money and a huge reputation. Myself, my family and every other taxpayer was punished, because we paid the costs of prosecution and incarceration. But the casino got to keep the money. Now that's extremely strange.'

In Sally Grossi's case, the National Australia Bank accepted responsibility for half the loss and refunded $879 000 to the Darlings. But if James Packer volunteered to match the bank's contribution, he certainly never advertised the fact. Nor is he likely to because by doing so he would open the floodgates to other claimants.

There have been at least a dozen Grossis, Jamiesons and De Stefanos through the Victorian courts in the last ten years. And there is no doubt that a lot more stolen money and black cash has passed through Crown undetected. If the casino was forced to pay all this money back to its rightful owners, it would find itself in danger of going out of business. Nor is Crown likely to turn away compulsive gamblers, because people like Kate Jamieson, Frank De Stefano and Sally Grossi deliver a large slice of its annual winnings. According to gaming analysts Crown brings in around $1 billion gross revenue a year, of which roughly two-thirds comes from its poker machines. And official estimates suggest that at least 40 per cent of this money is lost by people with a gambling problem.

So what does it mean to have a 'gambling problem'? The experts say you have one if gambling disrupts your life. In nine out of ten cases, it will make you depressed, stressed and anxious. In one in three cases you will think of suicide; in one in six cases you try to kill yourself. You will probably be sent broke, lie to your friends and family, and wreak havoc with your relationships.

Official estimates from the Australian government's Productivity Commission, which published a landmark report on problem gambling in 1999, put the number of problem gamblers in Australia at 330 000, or about 3 per cent of the adult population. But when friends and family are added in, some 2 million people are affected by this addiction. More worryingly, this hard core of addicts is said to constitute between 25 per cent and 40 per cent of 'regular' gamblers, most of whom are addicted to the pokies, which are described by experts as 'the crack cocaine of problem gambling'.

In 2007, Professor Natasha Schull from the Massachusets Institute of Technology explained to an official inquiry in the United States why poker machines are so addictive.

Every feature of these machines, from their mathematical structure, to their graphics, to their sound dynamics, even to their seating and their ergonomics is geared to what game developers call 'time on device' and to encouraging what they call 'playing to extinction'.

What this means is that poker machines are designed to get people to stay at the machine for as long as possible ('time on device') and keep them there till they run out of money ('play to extinction'). 'The reality for most people, problem gamblers included,' says Charles Livingstone, one of Victoria's leading gambling researchers, 'is that they normally lose everything when they play. They're cleaned out in every session.'

Problem gamblers talk of being 'in the zone', where they shut out everything in the world around them. And casinos do their best to keep them in this trancelike state. It is what the music, the pulsating lights and the chinging of the machines are designed to achieve. As is the absence of windows, clocks and anything else that will alert them to the passing of time.

In the United States casinos go to great lengths to stop gamblers leaving their machines for anything other than a toilet break. Drinks and cigarettes can be summoned with the press of a call button, as can a mobile ATM if they run out of cash. Some machines even connect gamblers to their bank account so they can transfer money into gaming credits as they play.

But maximising 'time on device' is not the sole aim of poker machine designers. They also want people to play faster so the casino can win more. Pulling a handle on the old one-arm bandits used to deliver a maximum of 300 games an hour. Nowadays, pressing a button brings that rate closer to 600. Putting coins in the slot also wasted valuable time, so modern machines load bank notes by the wad.

Poker machines are also configured to convince punters they're about to strike it rich. The odds of hitting the jackpot on most machines are 1 in 80 million, which is five times more spins than the average machine makes in its life. Yet players can feel like they keep coming close because it's so easy to get three out of the five reels right (and almost impossible to get the other two).

Pokies are also set up to deliver a large number of small wins that are smaller than the amounts staked. This is called 'cherry dribbling'. But psychologists know it better as 'operant conditioning', a technique designed by American psychologist B.F. Skinner in the 1930s to make rats in cages keep pressing levers to get a dose of sugar. One of the foundation experiments of modern behaviourist theory, it is well known to poker machine experts. There is a famous film clip of Skinner from the 1950s in which he describes Las Vegas's one-armed bandits as the 'perfect operant-conditioning device'. That description still applies today, except that Skinner's 'perfect' machine has been made a whole lot better and a whole lot more potent in its ability to make gamblers keep pressing those buttons.

So does James Packer lie awake at night and worry about such things? Does he lose sleep over the damage his huge casinos do to people's health, wealth and relationships? Clearly not, or he wouldn't be investing his family fortune in building more and more casinos. And he wouldn't allow Crown to behave as it does.

CHAPTER 24
THE TROUBLE WITH HARRY

This is going to be a war, a mighty war . . . I'm going to
fucking crush them.

Like Kate Jamieson, Chia Teck Leng has never met James Packer.
But it would be odd if James didn't know his name because he was
a huge gambler at Crown Casino until September 2003 when he
was arrested by Singapore's Commercial Affairs Department and
charged with one of the biggest frauds in the nation's history. Chia is
now serving forty-two years in Changi Prison after being convicted
of defrauding four banks of $100 million and losing the money in
casinos around the world, with Crown chief among them.

Chia was not a rich man but he had access to huge amounts of
cash as finance manager at Asia Pacific Breweries, which sells Tiger
and Heineken beers in Southeast Asia. He started his gambling
on a cruise ship one lazy afternoon in the early 1990s and did well
for several years until he lost $750000 in one big binge. He then
tried to recoup his losses and lost even more. Before long, the debt

collectors were after him and he became depressed and suicidal. As he later confessed in a letter from his jail cell:

> I began to take outrageous risks. I falsified bank documents in order to obtain funds. Alas, the more I borrowed, the more I lost. Soon, I was placing a million dollars bet a hand and winning or losing ten million dollars or more on every trip. At the point when I was arrested, I was purportedly the second-biggest casino gambler in the world.

Chia's favourite destination was Crown Casino in Melbourne, which rolled out the red carpet for him because he was one of its most valuable players. In the three years he gambled there, Chia was flown in on a private jet on more than fifty occasions at Crown's expense and put up in Room 3918 at the Crown Towers Hotel, which normally costs $25 000 a night. This luxurious 'villa' with its panoramic views of the city takes up the entire top floor and comes with a private butler and a twenty-four-hour 'host' to cater for guests' every whim. Chia lost his money gambling in a special private suite called Pit 88, where he was attended by croupiers trained to play his favourite three-card poker game. He would also have sat at his own custom-built table had he not been arrested a couple of weeks before it was ready for him to use.

During his time as a high-roller at Crown, Chia deposited $190 million into his account at the casino and another $30 million into an account at Westpac in Melbourne. How much of this stolen money he actually lost on the gaming tables was never revealed in court because he pleaded guilty to the fraud charges. And no one came knocking on the casino's door to ask for the money back. But the *Herald Sun*'s Michael Warner was told Chia would lose anything up to $10 million a day at Crown. 'He'd just go flat out . . . it was crazy,' Warner quoted one casino staffer as saying.

As far as we know, Crown's executives never asked where Chia's riches were coming from, or how a mere finance manager could get hold of $100 million. And they had no incentive to discover the truth, because hooking on to high-rollers such as Chia is an extremely profitable part of the casino's business.

Euphemistically called 'player development', it involves paying teams of agents to find and schmooze the world's biggest gamblers, so they can be made an offer they can't refuse. Sometimes, this process is spectacularly successful, as with George Lu, who was targeted in Las Vegas and persuaded to make Crown his casino of choice for a couple of years. The mysterious Mr Lu, who has not been seen in Australia since 2002, ended up leaving $93 million on the baccarat table in Pit 88.

At other times, however, the hunt doesn't end so well, as in the case of Ko Kon Tong. Spotted in Las Vegas by Crown's talent scouts, Ko was persuaded to relocate to Melbourne's Crown Towers Hotel, where he ran a heroin-importation business from his free luxury suite on the 27th floor until the National Crime Authority caught up with him.

And occasionally, things go completely pear shaped, as they have with Harry Kakavas, a Gold Coast property developer who is suing Crown to recover $20.5 million he lost playing baccarat at the casino in 2005 and 2006. Kakavas's statement of claim in the Victorian Supreme Court asserts Crown knew he was an addict who couldn't control his gambling and knew he was barred from every major casino in Australia, yet nevertheless conspired to lure him back to its tables so it could take his money.

It should be said from the start that Harry Kakavas is no

paragon of virtue. He's a compulsive gambler with a conviction for fraud. It should also be said no one has ever won damages in such a case. In a similar British action in 2007, the judge found in favour of the plaintiff but refused to give him his $2 million back because he was a pathological gambler who would have lost his money anyway. However, there is a wealth of evidence to back up Kakavas's case—which alleges Crown behaved illegally and unconscionably in breach of the Trade Practices Act—and there is a real possibility he will make legal history.

In mid-2008, I went to meet Kakavas in his lawyer's office in Melbourne to get a look at the man who has dared to take Packer on. With his wide, flat face, narrow eyes and straight, close-cropped hair, he reminded me of a Russian billionaire or perhaps a member of the Russian mafia. Dressed in white jeans and white T-shirt underneath a grey, pinstriped suit jacket, he was sporting a diamond-studded platinum Rolex, and he was agitated. He sat in his chair fidgeting constantly, every so often jutting his chin forward and rotating his neck like a boxer getting ready for a fight.

'This is going to be a war, a mighty war,' he offered without preamble. 'And they couldn't have chosen a worse person than me to fight. I'm going to fucking crush them. The facts will crucify them. They've got no hope, they can't win.' Perhaps ten times in the course of the next hour he told me, 'It's my money. It's my fucking money. And I fucking want it back,' becoming more vehement every time he said it. I was left with the impression that he was not a man to mess with—which was no doubt the message he was trying to send to James Packer.

Kakavas does have a criminal record, but not for violence. He served four months in jail in the 1990s for fraud, having stolen $286 000 from the finance company Esanda to finance his gambling at Crown Casino, and was charged in 1998 with the armed robbery of a Melbourne restaurant but found to have no case to answer. Nowadays, he makes his money, and lots of it, selling real estate on the Gold Coast.

Kakavas's solicitor, Andrew Joseph, is the chalk to Harry's cheese. A respected, old-school lawyer whose office is full of French clocks, antique furniture and cricket memorabilia, he could hardly be more different to his client. Founder of the Cricket Society in Australia, Joseph claims to be the only man in the world with three complete sets of *Wisden* dating back to the mid-1800s. His walls are covered with cartoons, blazers, sweaters and caps worn by famous Australian cricketers down the ages.

Joseph, who is smooth, suave and well-spoken, and more English than the English, told me he did not expect the facts of the case to be disputed. He was less certain whether the court would give Kakavas his money back.

Kakavas's statement of claim says he began trying to control his gambling in the early 1990s to stop himself racking up bigger and bigger losses. In 1994 and 1995 he asked Crown for help, telling its managers he was an addict who had committed fraud to pay off his gambling losses at the casino. Certainly, there is no dispute that in November 1995 Crown advised him to apply for a self-exclusion order which barred him from entering the casino until further notice.

Three years later, in 1998, Crown accepted Kakavas's request to revoke this self-exclusion order, but simultaneously banned him from the casino, whether he wanted to gamble or not. Crown claimed in court in 2009 that it withdrew his licence to enter the premises (which is what was technically involved) because Kakavas was facing armed robbery charges and had threatened one of the casino's VIP gamblers who owned the restaurant where the robbery took place. Whether this was Crown's real motive for withdrawing the licence is debatable but it is not a central issue in the case.

Shortly before revoking Kakavas's self-exclusion order, Crown's Community Affairs Manager Bill Horman, a former deputy-commissioner of police in Victoria, swore a statement about Harry's gambling problems. In this statement—used by the defence in Kakavas's 1998 fraud trial—the ex-police chief admitted he had personally referred Kakavas to Dr Jack Darmody, a counsellor employed by Crown Casino who specialised in the treatment of gambling disorders. Horman also admitted he was seriously worried about the gambler's sanity: 'On a number of occasions, he talked to me about committing suicide. Later, even when I understand he was obtaining some psychiatric assistance, I had concerns about his well-being.'

In September 2000, two years after Kakavas was banned by Crown, the New South Wales police also banned the gambler from entering Sydney's Star City Casino. By this time, his addiction was so bad he was asking Jupiters Casino on the Gold Coast, Burswood in Perth and the Treasury in Brisbane to prevent him from gambling in these venues as well. Consequently, by 2001 Kakavas was effectively self-excluded or banned from every major casino in Australia.

Of these, the Star City ban was the most significant because it had the status of an Interstate Exclusion Order, which made it illegal under Victoria's *Casino Control Act 1991* for Kakavas to gamble at Crown. This order also made it illegal for Crown to allow him onto the premises or give him his winnings if he gambled there.

However, the bans did not stop Kakavas feeding his addiction. Nor did they prevent Crown from getting him back to gamble.

By early 2004 Harry was flying to Las Vegas and losing millions of dollars, and news of his jaunts was filtering back to Crown in Melbourne. According to Kakavas's statement of claim, the casino then began trying to haul him in. In October 2004 he was contacted by the vice president of Crown's VIP gaming services, Ishan Ratnam, who told him the casino's chief operating officer, John Williams— stepson of Lloyd Williams—was prepared to match whatever he was getting in Vegas in an effort to secure his business.

> John Williams has asked me to give you a call. He's heard you're betting in Vegas and wants you to give our property a chance. You don't need to fly sixteen hours to Vegas when you have a two-hour flight to Crown. We know the type of deals you're getting at Bellagio and we can give you better incentives. Johnny Williams said that we will let you bet up to $300 000 a hand and we will give you a 20 per cent rebate on losses.

A couple of weeks later Kakavas received a second call from Crown's manager for interstate marketing, Richard Doggert, who emphasised how keen the casino was to get him gambling again. According to Kakavas, this call was also on behalf of John Williams:

> Doggert: What do we have to do to get you to come back to Crown? Johnny Williams really wants you back.
> Kakavas: What do you need to let me back in?
> Doggert: We need a letter from a doctor giving you the all-clear to gamble. We need the doctor to say that you're over your gaming problems.

The request for a doctor's letter is of crucial importance, for why would Crown's officers demand one unless they were aware Kakavas had a gambling problem?

Crown denies these two conversations took place. It also maintains it was Kakavas who contacted John Williams, begging to be allowed to gamble again and claiming he was rich, reformed and back in control. But whichever version is correct, there is no doubt that Crown set about getting the gambler back to the tables.

According to Kakavas, Crown drafted a letter for him in October 2004 requesting his ban be lifted and claiming his gambling problems were a thing of the past. Crown then flew Doggert to the Gold Coast to get Harry to sign it. The letter, which is filed with the court, says Kakavas is enclosing an opinion from his psychiatrist/psychologist in support of his application.

In fact, Kakavas did not get a professional opinion until two weeks after this letter was delivered. According to his statement of claim, the psychologist who had treated him in the 1990s refused to give him an all-clear without 'conducting extensive consultations'. Kakavas claims he relayed this problem to Doggert, who told him, 'Just get a letter from any psychologist. Try someone on the Gold Coast.'

Kakavas duly went to see a psychologist at a shopping centre near his home in Broadbeach who apparently specialised in marriage and family counselling. Janine Brooks had never met him before and certainly never treated him for a gambling addiction, and she made this quite clear in her letter to Crown, which began:

> This is the only time I have had contact with Mr Kakavas, as prior to this meeting he was unknown to me. Therefore, I am unable to do an assessment of his suitability for readmittance to the Crown Casino.

But despite this failure to get Kakavas declared fit to gamble, Crown went ahead and revoked its 1998 ban without seeking a further professional opinion. The key person involved in this decision was Bill Horman, who had testified about Kakavas's gambling problems and fragile mental health six years earlier and who had referred Kakavas to counselling in 1995. Crown's internal documents show he made other executives fully aware of Kakavas's history of gambling problems and self-exclusion.

Kakavas claims Crown and its officers knew at this point that he still had an uncontrollable gambling addiction, knew he was banned from all major casinos in Australia and knew he was subject to a legally binding Interstate Exclusion Order, so they were acting both unconscionably and illegally in bringing him back to the casino. Kakavas claims he thanked Williams for 'not letting all my other exclusions affect your decision about letting me back into Crown', to which Williams allegedly replied, 'Harry, we don't care about your other exclusions, we only care about your exclusions from here.'

With the paperwork supposedly in order, Crown invited Kakavas to visit the casino and be shown its facilities. In January 2005, it flew him to Melbourne to wine, dine and fete him in the style to which high-rollers are accustomed. He watched the finals of the Australian Tennis Open from Crown's private box and was put up at the Crown Towers Hotel under the pseudonym Harry Kay.

Eventually, all of Crown's hard work paid off. On Friday 1 July 2005 Kakavas came back to the casino to gamble, having put up $1 million in 'front money'. By early the next morning he had lost the lot, plus the extra $200 000 that Crown allowed him as a rebate on his losses. Despite the fact that the banks were now closed, Kakavas was directed by officers of the casino to a branch of the

ANZ Bank that opened on Saturday mornings. Here he obtained a bank cheque for $345 000, which the casino matched with a further $345 000 in credit, even though this was in breach of the Casino Control Act. By the end of the day all of this had also been lost.

Despite his bad start Kakavas soon returned to gamble again, staking up to $300 000 a hand on his visits and on one occasion losing $2 million in 43 minutes. In the next fourteen months he wagered a staggering $1.4 billion and eventually racked up losses of $36.7 million, which made a nice addition to Crown's annual profit. These losses were reduced to $20.5 million (for the purposes of Kakavas's legal claim) by an extraordinary array of rebates, commissions and inducements and complimentary services Kakavas received, which included free limousine travel, free drinks, free food, free accommodation, free twenty-four-hour butler service and free air travel.

During the fourteen months he gambled at Crown, the casino flew Kakavas backwards and forwards to the Gold Coast and to the Philippines in its private jet on thirty separate occasions. It also gave him bags or boxes of cash to gamble with. According to his statement of claim:

> On about six or eight of these occasions, on boarding the private jet, the chief pilot on behalf of Crown gave the plaintiff a box containing an amount of cash ranging from $30 000 to $50 000.
> On at least three occasions, Howard Aldridge on behalf of Crown delivered carry bags containing cash either to the plaintiff on his arrival at the casino or to the plaintiff's room at the casino hotel, and each bag contained an amount of cash ranging from $30 000 to $50 000.

Kakavas claims he was told by John Williams that these cash payments were authorised by James Packer himself but kept secret from Kerry.

> Williams told the plaintiff that the cash payments were authorised by James Packer. Williams told the plaintiff that if Kerry Packer found out about the cash payments on the jet he would 'kill us'. When the plaintiff asked Williams why, Williams said that the reason was that Kerry Packer was the biggest gambler in the world and he does not get cash given to him to play at a casino.

Needless to say, this claim is denied by Crown.

Crown's first response to Kakavas's lawsuit was to ask the Victorian Supreme Court to dismiss it out of hand. But in December 2008 Justice David Harper refused to do any such thing, ruling that Crown at least had a case to answer. 'Pathological gamblers ought to be protected from themselves,' said the judge. 'There's a social responsibility for operators of these establishments to ensure that they do not actively create harm by their commercial operations.

'Looked at in the light of ordinary concepts of fair and just dealings,' Harper continued, 'it is at least arguably wrong, morally and ethically, for a casino operator by conscious and deliberate policy to prey upon a patron known by the operator to be a compulsive gambler.'

In March 2009, two months before the hearings were due to start in Melbourne, the case went to mediation, but Crown was not ready to make an offer and Kakavas was likewise in no mood to settle. 'They think I'm going to be happy with ten million or twenty million,' he told me. 'Well, they're wrong. I'm not going to go away unless I get every cent I'm owed.'

Kakavas's final statement of claim, filed in October 2008 by a legal team that included Allan Myers QC, who is probably Australia's highest paid and most formidable advocate, revealed he had good reason to be confident. Kakavas had secretly recorded two conversations with Richard Doggert, Crown's interstate marketing manager, that had him admitting the casino's executives, including John Williams, knew about the Interstate Exclusion Order but didn't 'give a monkey's' about it.

Even worse for Crown, Kakavas had obtained emails and memos that showed the casino's managers knew of his gambling addiction, his self-exclusion orders from Crown and other Australian casinos, and his ban from Star City. These also revealed that Rowen Craigie, Crown Casino's chief executive in 2004–05 who is now in charge of James Packer's entire gaming business, also knew. Craigie's involvement made the Kakavas case a great deal more serious. If Kakavas's allegations were found to be true, it opened up the possibility of the Victorian Commission for Gambling Regulation taking away Craigie's licence and perhaps taking action against Crown Casino itself.

And Victoria's regulators were not the only ones expressing an interest in the case. In the United States, the Pennsylvania Gaming Control Board was still deliberating on whether Crown should be licensed to run The Meadows casino, thus putting approval of the US$1.8 billion Cannery deal in limbo. In February 2009 it decided to fly one of its investigators, Steven Tedrick, to Melbourne to talk to Kakavas and listen to his tapes. Tedrick also planned to cast an eye over the Frank De Stefano case and talk to some of De Stefano's victims, whose money had been lost at Crown Casino.

As it happened, Tedrick never got on a plane. By this time,

the global financial crisis was in full swing and a more immediate obstacle to the Cannery deal had appeared—one that involved the Packer family itself.

CHAPTER 25
THE BIGGEST LOSER

Is he in trouble? Shit, yeah. The casinos have been an
absolute disaster.

The financial crisis that shocked the world in 2008 started with
auto workers in Detroit and real estate investors in Miami who
couldn't repay their housing loans. But it was like the flapping of
a butterfly's wings that triggers an earthquake on the other side of
the globe. Before long, the tremors from America's subprime mortgage market were shaking the foundations of Wall Street, sending
stock markets crashing and toppling some of the world's biggest
and best-known banks.

Casino companies in the United States were also being rocked by
the upheaval because they had racked up towering debts that now
threatened to bring them down. By February 2009 shares in Sheldon
Adelson's Las Vegas Sands had fallen 99 per cent from their all-time
high of November 2007 and the world's third-richest man had lost
more than US$39 billion of his US$40 billion fortune.

It was in this climate of fear and uncertainty that James Packer was expected to complete the purchase of Cannery Casino Resorts, even though the company was now worth between half and two-thirds of the US$1.8 billion he had agreed to pay. And this was only the start of his problems—all his other bets in Las Vegas were also losing and there was a risk he could forfeit his entire inheritance.

In a little over a year Australian share prices had fallen by around 50 per cent, but James had done considerably worse. Since the market peaked (just as the Cannery deal was being negotiated) he had lost around two-thirds of his $6.2 billion fortune and waved goodbye to his title as Australia's richest man. His shares in three key businesses—casinos, media and financial services—had shed more than $4.0 billion in value. Sitting in front of his computer watching the markets fall, he had been bleeding wealth at the rate of $8000 a minute, $480 000 an hour, $11.5 million a day. And that was just the average. Some days it was even worse.

Understandably, James was worried and depressed or, as one of his old mates put it, 'in a complete mess' over how much money he was losing. As the crisis worsened, he cut himself off from friends and stayed up at Ellerston with his new wife and baby girl Indigo, or bunkered down in his Bondi apartment. When he did reappear in public he had put on weight and taken up smoking again, just as he had done eight years earlier when One.Tel collapsed.

James was not the only billionaire watching his fortune ebb away. Rupert Murdoch, who briefly bobbed to the top of Australia's rich list, had also shed half his wealth. But James was suffering more than any of his rivals because he took money so seriously. It was what drove him, what he lived for, what had always served as the scorecard of his success in the never-ending battle to beat his father.

Having often boasted that whoever dies with the most toys wins, James was now looking like a loser. Most of the toys he had acquired since Kerry's death were up for sale, including the brand new Mangusta 165 *Z Ellerston*, which he had barely used, and the fabulous Mayfair apartment, which he had owned for only a year. He had cancelled an order for a new Boeing Business Jet and was getting rid of the family's huge cattle properties in the Northern Territory, which his father had built up in the 1980s. Finally, he was selling the best polo ponies, quitting competition and relinquishing the lease on the polo fields near the family estate in Sussex that Kerry had levelled from ancient water meadows almost twenty years before.

There was a mix of motives in all of this. James was getting a good price for the farms and ridding himself of some of the things his father had cherished, perhaps deliberately. But there was no doubt he was also feeling the pinch. In November 2008 Crown tapped its shareholders for $300 million to strengthen its balance sheet, and James was forced to find $100 million from his own private bank accounts to maintain his stake in the business. Almost certainly it was this, and the prospect of a further call when the Cannery casino deal went ahead, that was making him cash up.

'He wouldn't be selling if he didn't need the money,' said someone who had known him for twenty-five years. Asked if James was in trouble, 'Shit, yeah,' came the reply. 'The casinos have been an absolute disaster.'

In Australia, James's gaming businesses were in fact doing fine because Crown's casinos in Melbourne and Perth enjoyed a monopoly in their respective markets and had been bought for knock-down prices. But the overseas casinos were a different story. Having pulled off a brilliant coup by selling half the Packer media empire at the top of the market, James had gambled almost A\$4 billion of the cash in Las Vegas (including roughly A\$2.7 billion earmarked for the Cannery deal). Just about everything he had touched was now turning to dust.

Las Vegas had been hit by the full force of the subprime mortgage crisis with thousands of home foreclosures and a near-50 per cent fall in house prices, making it the worst affected city in the United States. Speculators had bought there because houses were cheaper than in California and prices had been rising so fast. It was not uncommon to buy four or five houses off the plan, with no deposit, then sell them at a profit before they were finished. But investors were now walking away and mailing the keys to the bank, and the majority of the new, empty houses for sale were out in the suburbs where Cannery's casinos operated.

The financial crisis had also hit the Strip, where building activity had been just as fast and furious. In mid-2008 US\$30 billion worth of new hotels, casinos and apartments were under construction— or more than the city's entire current stock—and another US\$70 billion worth was on the drawing board. But much of it would not get built because projects were being abandoned every week as bank finance dried up and buyers disappeared. And the worst slowdown was in high-rise apartments at the north end of the Strip where James Packer's massive Crown Las Vegas tower was to be built.

This 4700 unit development was the first of James's bets to fail. With no prospect of raising the US\$440 million needed to buy the site—let alone getting US\$5 billion to build the tower—James and his Texan partner, Chris Milam, had no choice but to let their option lapse in June 2008. Crown had paid \$44 million in fees to keep the dream alive and got absolutely nothing in return, apart from a large dent in its reputation.

Packer's new Fontainebleau Resort also included 1000 high-rise apartments, but because the finance was in place and construction had started before the credit crunch began to bite, work was still proceeding as 2009 began. It was clear, however, that the project would hit trouble: selling the apartments would be impossible and the world's two biggest ratings agencies, Moody's and Standard & Poors, reckoned the group was likely to default. As it turned out, the end came sooner than expected.

In May 2009 Fontainebleau's bankers cut off money to the development, claiming the project was running US$1.5 billion over budget. Construction stopped, 3000 workers were laid off and several Fontainebleau subsidiaries were forced to file for Chapter 11 bankruptcy. As the legal battles began, Crown admitted it would lose the $333 million it had invested in the group and another $22 million it had lent to the project.

By this time, most other big casino projects on the Strip were also on hold or in trouble. A few blocks away from Fontainebleau, work had stopped in August 2008 on Boyd Gaming's US$4.8 billion Echelon development, with its shell half built, because two of its hotels and the shopping mall could not get funding. And by early 2009, MGM's huge US$9 billion City Center—the largest private construction project in the United States—was also in danger of running out of money.

But it wasn't just new developments that were in difficulty. Las Vegas was also facing a big decline in visitor numbers that was threatening to bankrupt several existing operators. 'Most casinos are now so empty you could shoot a cannon through them,' one analyst quipped. 'It's ugly,' said another. 'It's the worst ever,' said a third. And all agreed there was more pain to come.

Casino revenues had started falling in January 2008 for only the second time in thirty-eight years, and by December winnings on the Strip had slumped by a shocking 23 per cent. In deference to the global financial crisis and President Obama's attack on corporate excess, businesses were choosing less flashy destinations for their conferences or staying at home. Vacancy rates had fallen to 75 per cent from the low 90s, and room rates were being slashed. Luxury suites that would normally cost US$400 a night were going for US$100. Even the famous Mandalay Bay Resort was offering rooms at US$89.90 a night. According to travel agents, Las Vegas had 'never been cheaper or better value', but for one casino operator the competition was so 'devastating' it was pushing everyone to the wall.

In this economic storm, James Packer was not the only one in danger of being blown away. By early 2009, shares in MGM Mirage were down 97 per cent and Wynn Resorts by more than 80 per cent. Worse still, investors in Donald Trump's Trump Entertainment had lost everything as the company went bankrupt for the third time in its corporate life.

On Christmas Eve 2008 the world's largest casino operator, Harrah's, was forced into what Americans called a 'distressed debt exchange' to save the company from bankruptcy. Shortly afterwards, it reported a massive loss for the fourth quarter of 2008 and warned it might not be able to meet interest payments. There was little chance of Crown getting back any of the $172 million that James Packer and his shareholders had punted on its shares ten months earlier.

Things were even worse at Station Casinos, where Crown had whacked $242 million on the table for its 5 per cent stake. In December 2008 Station's owners tried and failed to persuade bondholders to accept 29 cents in the dollar on the billions they had lent the company. Two months later, Station missed an interest payment and filed for bankruptcy, forcing its creditors to take a savage haircut. Once again, Packer and his shareholders looked unlikely to recover any of their money.

This was confirmed two weeks later when Crown wrote off its entire investment in Station and announced it would take massive losses on Harrah's, Fontainebleau and Gateway, which owned its Canadian casinos and where gaming revenues were down 20 per cent and staff were being laid off. The write-offs came to $504 million, on top of $300 million Crown had already provided for in August 2008, which meant it had taken just eighteen months to wipe out almost all the $1 billion in cash James had laid out on these four companies. Further losses were inevitable at Gateway, where Moody's was predicting more trouble to come. (And sure enough these came in August 2009 when Crown wrote down the value of all these North American investments, including Gateway, by another $330 million, taking total losses to more than $1.1 billion and reducing their value to zero.)

This was bad enough. In fact it was awful. But of even more concern was that Cannery's three Las Vegas casinos operated in the same sector of the market as the now-bankrupt Station and were being hit almost as hard. Luckily, Packer had not yet handed over the US$1.8 billion purchase price because Pennsylvania's regulators had still not approved the deal. But he was committed to proceed, nevertheless, losing Crown a further $900 million if the purchase went ahead. This further loss might well threaten the group's survival and wipe out the remains of James Packer's personal fortune. It was in contemplation of this, it seems, that he went on his selling spree.

But then, by a huge stroke of luck, salvation appeared from a most unexpected source. In November 2008, Gretel Packer and three secretive Bahamas-based trusts, believed to represent her three children, asked the Pennsylvania Gaming Control Board (PGCB) to let them withdraw from the licensing process because they did not want confidential details of their financial affairs to be made public.

In fact, most of the details Gretel and the trustees wanted to keep secret had already been supplied to the PGCB, whose investigators had interviewed her in Australia when they were looking into James's application to acquire The Meadows. But she was worried that some of this information—including the names of the trusts and the extent of their shareholdings—would now be available on the net. As the trusts' lawyer told the gaming board's commissioners in a public hearing in February 2009, privacy was the most important consideration to his clients, and this information was not available anywhere else in the world.

As it happened, this claim wasn't entirely true because the existence of these trusts—Consolidated Custodians No. 6, Consolidated Custodians No. 8 and Genetout No. 6—and their role in ownership of the Packer business empire had been disclosed in documents supplied to the Australian Broadcasting Tribunal in 1991. And these could still be inspected by anyone who knew where to look.

It was clear from these documents—and a bit of leg work—that the three trusts had been set up as a tax dodge in 1954 by James's grandfather, Sir Frank Packer, just after he suffered a famous run-in with the Australian Taxation Office. Being a racing man, the old tycoon had named Genetout after the French racehorse that had sired his famous Caulfield Cup winner, Columnist, which he had bred at his Hunter Valley stud.

By 1991 the same three trusts had become the ultimate owners of the Packer business empire via a Bahamas-based company called

Consolidated Press International Holdings Limited, which owned all the Packer companies in Australia for tax reasons. By this time their main beneficiary was Kerry, and it is only reasonable to assume he had passed the baton to his son James when he died. If this was indeed the case, the trusts' determination to withdraw from the licensing process was a great deal more significant, because it was not just Gretel who was trying to sabotage the Cannery deal but James himself, a suspicion confirmed by the fact that the three trusts were the only entities the PGCB was being asked to license as owners of The Meadows casino.

Certainly, killing the deal is what Cannery's owners Bill Paulos and Bill Wortman believed to be the point of the exercise. As soon as the application to withdraw was filed, their lawyers sent a letter to the trustees in the Bahamas accusing Consolidated Custodians International and Gretel Packer of 'colluding with Crown for the purposes of preventing the closing of the transaction' and 'colluding with Crown as a pretext for reneging on the purchase agreement'. By the time this became public in late February they were threatening to sue for a 'significant' amount of money, thought to be around US$1 billion.

Meanwhile, Gretel and the Bahamian trustees were also taking legal action—in Wilmington, Delaware—to have themselves declared innocent of any such charge and to be excused from legal liability if the casino deal fell over. The dispute seemed destined to end up in a long and expensive court case, which would make it impossible for Crown to get licensing approval from the PGCB before its contractual deadline of 31 March 2009.

In these circumstances the Cannery deal would almost certainly fall through, so it was no great surprise when a compromise was reached in which James and Crown were allowed to wriggle out of the purchase. Three weeks before the cut-off date it was agreed that Crown would pay Cannery's owners US$370 million, including a penalty of US$50 million, to acquire shares in Cannery Casino Resorts. The settlement would give Crown a quarter of the company but not allow Packer to receive interest or dividends. It also left open the possibility that Crown could complete the original transaction (while still paying the US$50 million penalty) at any time up to March 2011 if the markets recovered.

News of Crown's dramatic, last-minute escape sent the company's shares in Australia soaring by 15 per cent and produced a chorus of approval from analysts, who reckoned that the arrangement had spared Packer and his shareholders around half the $900 million loss they were facing. More to the point, it had saved Crown from taking on an extra $2 billion worth of debt that could endanger the company's future.

But it wasn't all good news. Packer's push into Las Vegas had effectively been abandoned. His reputation had also been harmed, as had his dream of making Crown into a world brand. Describing the foray into the United States as 'a disaster', Credit Suisse told its clients, 'It may be difficult for Crown to do deals with potential sellers in the USA for some time.' Packer's handshake could no longer be relied on.

It was a measure of the huge relief James felt at his last-minute escape that he was prepared to accept such collateral damage. Now, thanks to the reprieve, Crown would be left with a strong business in Australia, manageable debt levels and a relatively secure future. More to the point, James would not lose the family fortune. Things might still be tough, but with luck the worst was behind him.

CHAPTER 26
DREAMS AND NIGHTMARES

James isn't following the strategy that made the Packers
great.

After the worst year of his life, James Packer looked happy at last.
At the grand opening of his new City of Dreams casino in Macau
on 1 June 2009, he stood alongside his pretty wife Erica at the
ribbon-cutting ceremony, clutched her hand and grinned like a
man who had just won the lottery. That night, at the gala dinner
for 600 VIP guests, away from the flashlights and TV cameras, he
hugged his builder, Wal King of Leightons, and put an arm round
his financier, Rob Rankin of Deutsche Bank. And it was not just
the free-flowing Dom Perignon that was making him smile.

The City of Dreams looked fabulous and the launch had gone
off without a hitch. Better still, as the last sparks from the spectacular fireworks display sank into the artificial lake, thousands of
Chinese gamblers had started streaming in through the entrance. By
morning, no less than 40 000 visitors had come through the casino.

No doubt James felt a great weight off his shoulders. His new casino had actually been built—unlike Crown Las Vegas or the ill-fated Fontainebleau—and he had escaped from the disastrous Cannery deal without losing his fortune.

Nevertheless, as he and Erica gazed at each other like a couple of newlyweds he would have known there was still a lot at stake, and not just in terms of the money he stood to lose. The City of Dreams was all that remained of the international gaming empire he had hoped to create and his last chance to salvage his damaged reputation. The $3 billion question was, would it succeed?

Certainly, it was a brave moment to be betting so big. After five years of stellar growth the Macau market had started to shrink in mid-2008, and Crown's first casino there had been forced to lay off staff, cut wages and ask employees to take unpaid leave. By mid-2009, gaming revenues in the territory had fallen 13 per cent and the other casino operators had all put their development projects on ice.

Less than 50 metres from the limousines dumping local film stars onto the City of Dreams's red carpet, the skeletons of two new casinos and 6000 hotel rooms testified to the end of a gold rush that had brought foreign prospectors flooding in. Originally supposed to open in September 2009, the half-built shells were now surrounded by strings of barbed wire atop corrugated iron fences. Work on the sites had stopped in November 2008, and 11 000 workers had been laid off when the developer, the now much poorer Sheldon Adelson, had run out of money.

A kilometre away from Packer's glitzy launch party, the bones of yet another huge, half-finished casino, the Galaxy Macau, pierced the dull grey Chinese skyline. Due to open in 2008, well before the City of Dreams, its owners had decided it was a lousy time to be punting on the future and had halted construction until business picked up again.

The good news for James amid all this gloom was that his would be the only new casino in the market in 2009. The bad news was he couldn't have picked a tougher time to be opening. Consequently, the City of Dreams was being pushed hard to Asian customers with a huge TV campaign and massive media junket for 500 journalists flown in from China, Taiwan, Korea, Singapore, Thailand and Vietnam and put up at the resort's new Hard Rock Hotel. By contrast, only three representatives of the Australian media had managed to wangle an invitation.

By opening day, Hong Kong's gaming analysts were optimistically predicting the casino would make a healthy $1 million a day in profit (before interest, tax and depreciation), and James's partner Lawrence Ho was telling the media that business was 'buzzing'. But weeks earlier he had described the opening of the new casino as 'crucial' and warned it would be the 'endgame' for the now renamed Melco Crown if it did not start well.

And a month after the opening, reality dawned. The casino confessed its first thirty days' trading had been disappointing: the public had come but not spent money. It had captured only half the 10 per cent market share Packer and Ho were hoping for, and several high-rollers had hit an unwelcome winning streak.

Analysts promptly slashed Melco Crown's profit forecasts by 80 per cent and pronounced it would lose money in 2010 and make next to nothing in 2011. By mid-August the company's shares, which had tripled to $7.00 in anticipation of the opening, were back to $5.00 again, and Packer and Ho were tapping shareholders for yet more cash. City of Dreams managers claimed bravely that business was improving every day, but if the casino was to make money it would either have to take more custom from its competitors, or the market would have to start growing again.

Like everywhere else, Macau had been battered by the global financial crisis. The nearest Chinese province, Guandong, was still reeling from an export slump that had closed 40 000 factories and bankrupted hundreds of millionaires. Gaming revenues were also being affected by the Beijing government's decision to cut back on exit visas from the mainland and restrict junket operators' access to the black-market banking system, which threatened to have an even more lasting effect on Macau's casino business. No one knew for certain why China's leaders were cracking down in this way, but there seemed to be two obvious motives. First, they apparently believed too much money was flowing out of China into the pockets of foreign operators like Adelson. And second, they were concerned that too much high-roller cash was coming from corruption.

Mainland newspapers carried regular accounts of the trial and imprisonment of local party officials, village chiefs and managers of state-run enterprises who had stolen money and gambled it away on the tables in Macau. One such case involved a woman called He Liqiong, head of the post office savings bank in the booming industrial city of Foshan, who stole $316 million from customers to pay gambling debts and speculate in real estate. She started visiting the casinos in Macau and lost heavily, then borrowed from loan sharks at high interest rates and tried to recover her losses, only to lose more. As the *Asia Sentinel* reported in November 2007, she was just one of dozens of officials who had hijacked public funds in this way.

A study of reports in the Chinese media by Professor Zhonglu Zeng of the Macau Polytechnic Institute uncovered ninety-nine similar cases of high-rollers whose gambling losses were funded by corruption. More than half were local government officials or managers of state-owned factories, who had embezzled an average of $2 million. Seventeen had been condemned to death and twenty given long jail terms, while another seven had committed suicide or been murdered. Such people, it seemed, made a significant contribution to Macau's casino profits.

Corruption had also spread to Macau, where at least one senior government official had been seduced by the huge amounts of money on offer. In early 2008 the territory's former Minister of Transport and Public Works, Ao Man-long, was sentenced to twenty-seven years in jail after Macau's biggest ever corruption trial found him guilty of forty counts of bribe-taking that had allowed him to hide US$100 million in secret foreign bank accounts. A year later he was charged with another twenty-eight counts of bribe-taking, money-laundering and abuse of power relating to the purchase of land for casinos that included Packer's Crown Macau and the City of Dreams.

But the Chinese government was not only concerned about its officials being corrupted. It was also becoming more hostile towards offshore operators. In mid-2008 China's Vice President Xi Jinping made a speech in Macau about the need to stand up to foreigners and not let them interfere in the territory's affairs. Shortly afterwards, the impeccably connected Stanley Ho urged local politicians and casino operators to speak out against foreign capital—and Sheldon Adelson in particular—so as not to be bullied. According to one of Adelson's rivals, Beijing was determined to force the American tycoon into accepting a Chinese partner for the Sands Macao and Venetian Macao and had engineered a crash in the market to achieve this. 'The rest of us are just collateral damage,' he complained. Whether this was fact or fantasy, the Chinese government's restrictions were undoubtedly hurting casino owners and there was a growing realisation that Beijing could not be trusted, which was a major concern for James Packer and his rivals.

There were other dark clouds on the horizon. In 2010 Macau was set to face competition from Singapore, where two huge new casinos were due to open. And longer term, there was a risk the Chinese government might end Macau's monopoly by legalising casinos on the mainland in order to grab some of the US$4 billion a year in tax revenue that Macau was raking in.

All in all, Macau was no longer looking like El Dorado. If things went well Packer and Ho might make money, but they were unlikely to strike it rich. It would be base metal not gold they picked off the streets. But if James's dream was not going to come true, it was also not going to turn into a nightmare. He could draw comfort from the fact that his financial engineering skills had ensured that little of his own money was at risk. Most of the US$5 billion invested in Crown Macau and City of Dreams had been put up by others: close to US$2 billion had been borrowed from the banks; another US$2 billion had been tipped in by Melco Crown's mainly American shareholders, while Packer and Ho (or their companies) had contributed only US$500 million apiece. And on this basis, the worst that could happen—in the unlikely event of a total wipeout—was a loss that would not sink James's mother ship back in Australia.

Packer and Ho were also in line for three-quarters of the profits, if Melco Crown ever made any, and were still ahead on their investment even though the shares had been hammered since the company was floated on the NASDAQ in late 2006. Those who had been dumb enough to stump up US$20 a share, however, had lost 75 per cent of their money.

But back home in Australia, some were already branding Packer a failure compared to his father. 'James tried to build a global brand in casinos when the assets were very expensive, and that's not the way Kerry did business,' one well-known Sydney entrepreneur observed. 'Kerry was a pessimistic, neurotic investor who always thought the sky was about to fall in; he was always cashed up and bought good assets when other people had problems. That's how he made his fortune. James isn't following the strategy that made the Packers great.'

In a rare interview in 1994, James had been asked why he wouldn't just put his father's billions in the bank and live off the interest. He had replied: 'If I sat back and decided to sell the product of my father and my grandfather's work, like a leech, you know I wouldn't be able to look at myself in the mirror at the end of the day.' Ironically, he would now be much richer had he done just that. If he had cashed up and gone to the beach when Kerry died in December 2005, as some suggested he wanted to do, he would have saved himself around $4 billion. But there was no chance of him walking away; he was driven by a determination to match his father's achievements and earn respect.

Back in 1994, James had also worried that the temptations of a playboy lifestyle would be too much if he abandoned his quest to increase the family fortune. But he hadn't succumbed to these either. A couple of close friends had fallen out with him because he was no longer up for fun and parties. Like his father, James now rarely went out in public—either to functions or for fun. Kerry had hammered into him the importance of staying out of the media, telling him, 'Don't get ya face in the papers,' and asking him, 'What'd ya fucken do that for?' if he did ever get his photo taken. This lesson had clearly sunk in. He now seemed more determined than ever to avoid the spotlight. And it wasn't just that he stayed home watching movies or cut himself off from friends by retreating to Ellerston, where Erica and Indigo spent most of their time.

At Crown's annual general meeting in October 2008, James went to great lengths to avoid the cameras by coming into the ballroom through the kitchen and banning TV and press from the meeting. At the launch of City of Dreams, he had little choice but to take part in the various ceremonies and photo opportunities, but he was surrounded by security and flunkies and refused to open his mouth. He ducked the morning press conference and would not say anything at the casino ribbon-cutting ceremony or guitar-smashing ceremony to christen the Hard Rock Hotel. The most he could offer was an awkward, 'Great, great' as he and Erica hurried away from a crafty ambush by Mark Burrows representing the Packers' old TV network, Channel Nine.

Just before this, I managed to attract his attention and get him to come to the edge of the security cordon in the brief moment of release after he smashed his rock guitar. It was strange for both of us. For two years he had refused to answer my letters or calls to his office, yet he knew I was writing about his life and I had heard from his friends that he was considering talking. So was he about to offer a private chat or chastise me for invading his privacy? Sadly, I never got to find out. 'Off the record, off the record,' he insisted as he bent down to shake my hand.

'I just wanted to ask you . . .'

'Off the record, off the record,' he repeated.

'I just wanted to ask you . . .'

Then he saw the TV cameras bearing down on him and broke away angrily, obviously thinking he had been set up.

It would have been easy for him to tell the world how thrilled he was with the City of Dreams and how well he expected it to do. But even this was too hard. Clearly, James Packer regards journalists like improvised explosive devices, ever ready to blow up in the face of innocents who come too close.

It is not only the media James has difficulty with. He is also uncomfortable dealing with the public. At the Packers' regular Ellerston polo tournaments Kerry was always happy to mix with the crowd, make visitors feel welcome and go from table to table to check they were okay. He loved social occasions and loved to chat. James, by contrast, choppers in and choppers out and rarely mingles with his guests. Most don't even know whether he's coming or not until he appears. Whether this is shyness, arrogance or plain lack of interest in others is hard to say. Most likely it's a mixture of all three.

But whatever the cause, this inability to talk to people doesn't just blight his private life, it also makes him less potent in business. Kerry in his heyday would have been able to pick up the phone to the Channel Nine stars and producers fighting with his network and charm or menace them back into the fold. James was incapable of doing this—or simply chose not to—and left it to his lawyers and underlings, who all seemed to manage it badly.

Yet it was not always thus. Back in the 1990s when the Super League war was raging he was good at making personal appeals to players who needed to be talked onside. So what has changed? Is he bruised by the way the world has treated him, by the burden of being a Packer, or has he become contemptuous of those who aren't loyal members of his tribe?

One man who knows James from those days says, 'I think hubris has taken over. At the time I knew him he was confident but always looking for information. Now he seems delighted with his own views and doesn't appear very interested in what anybody else might say. You might say Kerry was like that but he wasn't. He was always talking to people, listening and learning. I thought James was going to be absolutely terrific.' He shakes his head and sighs. 'Maybe he still will be.'

Similar shortcomings appear to have stopped James from heading off Harry Kakavas, whose lawsuit finally came to court in the winter of 2009. Kakavas maintains that an apology and an offer to settle would have avoided damaging publicity and possibly an even more damaging defeat. Kerry would have dealt with it quickly, man to man, Kakavas believes. But James has not been able to pick up the phone.

Perhaps this was because he didn't see the need. Perhaps his advisers were telling him Kakavas was a blackmailer who could not possibly win. Perhaps they were assuring him no casino had ever lost such a case so he did not need to worry.

All the same, Kerry would surely have asked why Kakavas and his highly paid legal team were going ahead with an expensive lawsuit if they truly had no chance of winning. He would also have interrogated his executives ruthlessly to discover whether Crown had behaved as Kakavas alleged. It was hard to believe that James had done either of these things. And, watching the trial unfold in a cold Melbourne courtroom, it was hard to comprehend why he had chosen to fight. The evidence provided by the company's own internal documents was so strong that Crown seemed to be denying facts that could not be denied. Even if Packer's company managed to avoid paying damages, it seemed certain to suffer a barrage of negative publicity.

The casino's defence was also remarkably undisciplined, with witnesses contradicting each other, denying claims made by Crown's QC Neil Young, and suffering disturbing lapses of memory. Former chief executive Rowen Craigie was nervous and unconvincing, and ex-chief operating officer John Williams was even worse.

The casino's head of community affairs Bill Horman was also unimpressive. The one-time traffic cop was clearly practised in the art of giving evidence, but he didn't convince the journalists covering the case that he was telling the truth, and some of his testimony was frankly incredible. He refused to admit knowing that Kakavas had a gambling problem, even though he had personally referred the gambler to Crown's counselling service in 1995 and had spoken to two of his doctors, who both believed Kakavas to be an addict. How did Horman explain his ignorance? He simply refused to accept the doctors' diagnoses, even though he was the first to point out that he lacked the qualifications to do so.

But Crown's Waterloo came when John Williams took the stand. It was Williams who had allegedly taken the decision to lure Harry back to gamble and Williams who had asked Horman to draft a letter for Kakavas requesting the ban on him be lifted. In his evidence, Williams insisted it was Kakavas who had badgered the casino to let him back to the tables and Kakavas who had set the whole process in motion. But it did not take long for Kakavas's QC, Allan Myers, to punch holes in Williams's story.

Williams was forced to concede that Crown's interest in Kakavas had been stirred in May 2004 by a phone call from Kerry Packer's friend, Ben Tilley, who was playing the tables in Las Vegas. Tilley had delivered a message that Kakavas was punting there and wagering huge amounts of money.

More calls from Las Vegas followed in October 2004, including one from casino mogul Steve Wynn and at least one more from Ben Tilley. Even more significantly there was now a call from Kerry Packer himself, demanding to know why Kakavas wasn't losing millions of dollars at Crown instead.

The language in which this question was expressed would have been colourful. And Williams would no doubt have reacted as everyone in the Packer fiefdom did to a call from Kerry. Shortly afterwards, on 27 October 2004, he sent out a four-line email to Bill Horman and the head of Crown's VIP gaming, Howard Aldridge, which he copied to Rowen Craigie:

> Harry Kakavas has apparently dropped between $3 million and $4 million in Vegas last week. Bill and Howard can you please get a draft copy of the letter in which it would take [sic] for Harry to be let back into Crown. I will then discuss with Rowen.

The process of hauling Harry back then began. According to Crown's phone records Williams rang the vice president of Crown's VIP services, Ishan Ratnam, who immediately made two attempts to ring Tony Khoury, a close friend of both him and Kakavas. Myers put it to Williams that he was asking Ratnam to find Kakavas's contact details so he could invite him back to the casino. Williams claimed to remember nothing about this, as the court transcripts show.

> Myers: You asked Mr Ratnam to get Mr Kakavas' telephone number for you, didn't you?
> Williams: I can't recall.
> Myers: Mr Williams, is that an honest answer?
> Williams: Yes.

Myers: Did you ever ask Mr Ratnam to get in contact with
Mr Kakavas?
Williams: Possibly.
Myers: Why do you say possibly; either you remember it or you
don't, sir?
Williams: I don't remember it, no.
Myers: Let me put a slightly different version of it to you: did
you ask Mr Ratnam on 27 October to get Mr Kakavas' contact
details?
Williams: Not that I can recall.
Myers: Do you deny that that happened?
Williams: I can't recall it.
Myers: Mr Williams, at any time did you ask Mr Ratnam to get
Mr Kakavas' contact details?
Williams: Not that I can recall.
Myers: At no time at all?
Williams: Not that I can recall.

But the very next day, Ratnam took the stand and filled the gaps
in his boss's memory, admitting that Williams had asked him to do
exactly as Myers had suggested. 'John Williams asked me to get
Harry's number. I rang Tony Khoury. He rang me back and he did
give me Harry's number and I did ring Harry.'

Listening to four weeks of evidence, it seemed pretty clear what
had happened. From 1995 to 2001, Crown had prevented Kakavas
from entering the casino and rebuffed all his attempts to be re-
admitted, whereupon he had essentially given up trying to get back
and gambled elsewhere. Then, in 2004, all this had changed with
the phone calls from Las Vegas and Kerry in particular. It seems fair
to speculate the Big Fella might have said something like: 'There's a

fucking Australian here called Harry Kakavas who's losing millions of dollars. Why the fuck haven't you got him at Crown?' And in the rush to do their master's bidding, prudence was abandoned. It's also fair to say Williams denies this is what happened.

Doubtless, Justice Harper won't allow himself the indulgence of speculation when he reaches his verdict, but even before Ratnam took the stand the judge was giving the court an insight into his thinking: 'I am presently of the view that there is evidence upon which I could conclude that Crown, knowing that Mr Kakavas was subject to an Interstate Exclusion Order, nevertheless allowed—went further than that—encouraged Mr Kakavas to enter the casino and gamble.' If Harper were to make such a finding he could also find that Crown knowingly broke the law, which would put Harry Kakavas well on the way to winning his case and making legal history. So what would happen then?

For a start, Crown could be ordered to pay more than $20 million in damages. It might also be pursued by the Victorian government for some of the $700 million gross it won from Kakavas. Worse still, the Victorian Council for Gambling Regulation (VCGR) might conclude that Crown was unfit to hold its casino licence. The VCGR was sufficiently concerned about the case to have someone in court taking notes throughout the trial.

Multi-million-dollar damages, big payments to the state and the loss of Crown's licence constitute a worst-case scenario, and it possibly won't come to that. Kakavas may well lose and Victoria's casino watchdog may be loath to bite the state's biggest taxpayer. However, even if Crown escapes unharmed, James Packer was surely unwise to expose his company to the risk of losing its livelihood. The Australian gaming business, after all, is the rock on which his entire fortune now rests.

It was also the worst moment for Crown to let the allegations about its business practices to be aired in public. In October 2009, Australia's Productivity Commission was due to deliver what threatened to be a damning report on how problem gambling could be reduced. With its potential to influence the political agenda, this was hardly the best time for Crown and Kakavas to be on the front page.

All in all, James's management of the Kakavas suit appeared to be another example of the poor judgment, overconfidence and lack of attention to detail that had been evident in the One.Tel disaster in 2001 and in his plans to double the family fortune by building an international gaming empire. Having lost $1 billion betting on casinos in Las Vegas and having narrowly escaped losing another $1 billion on the Cannery deal, and with his Macau venture still in the balance, James had allowed his hugely profitable Australian gaming business to be put into play.

It was not surprising, perhaps, that the team of analysts at online newsletter *The Intelligent Investor* listed Packer's management as a key reason not to buy Crown's shares. And they were not alone in their doubts. 'I don't think James will be the richest man in Australia in five years' time,' one of his old school buddies predicted. 'I think he'll be in the top ten. The others will have good growth rates and his will be mediocre.'

There are those, however, who remain confident that James Packer will still come good. 'He has been through some tough times but I think he's over them and in the next decade his contribution will be quite substantial,' says Jeff Kennett, Victoria's ex-premier, who continues to see James and counts him as a friend. 'The last ten years have been very difficult for him. Being part of the Packer family, which has been so dominant in Australian history, and being Kerry's son, I think it's been very tough for him personally. He's had a few learning experiences since then but I think they will stand him in good stead for the future.'

Even if James does bounce back, it is not clear he can recover the $2.6 billion he was still losing (in early September 2009) from the meltdown on stock markets. Nor is his future happiness assured. He seems destined to follow his father in so many ways. And he struggles with the same demons.

When he appeared at the City of Dreams in June, after nine months out of the public eye, it was a shock to see how much he had bulked up. With his puffy cheeks and deep-set eyes, he looked as large as Kerry had ever been. 'He has a shocking diet, he takes no exercise, he's very overweight,' says one of his close friends. 'He's just like his dad, who had his first heart attack at forty-six, and he won't do anything about it. He needs to go overseas and get away from the fishbowl. He hates being in the public eye because he doesn't like himself. And he's more vulnerable than Kerry because he has no protective shell.'

'He is very hard on himself. He feels a lot of pressure and at the moment he is under a lot of pressure,' says another friend who has known him for many years. 'I'm sure he's hating life at the moment. He's a nice guy and a good person. I feel for him.'

Like Kerry, James is a lonely man who is becoming increasingly reclusive. Like Kerry, too, he is obsessed with proving his worth. Perhaps even more than his father, he appears to believe in nothing except making money. He has no dreams of advancing technology, like Bill Gates of Microsoft, or of sharing his massive fortune like many American entrepreneurs. Nor does he crave power and influence like Rupert Murdoch. As far as can be told, he brings no emotion to the running of his businesses or the pursuit of his goals.

He is interested only in the numbers. He wants to be a billionaire and he wants the score to show he's a success.

So far, luck has not been on James's side. He inherited the Packer fortune on the eve of the biggest financial meltdown the world has seen since 1929. But despite a close call or two he is still in the game. And after all his billion-dollar losses and defeats, James Packer is doubly determined not to quit.

NOTES

PROLOGUE

Page 1: 'Is he in financial trouble? Shit, yeah', family friend of the Packers on James's asset sales, 2009.

Page 1: At the peak of the market in November 2007, James Packer's share holdings in his three key public companies—Crown Limited, Consolidated Media Holdings and Challenger Financial Group—were worth just under $6.0 billion. By November 2008, they were worth around $2.0 billion. He had also $170 million on his shareholdings in three other publicly-listed companies, Sunland, Ellerston Gems Fund and Magellan Flagship Fund. The value of his shareholdings declined further in February and March 2009, before recovering in April.

Page 3: 'In a way I'm sort of proud . . .', Gerry Harvey to author, 'A Perfect Storm', *Four Corners*, ABC-TV, 9 February 2009.

CHAPTER 1   MUMMY'S BOY

Page 5: 'I want them to know only one thing . . .', Kerry Packer in Terry Lane, ed., *As the Twig is Bent*, Dove Communications, Melbourne 1979.

Page 5: 'I think boarding school is very important for kids', Kerry Packer, *Parkinson in Australia*, ABC-TV, 1979.

Page 8: He was also quite definitely not dyslexic, despite the claims he and Kerry have made over the years. In 1998 James told the Australian

Broadcasting Authority, 'I am not trying to be a smartarse, I am dyslexic, I find it hard to remember what I did yesterday.' Australian Broadcasting Authority, *CPH, PBL, John Fairfax Holdings Limited,* Hearing Volume Number 2, 9 June 1998, p. 29.

Page 9: Malcolm Knox, 'Clive, Viv, Jamie and me', *Sydney Morning Herald,* 28 December 2007.

Page 19: 'There was this almost ridiculous obsequiousness around him . . .', Richard Guilliatt, 'Shadow on the son', Good Weekend, *Sydney Morning Herald,* 5 May 2003.

CHAPTER 2   FUCKING STUPID

Page 23: 'That's a fucking stupid idea . . .', Kerry Packer to James, circa 1990.

Page 24: 'nothing but trouble', Lindsay McLean to author.

Page 25: 'He hated the early starts and he hated washing in the turkey nests', Brian Nillson to author.

Page 26: The housekeeper took pity on him and did his washing, Liz Rae to author.

Page 26: 'one of the most well-mannered lads', Dick Wilson to author.

Page 27: 'There have been times when my pampering has been taken away . . .', Peter FitzSimons, 'James Packer: The interview', *Sydney Morning Herald,* 10 September 1994.

Page 28: 'beat him up and make his life a misery', Graham Lawrence to author; 'a good flogging', Peter Miller to author.

Page 31: 'I'm sending my fucking son over . . .', Rene Rivkin interview with Andrew Denton, *Enough Rope,* ABC-TV, 5 May 2003.

Page 33: 'I am not your friend . . .', Jasper Gerard, 'A blade who loves girls and gorillas', *London Sunday Times,* 22 October 2000.

Page 34: 'My life is over. I've broken up with Tania', Al Dunlap to author.

Page 34: 'My feeling was he hated it and wanted to know why the fuck he was here', Steve Wood to author.

Page 36: 'I liked Ros. She put up with a hell of a lot . . .', Judy Dunlap to author.

CHAPTER 3   HIS FATHER'S SON

Page 37: 'Jamie was a ludicrously gentle boy . . .', Phillip Adams, quoted in Muriel Reddy, 'In his father's footsteps', *The Sunday Age*, 9 May 1992.

Page 41: John Byrne, *Chainsaw: The notorious career of Al Dunlap in the era of profit at any price*, Harper Business, New York, 1999.

Page 45: 'James would not get in when others got into work . . .', Richard Walsh to author.

Page 46: 'the best of his parents' fine qualities', Reddy, 'In his father's footsteps'.

CHAPTER 4   CHIP OFF THE OLD BLOCK

Page 50: 'I don't *give* guarantees to governments, I *get* them', Kerry Packer to the NSW Casino Control Commission.

Page 51: 'He's doing a terrific job', *A Current Affair*, Channel Nine, 16 February 1995.

Page 54: 'The old man told me to ring . . .', Sally Neighbour, 'Packer and the Sydney Casino', *Four Corners*, ABC-TV, 7 April 1997.

Page 55: 'co-operate' and not 'fight', Neil Chenoweth, *Packer's Lunch: A rollicking tale of Swiss bank accounts and money-making adventurers in the roaring '90s*, Allen & Unwin, Sydney, 2006, p. 166.

Page 56: Pam Walkley, 'All eyes on the play for Sydney casino', *Australian Financial Review*, 25 May 1994.

Page 56: Soon afterwards, a manila envelope landed on her desk . . . According to the New South Wales Royal Commission into the Building Industry, Leighton Contractors received almost $3 million between 1985 and 1991 in secret commissions to forfeit building contracts. The fees were allegedly paid by other building companies as compensation to Leighton for submitting tenders that were deliberately priced to lose. Leighton's chief executive, Wal King, told the *Sun Herald*'s Karen Davey on 22 May 1994 ('Casino bid winner accused of collusion'): 'The allegation of collusive tendering is an assertion by the royal commission and that's never been proven either way . . . Virtually every major builder in NSW was participating in the practice which went on for many years.'

Page 57: Ian Verrender and Colleen Ryan, 'The biggest game in town', *Sydney Morning Herald*, 10 September 1994.

Page 61: However, he did bring down adverse findings against Wal King and Cyril Vella . . ., Murray Tobias QC, *Report of Public Inquiry pursuant to section 143 (4) of New South Wales Casino Control Act*, 1992, NSW Casino Control Authority, December 1994.

Page 61: 'broken the rules', and subsequent quotes, FitzSimons, 'James Packer'.

CHAPTER 5   THE BLOODING

Page 67: 'These are the words that sum it up . . .', Ken Arthurson, *Arko, My Game*, Pan Macmillan, 1997, p. 224.

Page 67: 'Son, I give you my assurance . . .', Arthurson, *Arko*, p. 5.

Page 69: 'I love the game', Federal Court of Australia, 1996, FCA 1813, Appeal Court decision, p. 54, 4 October 1996.

Page 70: 'I've been to see Kerry but I didn't get much joy . . .', Arthurson, *Arko*, p. 196.

Page 70: 'paper the wall with writs', Roy Masters, 'Bare-knuckled in the big league', *Sydney Morning Herald*, 5 July 1997.

Page 70: He told Quayle that News would go it alone . . ., FCA 1813: 'Super League is going to happen with you or without you people. It is entirely up to you.'

Page 70: Three months later, on 6 February 1995 . . . Cowley told the ARL meeting at Philip Street, 'Whatever happens, we will not start up a rebel league . . . there will never be a rebel competition', FCA 1813, p. 67.

Page 71: 'Secrecy, suddenness and deception . . .', *News Limited v Australian Rugby Football League Limited and New South Wales Rugby League*

Limited and Others, Federal Court of Australia, 1996, FCA 1256, Justice Burchett judgement, p. 24, 23 February 1996.

Page 71: They were given crib sheets instructing them to deny they had talked to News . . ., FCA 1813, pp. 77–8.

Page 72: 'Son, it's not like World Series Cricket where all you need is a couple of teams . . .', Geoff Cousins to author.

Page 74: 'Steve, you don't know me and I've never met you . . .', Mike Colman, *Super League: the inside story*, Pan Macmillan, Sydney, 1996, pp. 115–16.

Page 75: 'The ARL was back in the game', Colman, *Super League*, pp. 124–25.

Page 76: 'Richo was leader of the pack', Coleman, *Super League*, p. 128.

Page 76: 'It was a mad, bad time . . .', Arthurson, *Arko*, pp. 221–22.

Page 77: 'When we started we were . . . very behind and unplanned . . .', Peter FitzSimons, 'Hard yards in a tough game of political football', *Sydney Morning Herald*, 25 November 1996.

Page 78: 'It was a breathtaking piece of corporate treachery . . .', Arthurson, *Arko*, p. 11.

Page 79: 'The impetus for talking . . .', Glenn Burge and Sue Lecky, 'Bad blood', *Sydney Morning Herald*, 23 November 1996.

Page 80: 'Mr Packer spends his time travelling, playing polo and other activities . . .', Burge and Lecky, 'Bad blood'.

Page 80: 'I've told the world when people have come to me', interview with Jana Wendt, *Witness*, Channel Seven, 9 April 1996.

Page 81: 'All that any of us can do now . . .', FitzSimons, 'Hard yards in a tough game of football'.

Page 82: 'Business had come in through the door . . .', Arthurson, *Arko*, p. 10.

CHAPTER 6 UNFINISHED BUSINESS

Page 86: 'What the fuck have you said to Dad?', James Packer after the Star City bid was abandoned in April 1997.

Page 86: 'lurched from one disappointment to another', Sue Lecky, 'New casino boss dealt tough hand', *Sydney Morning Herald*, 31 August 1996.

Page 87: 'He implied a trust in me . . .', James Packer to Australian Broadcasting Authority, *CPH, PBL, John Fairfax Holdings Limited*, Hearing Volume Number 2, 9 June 1998, p. 12.

Page 89: Shortly afterwards Neil Gamble got a call from Kerry . . ., Neil Gamble to author.

Page 91: But he had wanted to conquer Fairfax for much longer than that . . ., Kerry Packer to Australian Broadcasting Authority, *CPH, PBL, John Fairfax Holdings Limited*, Hearing Volume Number 16, 27 October 1998, p.7.

Page 92: One story that caused him to go ballistic was a front-page article in the Fairfax-owned *Australian Financial Review* . . ., *Australian Financial Review*, October 1995.

Page 93: 'Well, Richard Coleman . . .', Richard Coleman to author.

Page 93: He bought more shares in February 1995 . . ., *A Current Affair*, Channel Nine, 16 February 1995.

Page 93: Days later, he made a similar pitch in the *Bulletin* . . ., Trevor Sykes and Elisabeth Sexton, *The Bulletin*, 28 February 1995.

Page 94: 'As a concerned member of the public . . .', Alan Kohler, 'Who gets Fairfax is the only issue', *The Age*, 15 November 1996.

Page 95: 'ludicrous' and 'outdated', Howard made similar comments in two interviews a week apart. See Anne Davies, 'Echoes of Packer as signal strengthens on media policy', *Sydney Morning Herald*, 25 April 1997; Anne Davies, 'PM attacks "ludicrous" media ownership laws', *Sydney Morning Herald*, 2 May 1997.

Pages 95–96: On 5 May 1997, the day before the changes were due to go to Cabinet, *The Age* published a letter from eighty prominent Australians . . ., Gervase Greene, 'Group warns PM on media', *The Age*, 5 May 1997.

Page 96: And the day after that, he braved a barrage of lollipops from Ray Martin . . ., *A Current Affair*, Channel Nine, 9 May 1997.

Page 98: 'We have always thought it would be fantastic . . .', Glenn Burge and Sally Loane, 'Packer's pitch for Fairfax', *Sydney Morning Herald*, 12 May 1997.

Page 98: 'The Packers were hot for it', Paul Neville to author.

Page 98: 'He was very blokey, very matey', Gary Hardgrave to author.

Page 100: Hearing that action was imminent, Rupert and Lachlan dropped in on the Prime Minister at Kirribilli House . . ., Gervase Greene and Malcolm Maiden, 'How the Packers missed out on Fairfax', *The Age*, 6 September 1997.

CHAPTER 7   DEATH'S DOOR

Page 102: 'Operations don't worry me a lot . . . I've had a lot of them and I believe I'm bulletproof', Kerry Packer to Australian Broadcasting Authority, *CPH, PBL, John Fairfax Holdings Limited*, Hearing Volume Number 16, 27 October 1998, p. 34.

Page 104: 'So what's the problem?' and following quotes, Neil Gamble to author.

Page 105: 'What are you doing up so early?', Mark Westfield, *The Gate-keepers: The global media battle to control Australia's pay-TV*, Pluto Press, Sydney, 2000. This has an excellent account of the Australis saga.

Page 107: Ross's relationship with Kerry, Nick Ross to author.

Page 108: 'One, I'm very hard to kill . . .', Dr Ian Bailey to author.

Page 111: Isom and his team were famous for taking the cases others wouldn't touch . . ., Candace Sutton, 'Surgeon in cowboy boots for Packer', *Sun Herald*, 26 July 1998.

Page 112: 'To be perfectly honest . . .', Australian Broadcasting Authority, Hearing Volume Number 16, p. 16.

Page 114: Packer's 27 October appearance before the ABA, all quotes from Australian Broadcasting Authority, Hearing Volume Number 16, p. 4

CHAPTER 8   THE CROWN JEWELS

Page 118: 'James is running PBL nowadays. This is his deal', Lloyd Williams commenting on the Crown takeover, December 1998.

Page 119: 'I don't think boards matter a damn as long as they don't do anything', Kerry Packer, evidence to Australian Broadcasting Authority, *CPH, PBL, John Fairfax Holdings Limited*, Hearing Volume Number 16, 27 October 1998, p. 20.

Page 120: A 'neat man . . .', Leonie Wood, 'Lloyd wakes from his casino dream', *The Age*, 19 December 1998.

Page 122: At first Williams assured the media . . ., Malcolm Maiden and Leonie Wood, 'Crown of thorns. Williams, unshaken but stirred', *The Age*, 1 November 1997. Also, Malcolm Maiden and Leonie Wood, 'High-rollers Savage Crown', *The Age*, 20 December 1997.

Page 122: With the announcement of the loss came news of a $200 million support package . . ., Richard Webb, 'Packer's $90m casino lifeline', *Herald Sun*, 20 December 1997. See also, editorial, 'Tarnished Crown', *The Age*, 22 December 1997.

Page 124: In September, the urgency increased . . ., Ian McIlwraith and Greg Thom, 'Packer's $425m casino bailout', *Herald Sun*, 12 September 1998. Also, Damon Johnston and Greg Thom, 'Kennett no to Packer', *Herald Sun*, 23 October 1998.

Page 124: Kerry made it abundantly clear that the Packers would walk away from the rescue unless they got what they wanted . . ., Terry McCrann, 'Kerry still finds it taxing to stroll into a casino', *Herald Sun*, 21 October 1998.

Page 125: By the time the third rescue bid was finally agreed . . ., Leonie Wood, 'Packer's big gamble', *The Age*, 15 December 1998.

CHAPTER 9   MASTER OF THE UNIVERSE

Page 127: 'Jodee, I love you . . .', James Packer to Jodee Rich, according to the affidavit of John David Rich, 27 March 2006, Supreme Court of New South Wales, ASIC v John David Rich and others, 5934 of 2001, para 713.

Page 137: Richard Guilliatt and Drew Warne-Smith, 'The son also rises, taking his place', *The Australian*, 9 December 2006.

Page 140: Kerry Stokes has given a hotly disputed account in the Federal Court of a conversation he had with James in late 2000 . . ., Federal Court of Australia, N1223 of 2002, Witness statement of Kerry Matthew Stokes, p. 10.

Page 141: 'He was thumping the table . . .', Graeme Samuel to author.

CHAPTER 10 PLAYBOY MODELS

Page 143: 'I'm a man's man. I hang out with the boys . . .', David Gyngell interviewed by Daphne Guinness, 'The good son, profile, David Gyngell', *Sydney Morning Herald*, 20 December 1997.

Page 146: Kate Fischer as *Dolly* covergirl, 'Face of 88: Cover Girl', *Dolly*, January 1988; on the front cover of *Vogue*, 'Star on the rise: Australian model actor Kate Fischer', *Vogue*, November 1993.

Page 147: Charlotte Dawson quoted in Kate Halfpenny, 'Lovely catch, that', *Who Weekly*, 14 July 1997.

Page 147: 'He was shy, awkward and reserved . . . the yin to James's yang. Yin is female, yang is male, but in some ways James and Kate's roles were reversed because yang is supposed to be active and yin submissive.

Page 147: In May 1997 . . ., *A Current Affair*, Channel Nine, 9 May 1997.

Page 148: 'They were very gooey and very much in love', quoted in Rachelle Unreich, 'A siren reborn', *Who Weekly*, 14 December 1998.

Page 148: Sellick has a very clear recollection of how the photo came to taken . . ., Robin Sellick to author.

Page 152: 'I just knew he wouldn't want me to write about it', Peter FitzSimons, *Nene*, HarperCollins, Sydney, 2004.

Page 152: 'James pays heartbroken Kate $10 million', Leigh Reinhold, 'James and Kate's $10 million split', *New Idea*, 17 October 1998. *New Idea*'s cover date is typically a week after first copies are distributed.

Page 153: 'Kate's friend Danielle Wallace told journalists . . .', Rachelle Unreich, 'A siren reborn', *Who Weekly*, 26 December 1998.

Page 158: 'Wedding of the Decade', *Australian Women's Weekly*, November 1999.

CHAPTER 11 A BIGGER BUNNY

Page 159: 'We're going to be Kerry's second Alan Bond', Paul Rizzo, former chief financial officer of Telstra, to author.

Page 162: 'We are all now on internet time . . .', Jennifer Hewett, 'At full speed, direction unclear', *Sydney Morning Herald*, 9 March 2000. See also Leonie Wood, 'Any portal in a storm: a corporate giant steps online', *The Age*, 15 January 2000.

Page 166: 'The brawl with the Packers . . .', Adam Shand, 'Packers versus Pretty: when deals go sour', *Australian Financial Review*, 24 May 2000.

Page 167: Ziggy Switkowski is convinced that the Packer camp was behind the attack, Switkowski to author.

Page 169: The younger Packer touched the politician's feet . . ., Neena Haridas, 'Uncle Kerry and brother James from Down Under taste Indian hospitality's thunder', *Rediff Business Special*, Rediff.com, 29 March 2000.

CHAPTER 12 HERO TO ZERO

Page 173: 'I just can't stand it anymore. Kerry gets sick but then he always seems to get better. I think he has nine lives', James Packer to Jodee Rich, Rich affidavit, Supreme Court of New South Wales, ASIC vs John David Rich and others, 5934 of 2001, para 1402.

Page 175: 'You're on a machine lying down in a bed for eight or nine hours a day . . .', Kerry Packer, 'Best of Friends', *Australian Story*, ABC-TV, 29 November 2001.

Page 180: In November 2000 he had dinner at James's Bondi apartment with Rich and Keeling . . ., Rich affidavit, para 930.

Page 181: 'more confident about One.Tel's prospects than [he] had ever been', reported by Paul Barry, 'James's cry from the heart', *Sydney Morning Herald*, 4 May 2002.

Page 182: 'Shithouse . . . Dad's very angry . . .', Rich affidavit, para 1306.

Page 182: All three quotes attributed to James Packer, plus James's alleged admission that Kerry would have to 'repay my borrowings' are from Jodee Rich's affidavit, para 1402.

Page 182: James denies saying this . . ., cross-examination by David Williams SC, reported by Anne Lampe, 'Nine lives of a billionaire dad', *Sydney Morning Herald*, 9 December 2005.

Page 183: Geoff Elliott, 'Back from the dead', *The Australian*, 10 May 2001.

Page 184: 'He told me I would have to go . . .', Rich to author, quoted in Paul Barry, *Rich Kids: How the Murdochs and Packers lost $950 million in One.Tel*, Random House, Sydney, 2002.

Page 184: Resignations Jodee Rich and Bradley Keeling, One.Tel board minutes, 17 May 2001.

Page 189: 'I may be a fuckwit but I'm not a liar . . .', Barry, 'James's cry from the heart'.

CHAPTER 13   THINGS FALL APART

Page 190: 'It's fascinating that he has buckled emotionally over One.Tel . . .', former Packer adviser on James's reaction to the collapse of One.Tel.

Page 192: 'James was completely fucked', Richard Guilliatt, 'Shadow on the son', Good Weekend, *Sydney Morning Herald*, 5 May 2003.

Page 192: 'James was so shocked by the company's failure he became dysfunctional . . .', Brian Powers to author.

Page 192: 'traumatised', Ziggy Switkowski to author.

Page 194: According to the *Sun Herald*'s gossip columnist Annette Sharp . . ., Annette Sharp, 'Why Jodhi called it quits', *Sun Herald*, 16 June 2002.

Page 195: Two weeks later James gave an extraordinarily frank interview. . ., Jeni Cooper, 'Pressures that drove James and Jodhi apart', *Sunday Telegraph*, 30 June 2002.

Page 196: And Richens later admitted as much . . ., Polly Graham, *Sunday Mirror* (London), 8 September 2002.

Page 196: *New Idea* laid out the photographs as a two-page spread . . ., Annette Sharp, 'James and the pictures that pulped a magazine', *Sun Herald*, 14 July 2002.

CHAPTER 14 XENU CALLING

Page 198: 'You find a religion that can take away the Packers' money and I'm going to convert', Brian Powers to author.

Page 200: 'I admire him enormously . . .', Jeni Cooper, 'Pressures that drove James and Jodhi apart', *Sunday Telegraph*, 30 June 2002.

Page 201: 'Immortal spirits who can control matter, energy, space, time, thought, and life . . ., 'What Scientologists Believe', *Beliefnet.com*.

Page 201: 'If life is a game, Scientology gives you the tools to play it with a stacked deck and win consistently . . .', from the Jason Beghe page in the 'Scientology Successes' section of 'What is Scientology?', official church website www.whatisscientology.org/html/part05/chp19/pg0317-a.html cited at www.adherents.com/people/pb/Jason_Beghe.html

Page 202: 'My experience personally is that . . .', the full Jason Beghe interview, lasting two hours, found at www.youtube.com/watch?v=KHb0BZyF5Ok.

Page 202: Kevin Victor Anderson QC, *Report of the Board of Enquiry into Scientology*, State of Victoria, 1965, Chapter 30, www.cs.cmu.edu/~dst/Cowen/audit/andrhome.html.

Page 202: Justice Latey's judgement, *Re: B & G (Minors) (Custody)*, High Court (Family Division), London, 23 July 1984.

Page 204: Ron Hubbard telling the Xenu story, www.youtube.com/watch?v=ZYYUBES8VnA, posted by www.youtube.com/user/TheEvilOfScientology.

Page 205: But Jason Beghe confirmed in a recent interview . . ., *Today Tonight*, Channel Seven, 4 February 2009, interviewer Bryan Seymour.

Page 205: 'The fact that members of the church apparently believe in inter-galactic travel . . .', Wensley Clarkson, *Tom Cruise: Unauthorised*, Hastings House, New York, 1998.

Page 206: 'The body he had used to facilitate his existence in this messed universe had ceased to be useful . . .' In early 2009 this could be found at Cultzone TV, www.youtube.com/watch?v=Nie-_r1z8D8.

Page 206: In presenting Cruise with Scientology's first-ever Freedom Medal of Valor in October 2004 . . . 'Tom Cruise Uncut: The Freedom Medal Award Ceremony', www.youtube.com/watch?v=ZD4KDOBBqno.

Page 207: The Church's online 'completion register' lists Erica Baxter as finishing two courses in 2004, www.truthaboutscientology.com/stats/ccint/celebrity355.html.

Page 208: Koop is widely quoted as saying, 'My recommendation about detoxification is to keep away from it. You don't need it . . . It's dangerous. I don't think L. Ron Hubbard has credibility in the scientific world.' I have not been able to find the original instance. In January 1991 Dr James J. Kenney, PhD, who was on the US National Council Against Health Fraud with Koop, was equally damning: 'The purification program was created by L. Ron Hubbard's fertile imagination in the mid-1950s. It is part of the teachings of the Church of Scientology and lacks any credible scientific support. This purification or detoxification program is claimed to help clear the mind of toxins such as drugs, pesticides and chemical pollutants. It consists of large doses of niacin, vegetable oil, exercise and low temperature saunas. According to the followers of L. Ron Hubbard, the large doses of niacin work by stimulating the release of fat into the blood stream and this is accompanied by various toxins trapped in the body's fatty tissues. According to science, large doses of niacin actually block the release of fat from fat cells. This has been observed both at rest [*Acta Medica Scandinavia* 1962, 172(suppl):641)] and during exercise. [D. Jenkins, *Lancet* 1965, 1307] In other words, the scientific evidence shows the exact opposite of what Hubbard's theory predicts. There is no credible support for claims that large doses of niacin clear toxins from the brain, fatty tissue or any other part of the body. To make matters worse, large doses of niacin . . . can cause serious liver damage . . . trigger gout, raise blood sugar into the diabetic range, cause itching, flushing and a rash.

Page 210: According to a story in *Crikey* . . ., Stephen Mayne, 'Has KP fire-proofed the empire from the Scientologists?', 20 February 2006, available at Mayne Report, www.maynereport.com/articles/2008/07/14-1227-9924.html.

CHAPTER 15 THE BIG FELLA'S BACK

Page 211: 'I know more about gambling than anyone in this fucking country', Kerry Packer to Crown Chief Executive Officer, Ian Johnson, 2000.

Page 212: 'James would kiss his father . . .' and the quote that follows, Ian Johnson, interview with author.

Page 216: One high-class call girl who gave evidence . . .', John Horn, 'Australian media magnate was among Heidi Fleiss's customers', Associated Press, 14 July 1995.

Page 217: 'This is not someone else's money . . ., *The Australian*, 1 September 2000.

Page 218: Almost immediately, Burswood Casino in Perth came onto the radar . . . Other potential bidders were waiting for ratification of a new law that ended a prohibition on anyone outside Western Australia holding more than 10 per cent of the casino. PBL had been given legal advice it could jump the gun.

CHAPTER 16 KILLING NINE

Page 222: 'Who Killed Channel Nine? Kerry killed Channel Nine . . .', Steve Wood, former executive producer of Channel Nine's *Today*, to author.

Page 225: 'I'm bombproof . . .', Peter Lalor, 'All the king's men—inside the court of James Packer', *Daily Telegraph*, 12 January 2002.

Page 226: 'They have my absolute support . . .', Peter Lalor, 'All the king's men'.

Page 226: Widely known as Lord Farquaad . . ., Jane Cadzow and John Huxley, 'The Alexander technique', Good Weekend, *Sydney Morning Herald*, 18 September 2004.

Page 228: John Alexander profile, Mark Day, 'Power behind Packer', *The Australian*, 30 June 2006.

Page 233: 'I'm not sure whether JA was channelling Kerry or vice versa . . .', Peter Meakin to author.

Page 236: Gyngell's resignation, Cosima Marriner and James Chessell, 'Why the best man abandoned the Packers', *Sydney Morning Herald*, 10 May 2005.

CHAPTER 17 WHAM BAM, THANK YOU SAM

Page 238: 'He was an absolute fucking monster . . . I've never encountered anyone like that in my entire life', senior Channel Nine executive's verdict on Sam Chisholm.

Page 239: 'They transplanted my lungs not my personality', Christine Jackman, 'Sam Chisholm's second chance: A new set of lungs and a new outlook on life', *The Australian*, 11 October 2003.

Page 245: 'Well, there you are. Everyone has an opinion . . .', Sam Chisholm to author.

CHAPTER 18 A GREAT AUSTRALIAN

Page 247: 'He wasn't Mother Teresa . . . he could be a really tough bastard', Trevor Kennedy, January 2006.

Page 249: 'I can't eat what I want to eat. I can't do what I want to do . . .', 'Alan Jones speaks of friend Kerry Packer's final days', AAP, 27 December 2005.

Page 250: 'About ten days before Christmas . . .', Dr Ian Bailey to author.

Page 251: 'Kerry was very discreet about it, but Ros certainly knew', Nick Ross to author.

Page 253: Howard claimed the media mogul was a personal friend, Tara Ravens, 'PM calls Packer a generous Australian', AAP, 27 December 2005.

Page 256: 'I gather he died in your mother's arms', from *The Big Fella: The Extraordinary Life of Kerry Packer*, Channel Nine, 16 February 2006.

Page 257: The description of Russell Crowe is poetic licence. He was born in New Zealand, but he lives in Coffs Harbour and co-owns the South

Sydney rugby league club. Australians like to claim him as their own.

Page 258: James Packer's eulogy was published as 'My greatest fortune', *Sydney Morning Herald*, 18 February 2006.

Page 259: 'C'Mon Aussie, C'Mon' was written by Allan Johnston and Alan Morris in 1978, published by Warner Bros. Music, and originally performed by The Mojo Singers.

Page 260: Kate McClymont, 'How Packer lavished property on a friend', *Sydney Morning Herald*, 7 January 2006.

CHAPTER 19   THE SON ALSO RISES

Page 261: 'Kerry died a lonely man and he deserved to . . .', an old 'friend' of James Packer.

Page 261: Mark Drummond, 'Packer moves to conquer new investment frontiers', *The West Australian*, 25 March 2006.

Page 261: Pam Williams and Damon Kitney, 'My way', *Australian Financial Review Magazine*, December 2006.

Page 265: As Csidei admitted in his biography . . ., Norm Lipson and Adam Walters, *The Accidental Gangster: The life and times of Bela Csidei*, Park Street Press/Media 21 Publishing, Sydney, 2006.

Page 268: 'He is so ambitious', David Thomas, 'The odd couple', *Mail on Sunday* (London), 31 October 1999.

Page 269: 'I'll probably be less successful . . .', Drummond, 'Packer moves to conquer new investment frontiers'.

Page 270: 'Kerry would have you in there all night if he could', Peter Ivany to author.

CHAPTER 20   JAMES'S BIG GAMBLE

Page 273: 'It's a horrendous mass-market destination . . . I reckon they'll end up gutting it', an analyst's verdict on Crown Macau, 2007.

Page 276: 'The second was that this licence holder would inevitably be Lawrence's father, Stanley Ho . . .' Ho had been blacklisted by every jurisdiction in which he had ever applied for a casino licence, except Macau.

Comprehensive reports and dossiers are available at http://familyfocus coalition.org/pages.php. See also Dominic Kennedy and James Doran, 'Oxford takes gambling king's cash', *Times Online*, 26 May 2007; 'Casino connections part 2: Stanley Ho's house of cards', *Asian Pacific Post*, 22 July 2004; Matt Ward, 'Alleged confidential reports on Pansy Ho, Stanley Ho leaked online', *Las Vegas Business Press*, 27 February 2007.

Page 277: The opportunity to buy the sub-concession was a happy accident for James . . . Galaxy won one of three licences on offer in a consortium with Adelson's company, Las Vegas Sands. Each then decided to go their separate ways and Las Vegas Sands became a sub-concessionaire. That opened the way for the other two winners, Wynn's and Stanley Ho's Sociedade de Jogos de Macau (SJM), to sell sub-concessions themselves. Pansy Ho and MGM bought SJM's for US$200 million. Melco-PBL bought the other for US$900 million.

Page 278: 'Wynn says he only agreed to sell the sub-concession after being badgered by James for months on end . . .', Glenda Korporaal, 'Packer's helping hand', *The Australian*, 8 April 2006.

Page 282: After it's refit, Crown Macau did better. After big losses in 2007, in 2008 Crown Macau made US$163 million EBITDA before interest, tax, depreciation and amortisation. Melco-PBL lost money from 2005 with an operating loss of US$57.6 million in 2006, US$195 million in 2007 and US$2.5 million in 2008, by which time it had accumulated total losses of US$258 million.

Page 284: 'Forget about dating services . . .', Sheldon Adelson quoted in William Mellor and Oliver Staley, 'Macau builds a dream—to be Las Vegas on steroids', *Bloomberg*, January 4, 2007.

Page 285: Others were not so sure. Gabriel Chan, 'Macau gaming industry: destructive competition has already begun', Credit Suisse, 4 October 2007.

Page 285: This is where the junket operators come in . . . The house win at baccarat, the game played by most high-rollers in Macau, is assumed to be 2.7 per cent of rolling chip turnover, which is the amount wagered by high-rollers. Junket operators typically received 1.1 per cent of this turnover in commission, which worked out at roughly 40 per cent of the casino's win. Tax to the Macanese government took another 39 per cent of the win, leaving 21 per cent for the casino. Hence the junket operator took roughly twice as much as the casino, or two-thirds of the casino's gross revenue.

Page 286: But this fortune came at a price. Raising the junket operator's commission rate from 1.1 per cent to 1.35 per cent of rolling chip turnover almost halved the casino's take. Out of every $100 wagered at baccarat, there should be $2.70 in house winnings. The government took $1.05 in tax, leaving $1.65 for the casino and the junket operator to share. This divided $1.10 to the junket operator and $0.55 to the casino if the commission rate was 1.1 per cent, but divided $1.35 to the junket operator and only $0.30 to the casino if the commission rate was 1.35 per cent.

Page 286: 'The largest Asian-focused gaming company in the whole world', Lawrence Ho in Anne Hyland, 'High-stakes casino kings ready to roll', *Australian Financial Review*, 4 January 2006.

CHAPTER 21   JAMES GETS HIS ALAN BOND

Page 288: 'You only get one Alan Bond in your lifetime and I've had mine,' Kerry Packer.

Page 288: 'Faiman asked Audsley what he should do . . .', Peter Faiman to author.

Page 290: 'Nine is dying . . .', Posie Graeme-Evans to author.

Page 292: At the end of 2005, the two people behind the show . . ., Julian Cress to author and unpublished 'Affidavit of Julian Cress' June 2007.

Page 294: 'You need to be careful here, very careful . . .', this and subsequent quotes are from affidavit of Mark John Llewellyn, NSW Supreme Court, 23 June 2006.

Page 299: 'The implications are breathtaking . . .', Bruce Wolpe to Brendan Trembath, 'Nine launches legal attack on Fairfax', *AM*, ABC-Radio, 30 June 2006.

Page 299: 'Hard to imagine . . .', Monica Attard, 'Nine's gangsters', *Media Watch*, ABC-TV, 3 July 2006.

Page 300: 'Facing his biggest crisis since taking over his father's multi-billion-dollar empire . . .', Janet Fife-Yeomans, 'He's just sacked 100 staff, his network is a mess, and he's in England for tennis and polo. Home James', *Daily Telegraph*, 30 June 2006.

Page 305: 'It is impossible not to like her', Neil McMahon, 'Meet Mrs Packer', the (Sydney) magazine, *Sydney Morning Herald*, 12 June 2007.

Page 306: Erica completed her album . . ., Phillip Koch, 'Erica Baxter's star is shining', *New Idea*, 20 May 2007.

Page 307: 'Girls need clothes and food and tender happiness and frills . . .', 'Scientology Weddings: Frequently Asked Questions', *Beliefnet.com*.

Page 307: 'Baxter looked beautiful in a strapless, tiered, floor-length white gown . . .', Valkerie Mangnall, 'Packer's bride wore white—twice', AAP, 21 June 2007.

CHAPTER 22   BILLION-DOLLAR BETS

Page 309: 'He's got the scent of a guy who has just been let off the leash. It looks to me like he's overpaying for everything', Anthony Curtis, publisher of the *Las Vegas Advisor*, to author.

Page 312: 'We are extremely pleased to have such a renowned industry leader as James Packer's PBL as our cornerstone investor', 'Fontainebleau Resorts announces definitive agreement with Publishing and Broadcasting Limited', PRNewswire, Las Vegas, 16 April 2007.

Page 314: The figure of US$1.8 billion Crown agreed to pay for Cannery Casino Resorts (CCR) includes US$49 million acquisition costs.

Page 316: 'Probably 90 per cent of life is being at the right place at the right time', Liz Benston, 'Cannery partners did it their way', *Las Vegas Sun*, 13 September 2008.

Page 316: By selling out to James Packer, Oaktree appeared to have quadrupled its investment in little more than a year. It is hard to be precise because Packer was buying CCR debt free, so Oaktree's profit would be less than the bare figures suggest, but see David Carey and Ben Fidler, 'Oaktree gains big in Cannery deal', *TheDeal.com*, 12 December 2007.

Page 317: Another of CCR's Las Vegas casinos is the new Cannery Eastside . . ., details can be found at www.eastsidecannery.com.

Page 318: The day The Meadows opened for business in its temporary home . . ., Gary Rotstein, 'Meadows betting on extra perks to offset losing streaks', *Pittsburgh Post-Gazette*, 13 June 2007. The permanent casino, which was due to open in mid-2009, would have more than 3900 slot machines. Details at www.meadowsgaming.com.

Page 319: I saw one man feeding US$ 100 bills into a machine that had notched up 10 000 points . . . In US casinos video poker machines can be set to return anything from 88 per cent to 96 per cent to the skilful gambler. If you don't know how to play, the payout slumps to 34 per cent. Higher value machines (or playing multiple lines at a time) have a higher percentage payout.

CHAPTER 23   ILL-GOTTEN GAINS

Page 322: 'A river of stolen money flows into the pockets of the owners of Crown Casino . . .', Terry Lane, 'Want to spend some hot money?', *Sunday Age*, 15 December 2002.

Page 322: In seven years playing the pokies she racked up 10 million points and earned a truckload of freebies . . ., Kate Uebergang, 'Crown blamed for pokies debt', *Herald Sun*, 14 February 2006.

Page 323: 'There's one question they don't ask . . .', Jamie Berry, 'Lawyer points finger at casino in bank worker's $7m theft', *The Age*, 1 December 2006.

Page 324: 'If you need to demonstrate the evils of gambling . . .', Lawrence Money, 'Crown to turn tabs on punting elite', *Sunday Age*, 11 May 2003.

Page 324: But De Stefano's most tragic victim . . ., *Nexus PL v De Stefano and others*, Supreme Court of Victoria, 5499 of 2001. See also, Shaun Phillips, 'Victim lodges claim for gambler's losses', *Herald Sun*, 25 April 2001.

Page 325: They also agreed to settle a second lawsuit . . ., *Global Issues Pty Ltd and others v De Stefano and others*, Supreme Court of Victoria, 5148 of 2000.

Page 326: Like many addicts, Sally Grossi started playing the pokies to escape from depression and an unhappy marriage, *The Queen v Sally Grossi*, County Court of Victoria, 206 VCC 1622, Sentencing Remarks, Dyett J. See also, Jamie Berry, 'Society couple fleeced of $1.7m to fund gambling', *The Age*, 30 November 2006.

Page 327: The head of New Zealand's Problem Gambling Foundation John Stansfield, made a similar observation . . ., Damien Carrick, 'Casino punished', *The Law Report*, ABC Radio National, 24 October 2006.

Page 328: Official estimates from the Australian government's Productivity Commission . . . The Productivity Commission estimated in 1999 that 42 per cent of poker machine revenue comes from problem gamblers, *Australia's Gambling Industries*, Inquiry Report, Australian Government Productivity Commission, 16 December 1999, www.pc.gov.au/projects/inquiry/gambling/docs/finalreport.

Page 329: 'Every feature of those machines . . .', Professor Dr Natasha Schull, testimony to Joint Committee on Mental Health and Substance Abuse, Massachusetts Legislature, 31 October 2007. Schull is the author of *Machine Zone: Technology and compulsion in Las Vegas* to be published by Princeton University Press in 2009.

Page 329: 'The reality for most people, problem gamblers included . . .', Charles Livingstone, Senior Lecturer in Health Science at Monash University, to author. Livingstone has published extensively on electronic gaming machines.

Page 330: 'cherry dribbling' and 'operant conditioning', see David Espar (producer), *Discovering Psychology*, WGBH TV, Boston, in association with the American Psychological Association, 1989. See also, B.F. Skinner, 'A brief survey of operant behavior', B.F. Skinner Foundation, www.bfskinner.org.

CHAPTER 24   THE TROUBLE WITH HARRY

Page 331: 'This is going to be a war, a mighty war . . .', Harry Kakavas to author, 2008.

Page 332: 'I began to take outrageous risks . . .', Chia Teck Leng's thirteen-page confession was released by Singapore's Home Affairs Ministry during debate about whether the nation should allow casinos. It is widely available on the internet, and can be found at *GlobalGaming-News.com*, Chia Teck Leng, 'Taming the casino dragon: The only certain thing in life is its uncertainty', www.globalgamingnews.com/news_asia/taming-the-dragon.html.

Page 332: 'He'd just go flat out . . .', Michael Warner, 'High-roller lost millions', *Herald Sun*, 23 October 2003. Also, Michael Warner, '$190m high roller jailed,' *Herald Sun*, 16 October 2003.

Page 333: 'Kakavas's statement of claim in the Victorian Supreme Court . . .', and all quotes from the statement of claim that follow, *Harry Kakavas v Crown Limited and John Williams and Rowen Craigie*, Supreme Court of Victoria, 4964 of 2007.

Page 336: 'Shortly before revoking Kakavas's self-exclusion order . . .', statement given by Bill Horman on behalf of Crown Casino in criminal proceedings against Kakavas on 19 January 1998, cited in Second Further Amended Statement of Claim, October 2008.

CHAPTER 25   THE BIGGEST LOSER

Page 344: By February 2009 shares in Sheldon Adelson's Las Vegas Sands had fallen . . . Las Vegas Sands shares hit rock bottom at US$1.42 on 9 March 2009.

Page 345: In a little over a year Australian share prices had fallen . . . The ASX All Ords hit a low of 3090 in early March 2009, 55 per cent down on its November 2007 high.

Page 347: In mid-2008 US$30 billion worth of new hotels, casinos and apartments under construction . . ., Jeremy Aguero, Applied Analysis, Las Vegas, to author.

Page 348: By this time, most other big casino projects on the Strip were either on hold or in trouble. These casino financing and construction stories have been widely covered, particularly by the excellent *Las Vegas Review Journal*, but also by the *Las Vegas Sun* and *Las Vegas Business Press*.

Page 349: On Christmas eve 2008, the world's largest casino operator, Harrah . . ., 'Harrah's: cash flow may not service debt', Reuters, 17 March 2009.

Page 350: This was confirmed two weeks later when Crown wrote off its entire stake in Station . . ., 'Crown Announces half-year results', ASX media release, 27 February 2009.

Page 350: Luckily, Packer had not yet handed over the US$1.8 billion purchase price . . . At best, the properties were now worth two-thirds of what Packer would have to pay for them—which would leave Crown with a further $900 million loss. The cost was US$1.8 billion, which, in March 2009, was roughly $2.7 billion.

Page 350: In November 2008, Gretel Packer and three secretive Bahamas-based trusts . . ., Carly Crawford, 'Gretel Packer seeks to end role in James' Nevada gaming push', *Daily Telegraph*, 23 February 2009.

Page 351: But she was worried that some of this information . . . Some of this information still is, in Pennsylvania Gaming Control Board, Application Status Report, 23 March 2009.

Page 351: As the trusts' lawyer told the gaming board's commissioners in a public hearing in February 2009 . . . Pennsylvania Gaming Control Board, public meeting minutes, 20 February 2009.

Page 351: As it happened, this claim wasn't entirely true . . ., see ABT File IO/91/2, document 46. Also Paul Barry, *The Rise and Rise of Kerry Packer Uncut*, Bantam, Sydney, 2007, p. 414.

Page 352: 'Meanwhile, Gretel and the Bahamian trustees were also taking legal action . . ., *Consolidated Custodians International Limited (a Bahamian corporation) and Gretel Lees Packer v Millenium Gaming Inc and others*, case 4388, Court of Chancery State of Delaware, Verified Compliant for Declaratory Relief, filed 23 February 2009. Inter alia, the document details legal threats by Millenium/Cannery to sue Consolidated Custodians International Limited and Ms Packer.

Page 352: Three weeks before the cut-off date it was agreed that Crown would pay . . ., 'Cannery Casino Resorts and Crown terminate merger agreement; Crown to make investment into CCR, Cannery Casino

Resorts to Receive US$370 Million', *PRNewswire*, Las Vegas, 12 March 2009. Also, 'Update on Cannery transaction, Crown Limited', ASX media release, 13 March 2009.

Page 353: News of Crown's dramatic, last-minute escape pushed up its shares in Australia by 15 per cent . . ., 'Crown cans Cannery', ABN Amro research paper, 13 March 2009.

Page 353: 'a disaster' and 'It may be difficult for Crown to do deals with potential sellers in the USA for some time', Vanda Carson, 'Cashed-up Crown to pounce', *Sydney Morning Herald*, 16 March 2009, pp. 6–7.

CHAPTER 26   DREAMS AND NIGHTMARES

Page 355: By mid-2009, gaming revenues in the territory had fallen by 13 per cent . . . Revenue figures are published quarterly by the Gaming Inspection and Co-ordination Bureau in Macau, www.dicj.gov.mo/.

Page 357: As the *Asia Sentinel* reported in November 2007 . . ., Mark O'Neill, 'Macau's perilous lure for China's cadres', *Asia Sentinel*, 19 November 2007.

Page 357: Professor Zhonglu Zeng, 'High rollers from China—a profile based on 99 cases', Macau Polytechnic Institute, January 2009.

Page 358: Corruption had also spread to Macau, where at least one senior government official in Macau had also been seduced . . ., Irina de Carvalho, 'Round two, Ao back in trial', *Macau Daily Times*, 19 February 2009.

Page 358: Shortly afterwards, the impeccably connected Stanley Ho urged local politicians . . ., 'Stanley Ho turning up the heat on Las Vegas Sands', *Macau Daily Blog and News*, 10 March 2009. Also, 'Las Vegas Sands competitor cancels Macau purchase', www.casinogamingstock.net, 20 March 2009.

ACKNOWLEDGEMENTS

The Packers never like being written about, and James is no exception to the rule. So I did not get to sit down with the subject of this book and talk about his life. But unlike his famous father, James never told his friends not to speak to me and never threatened to sue everyone I spoke to. So my first and biggest thank you is to James Packer. I hope I've been fair to you and I hope I've done you justice. It's a great responsibility to write an unauthorised biography of a living person, and I hope I have not been too harsh.

This book has taken more than two years to write. During that time I have spoken to a couple of hundred people who have known James or his father as friends, acquaintances, employees or rivals in business. Some agreed to be named; far more preferred to remain anonymous. I would like to thank all for their contribution. Many showed great generosity and trust, and I hope I have done their stories justice too.

In the internet age it is possible to sit at one's desk and read hundreds of articles, columns, blogs and books relevant to the task, and I would like to thank all those whose work I have drawn on. Where I have quoted or relied on them, I have tried to acknowledge the author in the text or the endnotes, but I'm sure there are some I have forgotten, and for this I apologise.

Books need publishers, too, and Allen & Unwin has been a joy to work with. My thanks in particular go to my editor, Rebecca Kaiser, for her guidance, patience and eagle eye. Thanks also to Sue Hines, the publishing director, and to our legal advisor Richard Potter, for their calmness and wisdom. And to Richard Walsh, who encouraged me to do this book in the first place and nudged me gently but firmly towards the finish line.

Finally, I want to thank my family, who had to endure my locked door and constant absences from daily life. It's a lonely job being a writer, but it's just as hard for the people they live with. Daniel sat on my lap while I wrote, while Leo and Lotte asked constant questions, like 'When are you going to finish?' as they queued to use the computer. Lisa gave me space, ran the house, wrangled the children, worked and took the strain. She also read the final manuscript and proved to be my best critic. She deserves the biggest thank you of all, and I dedicate this book to her.

But I also want to say a special thank you to my eldest son Alex, now busy making documentaries, who spent several months at the beginning of this project as my researcher. He was great at finding people, excellent at winning their trust and meticulous in reporting what they had to say. Sadly, other employers soon discovered how smart he was and snatched him from me.

INDEX

JP refers to James Packer
KP refers to Kerry Packer